Before Whispers Become Silence

A MEMOIR

For Dianne
Enjoy!
Judy

A MEMOIR

Andrew Clyde Little

Before Whispers Become Silence

PENUMBRA PRESS

Published by PENUMBRA PRESS
Printed and bound in Canada.

NATIONAL LIBRARY OF CANADA CATALOGUING IN PUBLICATION

Little, Andrew, 1936-
Before whispers become silence / Andrew Clyde Little.
ISBN 1-894131-39-8
1. Little, Anna Gertrude. 2. Little, Andrew, 1936- --Family. 3. Cameron, Ewen, 1901-1967. 4. Psychiatric hospital patients--Quebec (Province)--Montréal--Biography. 5. Suicide victims--Quebec (Province)--Montréal--Biography. 6. Montréal (Quebec)--Biography.
I. Title.
RC464.L58L58 2003 616.89'0092 C2003-905754-2

Canada

ONTARIO ARTS COUNCIL
CONSEIL DES ARTS DE L'ONTARIO

Canada Council for the Arts

Penumbra Press gratefully acknowledges the Canada Council for the Arts and the Ontario Arts Council for supporting its publishing programme. The publisher further acknowledges the financial support of the Government of Canada through the Book Publishing Industry Development Program (BPIDP) for our publishing activities. We also acknowledge the Government of Ontario through the Ontario Media Development Corporation's Ontario Book Initiative.

INTRODUCTION

It is 4:00 a.m. and Nature is calling ... calling collect. At my age this middle-of-the-night wake-up call no longer comes as a surprise, and I rise and grudgingly grope my way to the bathroom. By now I know this nocturnal ritual so well I can usually complete it in the dark and be asleep again within minutes. There are some nights, however, when back in bed I discover I have relieved myself not just of discomfort but the capacity to get back to sleep as well. When this happens, I lie there awhile, enviously listening to the regular, deep breathing coming from my wife's side of the bed. Eventually I surrender and get up.

In the kitchen, shielding my eyes to minimize the shock, I switch on a light, pour a bowl of Spoon Size Shredded Wheat, add two-percent milk, and start the coffee. I carefully peel and section an orange. At the dining room table I eat it slowly, savouring each piece. The scent of the orange gives way to the aroma of freshly brewed coffee. If I am to be denied sleep, there is at least the compensation of food. By now the cereal is soggy, just the way I like it. With the first clink of the spoon on the bowl, Moiria purrs. For the moment she is content to watch me through half-closed eyes from her favourite spot on the sofa, but when I finish the cereal she stretches and casually crosses the room to a position at my feet, where I deposit the bowl. I am well trained. She first sniffs suspiciously, as if the leftover milk might contain something offensive to her delicate cat's palate. Finally satisfied the offering is worthy, she begins to lap it up.

Moiria is not really mine. We inherited her from our son, Kip. When asked why he had called her Moiria, he would smile his enigmatic smile and say simply that he liked the name. We were sure there was more to it than that, but if there was, it remained a mystery. Kip was like that; there are things about him we will never know.

Back at the stove, I pour my coffee and turn off the light. With soothing darkness restored, I settle into my favourite chair in the living room, overlooking the ocean. Cradling the cup to my chest, I welcome its warmth. Moiria finishes the leftover milk and, after some unnecessary grooming, makes her way like a slow-motion heat-seeking missile to a favourite position on my lap. I stroke her fur and am rewarded with a deep, vibrant purr.

Most people get Moiria's name wrong; they call her Moira. Kip would always gently correct them. Getting names right was important to him. So I still correct anyone who makes the mistake.

"It's not Moira, but Moiria," I say. "The more-ya see her, the more-ya love her."

I do this because Kip would have appreciated it. Word play and puns amused him. Wherever he went, he always took his sense of humour along. He often joked he was the victim of a too-functional family. His childhood had been happy and he worried that things came so easily to him. He feared he could never be the serious writer he wanted to be because his young life was trouble-free, unscarred by tragedy. Then, one winter afternoon on an icy road north of Montreal, Kip was killed in a car accident. He was twenty-nine.

Along with the sorrow and loss, we inherited Moiria. She has become our sacred trust, a living link to the past. There is a profound sense of comfort knowing that the cat on my lap is the same cat Kip stroked so many times. Moiria and I sit, together in the dark, sharing more than just each other's warmth.

Outside, night shrouds the view from the window, but it can't muffle the sound of the surf or the periodic moan of the foghorn. I listen, absorbed by these sounds, waiting for dawn. I sip my coffee. With each swallow the sky lightens, the change gradual, the shift powered by Moiria's purring. I put my empty cup aside, scratch her behind the ears. Her purring drops an octave, our breathing synchronizes and we doze.

By now the window is a grey wash of fog. Outside, stalks of sea oats emerge from the gloom, survivors of a recent storm that eroded much of the beach. There are six of them, thin brushstrokes of blackness, leftover remnants of the receding night. They form a ghostly tableau, silent and still, huddled just beyond the window. They seem to be waiting out there. Waiting for what, I wonder? I half close my eyes, squinting to deliberately distort their already blurred image, looking for a meaning. They seem to be posing, as if for a group photograph.

I close my eyes completely, going back into the darkness, searching. Moiria's purring has stopped, as if she too is seeking something. The only sound now is the surf. From deep inside me an idea rises like a bubble, slowly breaking the surface of my consciousness with a soft pop of recognition.

The last time I talked to Kip, two weeks before his death, he'd asked about my family. He had never met any of them and by then it was too late; they were no longer alive. I promised him that some day I would write their story.

Now I understand. Those surviving sea oats stand like my parents and grandparents, waiting for a story – their story – the one I promised Kip.

I open my eyes. A gentle offshore breeze has swept away the last of the fog. Before me the sea oats begin to sway, dancing in the first shafts of light from the rising sun. I glance at my watch. In a few hours I'll be flying home to Ottawa and I promise myself that tomorrow morning I'll begin writing. Morning seems the right time to start because it certainly won't be a bedtime story.

CONTENTS

PART 1

"The thing which prompts you to sit down and write must be something which haunts you."
—Jane Frame, *In the Same Room*

SHERBROOKE, QUEBEC, OCTOBER 1953

IT SHOULD HAVE BEEN a grey day, overcast and raining, because that was how I felt. Instead, the hills of the Eastern Townships were bathed in sunlight, awash with wave after wave of autumn colour. Those hills mocked me; I wanted them dressed for mourning, not for celebration. I wanted to feel the first chill of winter in the air, not the warmth of an Indian Summer.

Just ten days ago my mother died suddenly and I guess you could say unexpectedly. The funeral was a private affair. A closed coffin, just six people at the service: three of her sisters, my grandmother, my father, and me.

Now, back at university, I was trying to distance myself from the reality of her death. It was my plan to let the grief out in small, manageable doses, to deal with the loss in my own way, at my own pace.

Then yesterday Dad called. "I thought I might come down this weekend," he'd announced. "You could show me the campus, we could spend Thanksgiving together." I'd stared at the pay phone on the wall of the third floor of the Norton Hall residence. I didn't want my father here. I'd just begun my freshman year at Bishop's. This was my world, my sanctuary. His visit would be an invasion; it would force me to face our loss on his terms, not mine.

I'd swallowed my resentment. "Okay." I knew he was trying to do the right thing, trying to fill some of the vacuum left by my mother's death. "When will you be getting in?" I'd tried to keep the annoyance from my voice. Didn't he understand? I just wanted to be left alone.

"Tomorrow," he'd said. "The noon train."

At the railway station in Sherbrooke everyone seemed to be smiling, people were starting the long holiday weekend, talking in the excited, conspiratorial tone of kids let out of school early. Flashes of my mother appeared everywhere—in the way one woman walked as she moved along the platform, the laugh of another as she bought a ticket—the slightest gesture and for a tiny fragment of time Mom would be there. And just as quickly she'd be gone, like the snapshot missed in the time taken to focus a camera.

On one of the wooden benches on the station platform a middle-aged lady rummaged in her handbag and brought out a Cherry Blossom candy bar and a package of Du Maurier cigarettes. As she bit into the chocolate, a young boy on the bench next to her watched enviously. When she finished, she rolled the foil wrapper into a neat ball and put it back into her purse. The little boy lost interest. She licked her fingers and lit a cigarette.

My mother smoked Du Mauriers. Not that she was a big smoker. To her, a cigarette had been a prop, an accessory she chose with the same care she used when selecting a piece of jewellery or a scarf. Smoking was something she did at parties, seldom at home. Even then she didn't inhale, but let the smoke languidly escape from her mouth.

This bothered my father. "Trudy, you're wasting a valuable commodity there," he'd say, and to make his point he'd deeply inhale the smoke from his own cigarette. His was a three-pack-a-day habit, each puff an athletic event as he drew the smoke greedily into his lungs. No sissy Du Maurier filter tips for him, his choice was a brand called Old Kentucky. The few times I'd swiped them as a kid they left me queasy and light-headed. My own choice was Sportsman, not on a par with the rough strength of Dad's Old Kentuckys, but stronger than Mom's Du Mauriers. On the station platform I lit up. The tobacco tasted stale. I took another drag but there was no satisfying hit when the smoke reached my lungs. I disgustedly flicked the butt onto the railway tracks, watched it pinwheel in a shower of tiny sparks.

I opened a copy of the local paper, *The Sherbrooke Daily Record.* The New York Yankees had won their fifth straight World Series, beating the Brooklyn Dodgers 4-3 in the final game. I read the opening paragraph three or four times without taking it in. It was no use; I couldn't concentrate. It was flat, meaningless, like the smoke from my discarded cigarette. Normally I would devour this stuff. Summer nights I used to lie awake listening to Yankee games on my bedside radio, the voice of Mel Allen's play-by-play commentary fading in and out from the faraway station in upstate New York. My father had won the radio in an office raffle, had brought it home after work one day and simply handed it to me. No consultations with my mother, no waiting for a special occasion, he just gave it to me with a smile, his way of saying I was old enough to have my own radio. I was nine; still young enough to believe my father had all the answers.

I used to challenge him. "You know everything," I'd say.

"No one knows everything," he'd modestly reply.

Then I'd ask him something I thought was really difficult.

"How come fishes can breathe under water and people can't?"

He would patiently explain the difference between lungs and gills. "Take a fish out of the water and it doesn't last very long."

It became a game we played. I'd ask—he'd answer. My object was not to stump him, but to prove he did indeed know everything. I don't know at what point I realized he didn't. Probably about the same time I began to think I had all the answers.

In that way, I was a lot like my mother. She always knew what to do; always did what was proper. "Don't point, Willis," she'd admonish my father, "it isn't polite." Or at dinner, "Elbows off the table, you're not at your mother's now."

Over the years she'd worn away whatever confidence Dad had in his own social skills, imposing her standards. In that struggle I'd often been an unwilling pawn, moved about according to her needs.

"You're slurping your soup again Willis," she'd complain. "Even your son knows better than that."

Now my mother was gone, the game had changed. Dad and I would have to work out new rules.

He stepped down from the train, Gladstone bag in one hand, briefcase in the other. The platform was crowded, steam hissed from the engine, and for a moment he didn't see me. His light tan topcoat seemed a size too big for him. He'd lost weight.

"Dad," I shouted. "Over here."

He turned and with a smile of recognition headed my way. He was the only man on the platform wearing a bow tie. He'd always worn one, it was a stubborn fashion statement, a badge that announced there were some things about him no one could change, not even my mother.

We didn't hug or shake hands.

"Want me to take your bag?"

"No, I'm fine," he said. "Why don't you grab us a cab and we'll drop these at the hotel."

"We don't need a cab. We can walk. I booked us into the Lasalle." I pointed across the street. "It's just over there."

The Saturday traffic in Sherbrooke was heavy and Dad and I had to wait for a break to hurry across King Street. I held the hotel door open then followed him in. It took a moment for my eyes to adjust to the gloom of the lobby. It seemed that everything was maroon, from the faded rug to the stuffed chairs to the pattern of the wallpaper. The drapes, pulled tightly across street-level windows, were the only exception. They were a faded yellow, but of such heavy material that very little daylight managed to make it through. From the lounge at the rear of the hotel the smell of cigar smoke and stale beer rode out to meet us on the soundtrack of a TV western.

The lobby was empty; my father put his bag down and hit a small silver bell on the reception desk with the palm of his hand. A moment later a clerk materialized, smoothing back his hair as if he'd been summoned from some slightly disreputable act. He was wearing a maroon uniform.

"Oui, monsieur?" His glance took in both of us, but stayed on my father.

"We have a reservation," Dad said. "A double."

The clerk checked a box of file cards. "The name?"

"Little ... Willis and Andrew Little."

I would have preferred it if Dad had taken a single room at the hotel and I'd remained at Norton Hall. But he'd swept aside that suggestion. "We'll see a lot more of each other this way."

He filled out the registration form in his precise draftsman's hand, then scrawled a signature at the bottom of the page: so neat and at the same time so sloppy. That was Dad, a paradox. As happy tinkering with the intricacies of the FM radio he'd built from scratch as he was spreading manure on the garden beside our house. Whenever I thought of him, my mother was always close by. Now, watching him check into the hotel I was seeing a different person: this man was formal, all business, the Willis-without-Trudy.

We rode the elevator to the third floor. The bellhop carrying the bags was a small, wiry man who whistled softly to himself. A jig or reel, I thought, but I couldn't put a name to it. He inserted a key in the door, swung it open, and ushered us in. I noticed that the maroon of the downstairs décor prevailed here as well.

The bellhop placed the luggage on a foldout rack at the foot of one of the beds. "Will that be all?" His words were flavoured with the faintest trace of an Irish accent. Dad handed him a dollar bill. "Much obliged." The smile he wore could have been part of his uniform. He put the bill into the pocket of his vest. "If you need anything else ... " He indicated the telephone on the bureau between the beds.

"Fine," my father said.

The man touched his hand to his cap and backed out of the room.

It was Dad's first visit to Sherbrooke, so we decided to spend the afternoon sightseeing. The fine weather I'd found so galling in the morning proved a blessing in the afternoon. By the time we were halfway up the hill on King Street, we'd shed our jackets. The October sun was behind us, warming our backs.

When we reached the top, Dad looked out on the valley below, the river, and the profusion of colour. "It's too bad your mother didn't like to travel. She would have loved this."

His words surprised me. Didn't like to travel? That was an understatement. I couldn't see Mom visiting me here at college, much less enjoying the view. About the only time I remember her taking trips from our home in St. Lambert were duty visits to relatives in Detroit and Windsor. Even those were undertaken reluctantly, made possible by an increased dose of the little blue and white capsules she took each night. The past Labour Day weekend we'd tried for a bit of a holiday at a friend's cottage in the country and Mom had been miserable, in bed most of the time. She not only hated travel, she didn't like it when Dad had to go out of town on business.

"You know," my father said, as if reading my thoughts, "there were plenty of times when Trudy could have come along with me on trips. I used to suggest it, but after a while I realized it just upset her, so I stopped asking."

I felt a stab of annoyance. "I didn't know that." My mother never mentioned this. She usually told me things like that. Or so I thought.

The sun slipped behind a cloud and suddenly it was cooler. Dad put his jacket back on. "Trudy was worried when your marks dropped last year," he said. "She was afraid you might miss the chance to get into university."

The wind shifted direction and now bore the sour scent of a distant pulp-and-paper mill. I had an uncomfortable thought. Had my mother really wanted me to go away to college? She didn't like it when Dad had to travel, but as long as I remained home she'd never been really alone. Bishop's changed that. Why had she encouraged me to go? I could have gone to university in Montreal. Would she have been alive today if I'd remained at home?

Thankfully, my father's next remark moved us away from the subject. "Most of the street names here seem to be English ... Wellington, King ... "

"A lot of the original settlers were Loyalists. They came here during the American Revolution."

I was glad it was my father's first time in Sherbrooke. I was only too happy for the chance to play tour guide. It provided a safe topic for conversation.

By late afternoon it was clear that our Indian Summer was over, and I seemed to be coming down with a cold. My nose was running and my sinuses were blocking up. We decided it was time for some supper. It was early and the restaurant in the New Sherbrooke Hotel wasn't crowded.

"Table for two, sir?" the maitre d' asked, and added, without waiting for an answer, "Right this way." His accent was French, his English impeccable.

He ushered us to a spot near a window. The high ceilings and thick carpets and drapes muted the conversations of the few patrons already seated. The clink of glasses, the occasional scrape of knives and forks on plates were the only sounds that carried. The smell of food filled the room, but the identity of individual dishes was hard to distinguish. Turkey, of course, and something sweet.

Our table was set for two, but I knew there would be three of us for dinner: the father, the son, and the Holy Ghost. My mother's memory was always strongest at mealtime. It hovered over us as we self-consciously ordered. The etiquette was pure Trudy. Linen napkins carefully spread on our laps. No elbows on the table. Soup spooned away from (and never toward) the diner. Rolls politely passed (and never reached for). The right fork selected for the salad and, when the main course was complete, cutlery placed neatly across the centre of the plate to signal to the waiter we were ready for dessert.

We not only ate by my mother's rules that night, our conversation reflected her sense of decorum; no mention was made of the circumstances surrounding her death. Dad was trying to forge something new between us, but I felt he was using pieces that were left over from a life that no longer existed. He seemed unwilling to acknowledge that without Trudy, we simply didn't fit together. Not yet, anyway. It was hard to talk; my throat was sore now and I hoped I wasn't coming down with the flu. Dad suggested a little brandy after supper. I wondered if my mother would have approved.

We sipped Remy Martin and looked out the window. It was evening, and outside, collars were turned up against the wind. The tail lights of cars flared as they braked at the intersection. We didn't own a car. It was my father's conviction that taxis were cheaper. Whenever he was in a hurry and there wasn't public transportation available, he'd call a cab. We'd even taken a taxi to the cottage where we'd spent the Labour Day weekend. This evening I wanted nothing more than a cab ride to Bishop's and the sanctuary of my room.

"Still getting along with your roommate?" Dad had suggested we invite Carl MacCallum to dinner, but he'd gone home for Thanksgiving.

"Yes, Carl's great. He'll be sorry he missed this," I gestured to the table, "especially with cafeteria food the way it is."

"I guess that's one thing about college that hasn't changed," my father chuckled.

Dad and I had been careful with each other since Mom died, avoiding issues that might flare into disagreement. There had been many of those in recent years—my duck's ass haircut, pegged pants, and lackadaisical study habits. His insistence that I take Science, when what I really wanted was Arts. Now we were two icebergs floating side by side, hoping that time and small talk would wear down the rough edges, allowing us to exist without biting into each other.

SHERBROOKE, SEPTEMBER 1953

WE FINISHED OUR DRINKS and decided to call it a night. Dad paid the bill; we left the New Sherbrooke and hurried across the street to the Lasalle Hotel. Dad had to clamp his hand on his fedora to prevent it from blowing off. The maroon lobby welcomed us. Live music had replaced the TV sound filtering in from the lounge. A piano, backed by a bass and drums, was working its way through "A Foggy Day." Imitation Brubeck.

Inside our room I quickly changed into my pyjamas, brushed my teeth, and climbed into bed. I shuddered with chills. In a way I was grateful; they gave me an excuse for silence. Our room was standard issue, complete with the faint smell of sweat from previous occupants. Dad sat reading the newspaper and smoking in an easy chair. He'd opened the window a crack and I could hear the murmur of traffic from the street below. It mingled with the riffling sound of pages turning and soon I drifted off.

I dreamed I was back home in St. Lambert, swimming in the St. Lawrence River. My mother stood on the shore, calling me. She was afraid of the swift current and didn't want me venturing too far. I let the current take me downstream, my mother's figure getting smaller and smaller in the distance until I could no longer hear her voice. Suddenly a roaring sound filled the air. I sat upright in the darkness, the dream a memory but the sound still there. An empty glass on the bedside table vibrated.

"It's just a train Andy," my father said from the bed next to mine. "Go back to sleep." I could see the faint glow of his cigarette.

The whole room now shook with the rumble of the passing freight. The luminous dial on my watch read two-thirty. I wondered if the train had wakened Dad or if he had yet to fall asleep. I decided not to ask. He took a last drag, found the ashtray, and ground out his cigarette. I rolled over, faced the wall, and tried to get back to sleep, but as the sound of the train faded the memory of another rude middle-of-the-night wakening replaced it.

It happened three years ago. I'd gone to bed early, tired from working long hours as a summer lifeguard. I'd been locked in a deep dreamless sleep when there was a sudden crack, like a cannon shot. Had I heard glass breaking? I wasn't sure. I was awake, but still groggy. A figure pushed open the door to my room. It was Dad.

"Quick," he said. "I need you." There was something urgent in his voice, something I'd never heard before, a sense of fear around the edge of the words.

I tumbled out of bed and followed my father into the large upstairs hall. The frosted glass panel in the bathroom door had been shattered and light spilled out across the floor. There, face down on a small circular rug, lay my mother. She was naked. There was water on the floor and shards of glass everywhere.

"She ... she was taking a bath. She must have fallen asleep in the tub ..." My father looked at me helplessly, his hair tousled, his hands at his sides, dripping water and blood. "The bathroom door was locked, I had to break the window to get in."

I knelt down, pulled the wet hair from the side of my mother's face and checked to make sure she hadn't swallowed her tongue. Then I straddled her, my weight on her buttocks, my hands resting just below her shoulder blades. Her body felt cool beneath me. I was about to push down when she gave a slight cough. I felt her shudder under my hands as she tried to draw air into her lungs. She coughed a second time, then retched and vomited green bile onto the rug. I pressed down gently and counted to myself ... one, two, three, four ... then relaxed the pressure. Her back rose, her breath caught, sputtered, halted.

"Don't stop." My father knelt beside us.

I repeated the process. This time Mom's breath continued on its own, ragged at first, like a poorly tuned engine. The sour smell of the vomit mingled with the sharp scent of blood and I felt a wave of nausea. Gradually her breathing settled into a shallow but regular pattern. She shivered and I could see goose bumps on her back. I realized for the first time that I was naked too, had worn no pyjamas that hot summer night.

"Get a blanket, Dad," I said. "I think she's going to be OK."

In our hotel room the rumbling of the train had subsided; the only sound was my father's deep regular breathing as he slept. I tried to clear my mind of the memory of my mother on the floor bleeding, fighting for her life. It was no use; I had to let the sequence play itself out.

Dad and I alternated shifts at her bedside; the doctor insisted someone be with her at all times until she regained consciousness. On the second day after what we were now calling "the accident" my mother stirred and opened her eyes. For a moment she didn't say anything, just stared at the ceiling. Then, in a voice so low and raspy I had trouble understanding, she muttered something. I leaned closer. She spoke the words again.

"I'd like ... a drink."

I poured water from the pitcher by her bed into a glass and lifted her head from the pillow. She closed her eyes and sipped. Her lips were cracked and it was painful, but she managed to get some down. She motioned with her hand when she'd had enough and I let her head down gently onto the pillow.

By the next day she was able to drink soup and within the week she was back on her feet. That was it. We never spoke of the incident again. It was as if she'd merely had the flu.

I rolled over in the narrow hotel bed determined to get some sleep, but there was something still bothering me, something I couldn't quite bring into focus. I lay there trying to work it out. Then my father began to snore and at that moment I realized what it was. Not the memory of the awful night or the days that followed; it was the room I was sharing with my father. I didn't belong here.

One night not long after my eighth birthday I woke in my bed screaming. I'd had a nightmare, and while I couldn't remember what frightened me, I still felt the fear. I slipped out of bed and hurried across the hall to my parents' room, where I had always sought comfort on occasions like this.

Tonight it was different.

"You're too old to be running in here every time you have a bad dream," my father said angrily. "Go back to your own room and get to sleep. We all have nightmares, you can't let them upset you."

I returned, frightened and crying, to my bed.

From my room, I'd heard the whispered sounds of my parents arguing. I knew my mother was pleading my case. It was one of the few arguments she lost. From that night on my nightmares had to be endured alone. I didn't belong in their room.

I didn't belong in this room either, here with my father, but in time I did manage to get back to sleep.

I woke to the buzz of Dad's Schick shaver from the bathroom. There was a knock on the hotel room door. I swung my feet out of the bed and padded across the floor.

"Room Service," said a voice in the corridor. I turned the key. It wasn't the bellhop from the previous night. This man was younger and his face gave off the scent of after-shave lotion. He pushed a trolley into the room. "Would you like me to pour the coffee?"

"No thanks," my father said, emerging from the bathroom. He reached into the pocket of his pants, folded on the back of a chair, took out a five-dollar bill, and handed it to the man. "Keep the change."

"Thank you, sir." With the obligatory smile the bellhop left the room, closing the door gently behind him.

"Are you up for some breakfast?" Dad removed one of the silver warming covers from a plate of scrambled eggs.

"I guess so." I was surprised that I was hungry.

"How's the cold?" My father was pouring himself a cup of coffee.

"It seems better. The chills are gone." I was still stuffed up, but I no longer had a fever.

"Have some orange juice, it's fresh."

I sipped from the chilled glass—so much better than the canned juice we were served at college. "I guess I don't have the flu, it's just a cold."

"Well, eat up," he smiled. "Feed a cold, starve a fever." He forked some scrambled eggs into his mouth.

We ate in silence. It was a good breakfast. Crisp bacon, eggs decently scrambled, toast and marmalade. When we finished eating, we sat back and sipped our coffee. Dad lit a cigarette.

"What's the agenda for today?"

"I thought you'd like to see the campus." I moved to the window and pulled aside the curtains. "It's cooled off." The sky was overcast. "They say it may rain this afternoon."

"Well," my father said, "we'd better get a move on then."

LENNOXVILLE, QUEBEC, OCTOBER 1953

BISHOP'S WAS DESERTED; almost everyone had gone home for the Thanksgiving weekend and I was thankful. The fewer introductions I had to make the better. Dad simply didn't fit in here, wasn't part of the new life I was trying to make for myself.

"Great view." He was looking out the window of my room.

Below stretched the green of the quadrangle and beyond it McGreer Hall, a century-old red brick residence that had housed the university's first students. To the left was a newer building, the library. It had been grafted on to McGreer Hall and it had the not-quite-right look of an artificial limb. It was hoped that in time, when the ivy on the walls matured, it would blend in.

"I'm glad you've decided to stay on here," Dad said. "It's what Trudy would have wanted."

I'd offered to drop out of Bishop's after my mother's death. It was a reflex reaction, an attempt to console my father in his time of need. It was made in good faith, like so many other offers at the time, but it didn't have any staying power. Now, I had trouble believing I'd actually suggested it.

"Would you like to do the pictures?" I was trying to sound casual. "The darkroom is downstairs."

My father turned to face me, his figure silhouetted against the window. "Yes ... " he said quietly. He paused, as if he'd been searching within himself, then repeated, " ... yes, I would."

It was going to be a bittersweet experience. The pictures, taken the day I left for college, had not yet been printed. I'd used a Voigtländer Bessa II, my high school graduation gift. They'd been shot that last morning in front of our house on Merton Avenue.

As I opened the door to the college darkroom we were greeted by the familiar vinegar smell of acetic acid. Inside I hit the light switch.

Dad took in the dimensions of the room. "You have a lot more space here than at home."

"We need it," I said. "The college paper prints its pictures here and so does the yearbook. It can be a pretty hectic place at times."

From beneath a table I pulled out the wooden butter box I used to store my photographic chemicals. I took the bottles I needed and placed them on the shelf above a long stainless steel sink. "I miss having my own darkroom." I turned on the hot water tap. "Some of the people using the equipment don't know much about photography." I rinsed out three white enamel trays. "I'm a little nervous when I develop anything here. We are supposed to use our own chemicals, but it doesn't always work out that way."

I ran water into a glass beaker, added Dektol paper developer, and poured the solution into the first tray. "I don't really mind people borrowing, as long as they know what they're doing." I added an ounce of the pungent acetic acid to a quart of water in the second tray. "If they forget which chemical is which when they pour them back, you've got a big problem." I added pre-mixed hypo to the third tray and ran my hands clean under the tap. As I towelled them dry I turned to look at Dad. "Can you get the lights?" I wasn't sure if he'd been listening. "The switch is beside you on the wall."

"Oh, sure." He flicked them off and we waited a few seconds to let our eyes adjust to the darkness, then I turned on the safelight. The darkroom was suffused with a soft red glow.

"I developed the negatives last week with fresh chemicals and they look pretty good." I selected one from an envelope and slipped it into the enlarger. A foot switch sent light through the film and the enlarger lens onto the easel below. I adjusted a knob and an image of my mother and I snapped into focus, its black and white tones reversed. Dad moved beside me and we both stood, staring down.

"What do you think?" he asked, uncertainly.

"Exposure looks okay." I bent closer to fine-tune the focus. "Sharp as a tack." I reached for the lens. "We'll close down three stops." I was talking to myself as much as to my father. "We'll try twenty seconds at f-8." I hit the foot switch, the image disappeared, and I reached into a drawer beneath the enlarger for a box of 8 x 10-inch Kodabromide printing paper. My father moved back to a position behind me and waited. I took a sheet of paper from the box and slid it into the easel, pressed the foot switch again, and stood back. The only sounds were the faint hum of the enlarger fan and the tick of the timer, counting down the seconds. When the time was up the enlarger light snapped off and I took the paper from the easel. I slipped it into the developer and once again Dad moved beside me.

For a few seconds all we could see was a blank sheet, submerged in solution. Then, slowly, details began to emerge. Blacks first, then greys. I gently agitated the tray. In the photograph Mom and I stood side by side on the walk in front of our house. Dad had taken the picture. My mother's wan smile looked up at us, her black-and-white features bathed in the blood-red illumination of the safelight.

"Well? " I realized I'd been holding my breath.

My father stared down for a moment. "Trudy," he said softly.

I lifted the print from the developer, put it into the stop bath, and a few seconds later transferred it to the hypo. Behind me my father lit a cigarette, shielding the flame in the darkroom the way he would in the wind. I hit the lights.

We both stood at the sink, looking at Mom's picture. Her smile provided no hint of what she'd been planning. She'd always been good at hiding things.

LENNOXVILLE, 1953

I WAVED GOODBYE from the railway platform as Dad's train pulled away from the station, heading back to Montreal. As it receded in the distance, I felt better and better. I'd been tense during his visit. It was only when the last car disappeared around a bend in the track that my body relaxed completely. The locomotive gave two short blasts of its whistle and I turned and walked to the row of taxis waiting on Wellington Street.

"Bishop's," I said to the driver and slid into the back seat.

"The university or the school?" he asked.

"Oh, sorry. The university." I was a little annoyed that I'd been mistaken for a high school student. Bishop's College School was just across the St. Francis River from the university and this was a source of confusion to people unfamiliar with the Eastern Townships. To dispel any impression of my status I lit a cigarette and inhaled deeply. Out the window I could see wind ruffling the river's surface, sun reflecting flickering pinpoints of light. It was odd, I thought, how Dad and I were literally moving in opposite directions at this moment; he was on his way home to St. Lambert and I was bound for Bishop's. It felt good to be returning to the life I'd just begun. I wondered how Dad felt. Was he beginning a new life too, free from worry for the first time in years? I remembered a long conversation I'd had with my mother the previous summer.

"You know," she said, looking at her glass of lemonade, "I've often thought your father would be better off without me."

We were sitting at the table in the kitchen. I sipped my drink tentatively. I didn't know how to respond.

"In fact, I've told him so."

Throughout the house, shades were drawn and windows closed to keep out the heat of the summer sun. It worked; the old house had retained the cool of the previous evening, but at a cost. It was gloomy in the half-light and I felt closed in.

I rattled the ice cubes in my drink. "I haven't heard him complaining." I was hoping to move the conversation to safer ground.

"I wouldn't blame him if he started seeing someone else," Mom said softly, almost to herself. She was wearing white shorts and a pink cotton blouse, open at the throat. Her tanned legs were crossed and one sandal dangled loosely from a foot as she nervously swung it back and forth. "I haven't given him much satisfaction."

I shifted uncomfortably on my chair.

She looked up at me and, sensing my embarrassment, smiled. "I shouldn't be bothering you with this." She reached across the table and patted my arm. Her freshly painted nails were a perfect match for her lipstick.

"I never thought of you ... of Dad ... that way," I lied.

She smiled knowingly. She always knew when I wasn't telling the truth. "Oh, you'd be surprised," she said with a grin. This was better. The strongest link my mother and I shared was our sense of humour. It was occasionally beyond my father's comprehension, as if we'd developed a secret language, one he never understood.

In Lennoxville my taxi turned left at the main intersection, bumped over two sets of railway tracks, and coasted down a hill. I flicked my cigarette out the window. Ahead, just across a bridge, was the university. There was something welcoming about the cluster of old brick buildings that nestled comfortably at the junction of the Massawippi and St. Francis Rivers. To me it looked the way a university should, with its old-fashioned quadrangle, Victorian residences, and Gothic-arched chapel.

I paid the cab and entered Norton Hall. A column of windows fronted the stairs and each landing provided a slightly different perspective on the campus. I paused on the third floor. The sun had been playing a game of hide-and-seek with the leaden, rain-bearing clouds all afternoon. It broke through now, backlighting a line of spruce trees that rimmed the hills overlooking the university. It would have made an interesting photograph, but I had something more important to do.

In my room I shucked off my raincoat, turned on a reading light, and sat down in a chair by the window. I opened a copy of *The South Shore Courier.* My father had handed it to me just before he boarded the train. "There's a piece in it about Trudy," he said with a smile. "Let me know what you think."

I found the story. It was Syd Gross's weekly column. Syd's columns had never been popular in our house. My mother was fond of picking out the grammatical mistakes he made each week, while my father liked to count the typos. I began to read with mixed feelings.

> Just a guy talking to himself ... There must have been a couple of hundred folks in the stands at last Saturday's football game at Lesperance Field. Yet even if it had been Yankee Stadium and you had your choice of any seat in the Park, you still would have wanted to sit up there with the Lovely Lady who had charmed so many in the community-at-large. So, just as on dozens of other similar occasions, you sought out that Lovely Lady. There was no way of knowing at the time how precious those few moments

> would be. Two days later came paralyzing, unbelievable news that the lovely lady had passed on, that the brightest shining star in your own special world had sputtered out.

My eyes filled with tears. Someone was publicly acknowledging my mother's worth. There'd been no eulogy at her private funeral and the service had been held in Montreal, not St. Lambert where we lived. It was as if we were somehow ashamed of the way she died. Strange that the tribute came from Syd Gross, a columnist whose writing my mother disliked.

> Working under a far greater strain than any of us ever realized, she had been an inspired leader in the field she loved—the furtherance of healthful recreation for youngsters and a wonderful spirit of sportsmanship and co-operation ... among those of us who head the various groups.

Well, it wasn't elegant writing, but there was no doubt the sentiment was heartfelt. And it also acknowledged the dark side to my mother's life, the side she kept so well hidden from the public. I had never known her to let her illness get in the way of the things she undertook for the sake of the community.

> She did not seek roles—they sought her out. She would've preferred to help in a modest way while others more appreciative of the spotlight took the laurels. Time after time she sought to project others into major roles, only to be left saddled with many of the myriad of duties herself when less dedicated volunteers let her down.

When people disappointed my mother she often blamed herself, as if she were somehow at fault for failing to properly motivate them. But she hid the hurt well, wearing a smile along with her makeup any time she ventured out. My mother was good-looking. I knew from snippets of overheard conversations that more than a few of my male buddies harboured lustful thoughts about her. Syd Gross had clearly wrestled with the same problem.

> A trim little figure and pretty as a picture. You couldn't help feeling, as no doubt many others felt too, that somehow she was your own special girlfriend, who inspired only the noblest and finest sentiments of which you are capable. I have to go way back to my own beloved Mom, who also died before her time as we on earth figure things, to find a parallel for some of the things the Lovely Lady made me feel way down inside. (Wipe away that tear, you dope—you get paid for writing.)

Syd was never one to hide his feelings. I smiled in spite of myself. I'm not sure what my mother would have made of that paragraph. Dragging his mother into the column might have prompted something about how self-centred he always was. And I suspect my father would have objected to the part about wiping away tears. Crying was something men didn't do.

> Strangely enough, I was already working on a modest little memorial of sorts to the Lovely Lady while she was still with us. Time after time I'd seen her officiating in the cold driving rain which too often accompanies local swim meets, efficiently keeping records, handing out the prizes and so forth, her smile shining through the gloom.

I remembered those swim meets. She'd become involved when I developed an affinity for water. From the time I was eight until I turned twelve I spent virtually every summer swimming in the St. Lawrence River. I think her original involvement was personal. It was a way of keeping an eye on me. Raised on Lake Erie, she was never comfortable with the swift current of our river. For a long time she fretted about my venturing too far from shore. It was only when I began to win races that she finally relaxed. Gross brought up something else, something I'd forgotten.

> And remember the time I got the idea of trying to introduce figure skating in St. Lambert? I turned to the Lovely Lady first, even though the sport was strange to her. She lent her inspiring support and I knew it was a cinch from then on. Without detracting one whit from the effort of the other folks involved, I can safely say that without the Lovely Lady there would've been no figure skating and, directly or indirectly, this goes for the success of many other worthwhile efforts in town.

That would have been the first year St. Lambert held a winter Mardi Gras carnival. Mom blackened our faces with burnt cork. She went dressed as Aunt Jemima on skates, pushing a baby carriage. Just before the final judging she threw back the coverlet and I jumped out, her Little Black Sambo, and did a quick lap around the rink. I must have been ten. We won top prize and a lot of laughs.

> To the Lovely Lady's immediate family I won't even try to extend an awkward attempt at condolence. I wouldn't know how to begin. The loss to every single child in the Lovely Lady's own community and to the hundreds more who came within the sphere of her influence is an irreparable one. Her wonderful

> kindly spirit was electric. The inspiration of her cherished memory points the way to all of us to carry on, in the face of any and all difficulties, toward the same unselfish goals toward which she blazed the trail.

I put the newspaper down. Out the window the sun had set behind the ridge of spruce, the sky was pink, the clouds had gone, and the deserted campus was shadowed in darkness. Tomorrow night, when the rest of the students were back, lights would be on and things would return to normal. For now, I was grateful for the stillness of the moment.

I think my mother would have been happy with Syd Gross's tribute. Embarrassed at the attention perhaps, but probably more than a little proud. I know I was. I'm sure Dad was too. I bet this was one column where he hadn't counted the typographical errors.

LENNOXVILLE, OCTOBER 1953

A CLUSTER OF STUDENTS made their way across the quadrangle, their black gowns billowing behind them as they hurried through the dying sunlight, racing their own long shadows along the paths to the chapel.

"Must be Divines," I said.

Carl MacCallum moved to the window of the room we shared in Norton Hall. He was tall, just over six feet, and had a reserve that I hadn't yet penetrated. Two years older than I was, he seemed a great deal more sophisticated. We watched the last of the gowned students disappear through the back entrance of the chapel. "They look like a flock of ravens."

"Nevermore," I cracked, "with apologies to Edgar Allan Poe."

Carl laughed. Behind the reserve I'd detected a well-developed sense of humour.

"Never-me, you mean," he said. "Can you imagine mandatory chapel attendance?" He shook his head. "Those poor buggers." He looked at his watch. "Well, while they are praying, I'll be eating." He crossed the room and opened the door to the corridor. "Coming?" He paused at the door

"No, you go ahead." I remained at the window. "I'll catch you later." The door closed and I was alone in the room.

The last echo of the chapel bell faded, replaced by the sound of a hymn floating across the quad. "Rock of Ages." Divines, young men studying for the Anglican priesthood, made up a quarter of the student body at Bishop's. The chapel was a focal point of their university life. Mine seemed to be the gymnasium. It was there that I went each day to grieve for my mother. While the Divines lit candles, I shot baskets.

It was a ritual developed by chance. Wandering the campus a few days after my mother's funeral I discovered that the door to the gym was unlocked. The building was empty, the basketball court deserted. The parquet floor, polished to a high sheen, was bathed in the natural light that poured in through a bank of windows. I bounced a ball a few times and the sound had a hypnotic effect. It filled some of the emptiness I felt. I moved to the foul line, lined up a shot, and let it go. It banked in off the backboard. I moved to a new spot and shot again and again, not moving to the next position on the floor until I made a basket. In time, I worked my way around the court and was back where I started. The routine had a soothing effect on me and I resolved to return.

In this way, the gym became my church. Since most of my classes were in the morning, I'd head there after lunch. I always began the ritual at the same place—the foul line. I'd shoot until I made a basket, then move and shoot again. My attention would switch back and forth from concentration on the ball as I lined up the shot, to memories of my mother as I retrieved it. As I worked my way around the court, the lines on the floor became the threads of my personal rosary, the basketball shots the beads. It didn't matter how long it took to make them; it was the routine that counted.

The ball arced through the air, rimmed out, and rolled to the wall.

What had been the exact nature of my mother's illness?

"Anxiety neurosis" was the term she used. There had even been a certain degree of pride in her voice. "It's nothing common," she'd said, "not something you can cure with antibiotics."

It took me two tries to sink a reverse lay-up. A difficult shot.

What were my father's feelings about Mom's illness?

"Trudy suffered a nervous breakdown," he'd explained, as if he was describing the failure of a piece of electronic equipment. It was seldom discussed.

I dribbled the ball out past the key, took a deep breath to relax myself, and let it go. Swish. Nothing but net.

When did I realize there was "something wrong" with my mother?

We were packing for our move from Ottawa to Montreal. I was seven, sitting on a steamer trunk while my parents piled up cardboard cartons near the door.

"I thought we'd be going back to Toronto," my mother complained. "You never mentioned Montreal." She spoke the word "Montreal" as if it left an unpleasant taste in her mouth.

"Well," my father countered, "Montreal does have some of the best doctors in the country."

"For what?"

"For your ... " he paused, seeking the right word. " ... for your condition."

"Is that what I am, Willis?" My mother was really angry now. "Is that what I've become? 'A condition?'" she snarled. "YOUR ... condition?"

It was time for some movement. I dribbled the length of the court, pulled up just outside the foul line for a fade-away jumper. It hit the side of the backboard with a clang and bounced harmlessly into a corner of the court.

"Shit." I heard my voice echo in the empty gym.

Was anyone responsible for my mother's condition?

I was nine the summer I accidentally overheard my aunts talking during a vacation by the lake. They were on the porch, drinking gin and tonic in the fading evening light. I was supposed to be swimming with my cousins, but I'd come back to get a dry towel in the room just off the porch.

"Isn't there anything we can do?" I recognized Aunt Claire's voice.

Another voice: "I don't know, she's seeing a very good doctor." This would be Aunt Alice, a nurse. "He says these things take time."

"Time?" a third voice queried. "It's been nine years, for goodness sake." It was Doris speaking now, my mother's oldest sister.

"She used to be so much fun," Alice sighed, "always the life of the party. I just wish she'd get back some of that spark."

"You know, she's never been the same," Claire said, "not since Andy was born."

I had heard enough. I slipped quietly from the cottage and headed down to the lake.

It was getting late and I wanted to get in some lay-ups with my left hand before calling it a day. I did a crossover dribble, then drove for the basket, jumped, and let it go. The ball caught the rim and dropped through. A good way to end the session. As I slipped into my Bishop's windbreaker I was aware of the faint smell of sweat lingering in the gym. If I'd been in the chapel it might have been incense.

LENNOXVILLE/ST. LAMBERT, QUEBEC 1953

AT THE END OF OCTOBER I reluctantly went back home for the first time since my mother's funeral. Reluctantly, because I liked the way my new life at university was giving me control over my grief. No one at Bishop's had met my mother; in St. Lambert it seemed everyone knew her. There would be more condolences and more questions.

The train picked up speed as it pushed north through the farmland of the Eastern Townships toward Montreal. A heavy rain the previous night had washed the last of the fall colour from the trees and stained the exposed soil a deep, rich shade of brown. From my seat in the coach I watched a yellow school bus make its way slowly along a muddy road, the driver being careful to avoid the deepest ruts. I, too, was going back to school, back to St. Lambert for my high school graduation.

I took a pint of Seagram's VO from my jacket pocket, broke the Quebec Liquor Commission seal with my thumb nail, unscrewed the cap, and tilted the bottle to my lips. Straight rye whisky always caught in my throat when I swallowed it and I liked the instant hit it provided. Mixed with Canada Dry ginger ale, it was Dad's favourite drink and it had been the first hard liquor I'd tasted. I was taking another pull on the rye when the door at the near end of the car opened, engulfing us in a blast of cool moist air. The conductor pushed his way in and the door slammed shut behind him. I slipped the bottle back into my pocket. Had he seen me?

"Tickets please, billets, s'il vous plaît," he called as he made his way along the aisle. When he reached my seat he bent to look out the window. "Nasty out there."

Sheets of rain pelted the glass and beads of moisture danced along the pane. The conductor's heavy blue uniform was damp and smelled of wet wool and stale cigar smoke. "You know," he said as he punched my ticket, "you can buy drinks in the club car." He handed my ticket back with a wink and moved on. I decided to take his advice; I rose from my seat and worked my way back along the swaying train.

The club car was almost deserted. It smelled of polished wood. A few middle-aged men sat reading papers. It was so quiet I could hear the chatter of ice as the bartender at the other end of the car mixed a martini. Individual leather chairs lined the interior. I sank into one and swivelled it for a better view out the window. A white-jacketed waiter materialized.

"Rye and ginger."

"Yes, sir." He was back within minutes with my drink. He placed a glass tumbler on the lacquered tray that folded out from the window frame. In the bottom of the glass two fingers of rye trembled with the vibration of the train. The waiter used tongs to add ice, then with a flourish produced a small bottle of ginger ale, uncapped it, and began to pour, watching me for the signal to stop. The train lurched, but the waiter didn't break eye contact, shifting his weight effortlessly, retaining his balance as well as his composure.

"That's fine." I reached into a pocket for money.

The waiter raised a palm in protest. "You're going to Montreal?"

"St. Lambert."

He nodded as if this was knowledge he already possessed. "We can settle up later then." He placed what remained of the ginger ale on the tray. "Will that be all?" he asked, and when I nodded he was gone.

I spent the rest of the trip in the comfort of the club car. I looked through a copy of *The Montreal Star*, scanning the headlines. Korean peace talks dominated the front page. I looked for the sports section. The main story was about a football game played in the rain. The Montreal Alouettes had beaten the Toronto Argonauts in a mud bowl at Delormier Stadium. It was too early in the season to take hockey seriously, but I did read Red Fisher's column on the new crop of rookies in the NHL.

From time to time the rain chattered at the windows and the dozing passengers shifted in their seats. I discovered that to order another drink I had only to press a tiny pearl button embedded in the panel beside my chair.

ST. LAMBERT, OCTOBER 1953

OUR HOUSE ON MERTON AVENUE was a side-by-side semi-detached, set back a good twenty-five feet from the street. Built in the twenties, it was a simple shoebox of brick, divided down the middle to accommodate two families. A hedge of yew separated our front lawn from the neighbour's. It thrived in the shade of the Norway maple that grew on our side of the yard. High up on the trunk of that tree, out of sight, were my initials, etched into the bark. I'd carved them the day we moved in, ten years ago, with a new pocketknife. The tree was bare now and its branches reached beyond the house and into the overcast sky. In the hedge tiny red berries, wet from the recent rain, glistened like points of fire.

Looking at the house I sensed a change. What was it? It hadn't been freshly painted; the wooden veranda was still the same durable shade of brown. The lawn was mowed to a uniform height; the hedge to the left of the property had been clipped. There'd been no new features added. Nothing was out of place. What was it that was different?

I mounted the steps, put the key into the lock, turned, and pushed inside. I stood for a moment in the entranceway, listening. The only sound was the faint hum of the refrigerator. I stifled the urge to call out a hello. I knew there would be no reassuring reply from my mother. No, of course not. I put down my suitcase, hung up my raincoat, and moved through the large interior hall, with its open fireplace, into the dining room. A hand-written note was propped against a glass on the table. It was from Dad.

"Welcome home," it read. "I'll try to make the five-thirty train. Supper at six?"

I looked at my watch. It was four-thirty. Plenty of time. In the kitchen I took a half-full bottle of Seagram's VO from a cabinet over the sink and poured a shot of rye into a glass. Then I turned on the tap, measured out an equivalent amount of water in another glass and carefully poured it back into the bottle, topping up the VO to its previous level. It was an old trick and a good one, as long as you didn't get greedy.

The kitchen was spotless, everything in place. In the refrigerator there was a can of Carnation condensed milk, a half-dozen eggs, some Maple Leaf bacon and a tin of grapefruit juice, its top punched open with twin triangular perforations. On the bottom shelf were two quart bottles of O'Keefe's Old Vienna beer. No ginger ale. I decided to drink the rye neat.

In the living room I sat and sipped in my father's favourite spot, an over-stuffed easy chair. I put my feet up on the coffee table. It used to be against the rules, but my mother was no longer around to enforce them. I switched on the radio and Mozart flooded the room. It was no surprise; Dad worked for the CBC and while he didn't particularly care for classical music, he kept the radio tuned to CBM out of loyalty. I turned the dial to CJAD and *Make Believe Ballroom Time.* The radio had been the subject of a running and sometimes heated debate between my parents for years. I looked down at the exposed maze of coloured wires, calibrated dials, and glowing tubes. No cabinet, just a metal base. Dad liked it that way; he was forever soldering in new connections, trying out new tubes—it was a work in progress. My mother didn't agree.

"It's ugly, Willis," she argued. "I'm embarrassed when we have people in."

"Well, it's what I do, Trudy. If it bothers you that much maybe we're inviting the wrong people."

The next day Dad bought an expensive new part for the radio.

"Willis," my mother said, shouting this time, "do you realize what we could have done with that money? Look at this room. We need new slipcovers for the furniture. The carpet is falling apart ... "

As usual she was exaggerating. And to my father's credit he didn't mention the cost of my mother's drugs or her medical bills. He just shook his head and began tinkering with the radio while she glared at him.

"Damn you," she said, and strode angrily from the room.

Dust had collected on the wires of the radio. Mom was right, it was ugly. But it had stayed in the living room—a victory for my father. And it was still here, tubes glowing, music pouring forth.

Fly the ocean in a silver plane,
See the jungle when it's wet with rain.

Jo Stafford was singing her latest hit. The radio did produce great sound. I wondered if Dad still considered its presence in the living room a victory?

I finished my drink and got out of the chair for a refill, but I'd had more than a few on the train so I decided I'd be better off with coffee. A battered aluminum pot sat on the back element of the stove. I emptied the used grounds into a garbage pail beneath the sink and spooned fresh Maxwell House coffee into the percolator. The slogan on the side of the tin read "Good to the Last Drop." Was there a statute of limitations on coffee freshness, I wondered? I added water, turned on the element, and sat down at the kitchen table to wait.

The "something" that had been nibbling at the edges of my consciousness ever since the taxi dropped me off was still there. The place felt different somehow and it wasn't just my mother's absence. I couldn't put my finger on exactly what it was and the booze hadn't helped. Out the window I could see a new apartment building going up a few streets over. Workmen moved back and forth in the fading light. The vacant lots of my childhood were filling up. When the coffee stopped bubbling I poured myself a cup, added some Carnation and stirred. The refrigerator motor shut down and the house was truly quiet for the first time since I'd arrived.

Suddenly I knew what had changed. The silence held the answer. Coming home, opening the front door, there'd been no sense of apprehension. For as long as I could remember the return-from-school ritual had been the same: uncertainty as I entered the house and announced my arrival. The few seconds that followed my "hello" were always a frozen frame of time for me, a moment when everything stood still—my life suspended. It was like those Saturday afternoons at the movies when the projector jammed but the image remained on the screen. Would the projectionist turn off the lamp in time or would the film melt, the picture dissolve before us? When my mother replied from the kitchen, from upstairs, or from the basement, the action would resume. I could get on with whatever I was doing.

This time coming home had been an entirely new experience. There had been no apprehension. No moment of doubt coming in the door. She was dead; it was over. There was sadness now, but at least the uncertainty was no longer there.

The change hadn't been in the house; it had been within me.

Upstairs, I unpacked my suitcase, put on a fresh shirt, and tried to decide which tie to wear for my graduation that night. I'd narrowed the choice down to two possibilities. In the bathroom I checked them out in the mirror. Would it be the new tie in the purple-and-white Bishop's colours or the one my mother had given me last Christmas, grey with blue stripes? I compared them and knew at once it was no contest—my mother's was the winner. Another wave of sadness swept over me and I sat down on the edge of the bathtub. This was the tub where she had tried to end it with sleeping pills just three years earlier.

It had been a humiliating experience for her and she had learned from it. There was to be no mistake the next time. I tried to picture how she'd spent her final hours here, just one month ago.

The stream from the showerhead pulses down as she washes one last time, adjusting the tap, getting the water temperature just right. She is usu-

ally a little uneasy when she is alone in the house, but not today. Her mind is made up and she is at peace. She sways slightly, humming softly to herself as the warm jet massages first one shoulder, then the other. This slow dance continues until the stream begins to cool and she realizes she has used all of the hot water. She turns off the taps, steps from the tub, and reaches for a towel.

She pauses almost instinctively to check herself in the mirror of the medicine cabinet. The image is blurred, softened beyond recognition by the condensed steam from the shower. She rubs at it with her hand to clear the glass, but as quickly as she rubs, it clouds over again. It is as if she doesn't really exist at all.

I left the bathroom, walked into the hall, following her movements as I imagined them that day. The rug was no longer on the floor—it had been thrown out. The blood from her previous suicide attempt, like the memory, couldn't be washed away.

There are faint wet footprints on the hardwood floor. In the bedroom clean underwear, nylons, and a garter belt are laid out on the chenille bedspread. Her towel drops to the floor and she slips into the panties. Sitting down on the edge of the bed, she pulls on her nylons and fastens her bra. Then, crossing to the bureau, she opens the top drawer and takes out two foam rubber inserts, slipping them inside.

Standing there, I flashed back to an afternoon a year ago when I walked into my mother's bedroom unannounced. She was sitting on the edge of the bed, using cuticle scissors to cut the nipples from the falsies. Embarrassed, she said, "They were simply too prominent," and hurriedly put them away. I realized later that while she wanted to look attractive, she didn't want to look aroused.

At the vanity table, she applies Elizabeth Arden lipstick carefully, with particular attention to the upper lip, never full enough for her liking. She takes her best silk blouse from a bureau drawer and buttons it, leaving the neck open. In the closet she removes a skirt and jacket, fresh from the dry cleaner and still smelling faintly of solvent. It is a deep shade of brown, to match the colour of her eyes. She adds a strand of imitation pearls, a graduation gift from her mother. In brown and white patent leather pumps, she pirouettes before the full-length mirror, checking over her shoulder, making sure her seams are straight. She applies a dab of Tweed cologne to her wrists and neck, then from the drawer of her night table she takes an envelope, and with one last, quick glance in the mirror, heads downstairs.

I descended to the dining room. I noticed that Dad had set places for two.

In my mind I see my mother hesitate here, then prop the envelope against a salt shaker.

The name "Willis" is written neatly on it. Then she turns and goes down the stairs into the cellar.

I took a deep breath and continued on down into the basement. This used to be a favourite place, where Dad had his woodworking shop and I had my darkroom. My first prints were made here, using an empty Heinz tomato juice can and our old folding Kodak camera as a makeshift enlarger. But this was no longer a favourite place. It was where the unthinkable had happened. There were cartons of Christmas decorations on the shelf next to the furnace. That was where she'd hidden the Remington rifle.

From a box of shells she takes a single .22-calibre bullet, slips it into the chamber, slides the bolt into place, and clicks the safety off. Then she sits down on a small stool and without hesitation puts the rifle between her knees, taking the barrel into her mouth. The metallic taste is unpleasant, but she doesn't care. With her left hand holding the stock, she reaches down until her right hand finds the trigger guard. She inserts her thumb and pushes down on the trigger.

The bullet tears into the roof of her mouth, through the brain, out the back of her head, and buries itself in the wood of a ceiling beam. The force of the shot topples her off the stool. Dust, dislodged from the beam, drifts down through the gunsmoke, settling on the blood that trickles onto the cement floor from the tiny exit hole in her skull. The acrid smell of cordite mingles with the sweet scent of her cologne.

I don't know if anyone heard the shot. Probably not. The noise made by a .22-calibre rifle, fired in a basement, wouldn't have carried very far. Perhaps Mrs. Curry, the old lady who lived next door, heard something. If she did, she would have cocked an ear, wondering what it was. A car backfiring? When the sound wasn't repeated she would have gone about her business, dusting or washing or listening to the radio. About six o'clock the front door would have opened and my father's slightly off-key, three-note whistle would have broken the silence. It was the way he always announced his nightly return from work.

He hangs his gray fedora on the hook behind the door and leans his battered briefcase against the hall wall. He takes off his suit jacket and loosens his bow tie, then checks the desk beside the fireplace for mail or telephone messages.

"Trudy?" he calls.

No answer.

He walks through to the kitchen and looks out the window. She isn't in the back yard.

"Trudy?" he calls again, and listens.

Silence.

Then he notices the envelope on the table. He feels a prickle of fear as he tears it open. He reads, then rushes down into the basement. He is too late.

It was hard to believe this was where it happened, harder still to imagine how my father must have felt when he discovered her. He'd never given up hope that a cure would be found for her illness.

Upstairs, the front door opened and I heard my father's familiar whistle. I was startled. It was eerie, his arrival now, just as I was picturing how it must have been one month ago.

"I'm downstairs," I called, a little shakily. "I'll be up in a minute."

In the darkroom I ran the tap, rinsed out my mouth, splashed cold water on my face, and towelled off quickly. Then I moved past the furnace and up the stairs.

ST. LAMBERT, OCTOBER 1953

WHEN I TRY TO RECALL details from my high school graduation ceremony a few impressions remain, like half-melted ice cubes in a watered-down drink.

We were seated on the stage of the gymnasium, facing the audience. I know I received more applause than I deserved when the principal, E.Y. Templeton, handed me my diploma. I felt like such a fraud. The ovation wasn't for any academic achievement; the people were clapping because they felt sorry for me. I didn't want their pity.

A few minutes later, when the guest speaker literally turned his back on the audience, I wondered for one brief, alcohol-altered moment if he resented them as much as I did. Then I realized it was merely a gimmick. Wilson Pickett, a banker whose public speaking skills had been honed in a Dale Carnegie course, had dramatically repositioned the lectern to face us, the graduating class of 1953.

"You are the future," he announced, "and so it is to you that I address these words."

I couldn't see beyond the stage lights, but I sensed a ripple of disapproval out there. Nothing overt, just throats clearing nervously and some whispering as parents came to terms with Pickett's unorthodox approach. It was a calculated trick, this turning the tables on the audience, but it's what I remember best about the ceremony.

Pickett was a small man who rocked back and forth on the stage in a vain attempt to gain height. "Whenever you see a sign that reads, 'Don't Touch—Wet Paint,'" he said, sweat beading his forehead, "don't take someone else's word for it. Touch it. Check it out yourself."

He paused, his stare a challenge, as if he expected someone to argue the point. When no one did, he waved his finger at us and boomed, "Always ... Touch ... Wet Paint!"

Then he leaned forward on the lectern and in a voice that was now conversational repeated the phrase. He rubbed a finger and thumb together, examined them, then looked up at us. "It's only paint," he said, and smiled. "You can always wash it off."

When the ceremony was over, we spilled out of the school, our breath clouding the night air, everyone talking. Cigarettes were lit and we piled into waiting cabs and headed across the Victoria Bridge for Montreal. In our taxi we tried humming Elgar's "Pomp and Circumstance" without much luck, dissolving into laughter with each successive failure.

I still had the bottle of rye, thanks to the understanding train conductor and an accommodating club car waiter. I'd been sharing it with Bryce Weir, my best friend, not usually a drinker. But it was a special night for him—he had pulled off the highest marks in our graduating class.

Our first stop was the Chez Paree, a nightclub on Mountain Street. It was crowded and hot; spotlights of colours cut through the smoke-filled air, illuminating the stage. The Andrews Sisters were the featured act, and they had just come on stage as we reached our table.

Drinking rum and Coca-Cola,
Go down Point Khoomahnah
First mother and daughter
Workin' for the Yankee dollar.

It was a fine choice for an opening song and it prompted me to order a rum and coke. It had been my mother's favourite drink and I raised the glass to her in a silent salute. She'd liked the Andrews Sisters.

If things had been different, she might have been up there performing. Mom had been a pop singer in the thirties, before I was born. She had a trio and her own weekly radio show on CKLW, a station serving the Detroit-Windsor area. She put aside her career to have me. It was bad timing. A few months after she quit, my father, who was working as an audio technician for the same station, was laid off. In the midst of the Depression he couldn't find other work. When I was born, my mother suffered a nervous breakdown and never sang professionally again.

I drank down the remaining rum and coke and ordered another. "Make it a double," I said to the waiter.

The next clear memory I have of that night is getting out of a Veteran's Taxi in front of Bryce's house in St. Lambert. For the first time in his life my best friend was drunk—in fact he'd passed out in the back seat of the taxi. I asked the driver to wait, hoisted Bryce on my shoulders, and staggered up his front walk. His mother must have been waiting up for him, because as I approached, the front door magically opened and she ushered me in with a finger to her lips. I deposited Bryce on a sofa in the living room and smiled sheepishly at her.

"Thank you." Her Scottish accent was more pronounced when she whispered. A tiny, round woman, she was no stranger to the problems of drink. Her husband Ernie fancied his "wee drop" as well.

"Can I get you something? A cup of coffee?" she suggested hopefully.

"No thanks," I said. "The taxi is waiting."

I took one last look at Bryce, asleep on the sofa. He was on his back, his shirt collar open, school tie askew, snoring softly. His mother smiled indulgently at him. One of his legs was bent over the arm of the sofa, the other extended to the carpeted floor. His shoes no longer held the high gloss he'd worked so carefully to achieve just a few hours earlier.

Outside, the taxi driver honked. "Gotta go." I gave Mrs. Weir a quick kiss on the cheek. "Goodnight."

"You mean good morning," she laughed. She was right. The street lights had gone out and the sun was beginning its climb in the east. "Thank you again," she called after me.

"It's nothing. He'd have done the same for me."

Bryce had been the first to call on us the morning after my mother's death. He tried his best to console me, but without much luck. "I have to tell you there's a rumour going around." His tone was confidential yet curious.

I looked at him questioningly.

"They say that your mother ... " he paused, embarrassed, then pushed on " ... that she ... that it was suicide."

"That isn't a rumour, Bryce," I said. "That's what happened. She killed herself." It came out matter-of-factly, and I realized for the first time that my father and I were probably the only two people in town who weren't completely surprised by the act.

"Oh," he said, as if he'd been slapped. "Oh, Christ." His cheeks flushed. "Oh, Christ, I'm sorry ... so sorry."

ST. LAMBERT, DECEMBER 1953

IT WAS CHRISTMAS before I managed to get back to St. Lambert again. The term had finished and I dozed most of the train ride home, catching up on some of the sleep I'd missed pulling a series of "all-nighters" to cram for exams. This time I stayed clear of the club car.

At home the scent of pine needles greeted me as I opened the door, bags in hand, a pillowcase of dirty laundry in tow. In the centre of the living room stood a huge, undecorated Christmas tree. It was still thawing out and there were little puddles of water on the floor. Dad emerged from the basement carrying cartons of decorations.

"What do you think?" He put down the boxes on the coffee table, a little out of breath.

"Looks good," I said. "Big." The top of the tree was just inches from the ceiling. "Different." I circled the tree.

"Scotch pine," Dad said proudly. In the past our trees had always been spruce. "I thought it was time for a change." He looked at the tree and then to me, seeking approval.

"It's great." It was fuller than a spruce and would require fewer decorations. Just as well, I thought to myself, since decorating the tree had always been Mom's project.

"I just brought it in." Dad reached out and fingered a branch, testing for ice. "Needs a few more minutes to settle. How about some eggnog?"

"Sure," I said. "Sounds good. Just let me put my bags upstairs first."

In my bedroom I wondered how we'd manage this. Although Christmas Day had always been a difficult time for my mother, she loved the preparations leading up to it. Each year she erected a cotton batten snowman in the bay window, sticking tiny balls on the pane to create the illusion of snow. The presents she gave were wrapped with such care my father used to say it was a shame we had to open them. But the tree was her most significant creation, a work of art. Dad and I had never been more than just helpers.

Downstairs, my father handed me a cup of eggnog. He'd forgotten to add cinnamon, but I let it pass. We opened the dusty boxes that contained the decorations. "Let's work from the top down," he suggested.

"Okay." I reached for a string of lights.

It took us less than an hour to finish and I was surprised at how well we did.

"Not bad." Dad stood back from the tree. "Not bad at all." He stretched to straighten the star on the top branch.

"It looks terrific," I agreed, but not without a pang of guilt. My mother's role had been usurped too easily.

Christmas Eve I'd been invited to a party; I offered to stay home, but Dad insisted I go. He said he had some office work to finish up, but I think he just wanted to be alone. I headed for the party with a twenty-six-ounce bottle of Southern Comfort and a determination to renew friendships with people I hadn't seen since mother's death. By midnight I'd accomplished my goals, we'd finished the Southern Comfort, and I'd passed out on the sofa in the basement recreation room of a friend's house. It was 5:00 a.m. when I finally dragged myself home, determined to be there when Dad woke up.

As it happened, it was Dad who was there when I woke up—at noon on Christmas day. He smiled good-naturedly and made no reference to my obvious hangover. We opened our gifts with mock good cheer, the ritual a sad parody of previous Christmas mornings.

When the last of the wrapping paper had perished in the fireplace, my father took a cigarette from the silver case on the coffee table. "I have something to tell you." He lit up. "I don't want you to worry, but the doctors have discovered something is wrong with my shoulder." He exhaled.

"Something?" I wasn't sure what he meant.

"There's a growth there, a lump."

"What kind of lump?" My hangover suddenly seemed a lot worse.

"It's a tumour."

Now there was a lump in my throat. "A tumour?"

"They've done some tests, a biopsy, and its benign," he said, "but they still want to take it out."

I was in shock. The taste of Southern Comfort rose in my throat. "An operation?"

"Sometime in the New Year," Dad shrugged. "Probably the middle of January. I'll only be in hospital a few days." He took a last puff from his cigarette and ground it out in the ashtray.

"Maybe I should stay home until you have the operation." I was fighting a losing battle with fear.

"Don't be silly." Dad picked up the ashtray, walked to the fireplace, still smouldering from burnt Christmas wrapping paper, and dumped the cigarette butts. The smell made me want to throw up.

"I should be here," I insisted, swallowing hard.

"We aren't even sure of the date." Dad sat back down in his easy chair. "There's no point in you waiting around, missing school." He lit another cigarette. "Go back to Bishop's," he said. "You can come home for a visit when I get out of hospital."

I wanted to share my fear with my father, but that had never been our way. I didn't know how. We didn't talk about fear. If you didn't talk about it, it didn't exist.

LENNOXVILLE/ST. LAMBERT, FEBRUARY 1954

IT WAS THE MIDDLE of February before they operated. My father called me at Bishop's a few hours after the surgery. I hurried to the pay phone down the hall.

"Dad?" I said, a little out of breath.

"It's me."

"How are you?"

"Still in one piece," he paused. "Actually there's a little less of me. They took the tumour out this morning."

Nearby a door opened and the sound of the Duke Ellington orchestra spilled out into the corridor. "Take the A Train." Then the door closed and it was quiet again.

"But you're feeling okay?"

"Just a little groggy, that's all. They've given me something for the pain. I'll be going home tomorrow afternoon."

"What about the operation?" I probed. "How did it go?" Outside I could see snow swirling in the fading evening light. Another storm. We'd had more than our share of snow this winter.

"They say they got it all. They want to do some radiation, just to be on the safe side." There was a pause and a muffled sound as he covered the receiver with his hand. Then he spoke again. "The nurse is here with my supper," he said. "You coming home this weekend?"

"You bet."

"I'll tell you all about it then."

"Good night, Dad."

"Good night, Bub."

Dad always called me Bub when things were tough, whenever he wanted to buck me up. I replaced the phone on its cradle and instinctively checked the coin return.

Nothing.

It was still snowing the next day when my taxi pulled up in front of our house in St. Lambert.

"Bitch of a winter," the cabby said.

The walk was unshovelled, but someone had left faint tracks in the snow. The newspaper boy, I thought. I handed the driver a two-dollar bill and he reached for change. "Don't bother." I got out of the cab.

"Thanks," he called, and I closed the car door. With the collar of my overcoat turned up against the cold, I moved through the snow, following in the footsteps of the newsboy. I paused on the porch, watching the taxi fishtail slightly on the slippery street, then disappear. I stamped my feet on the Welcome mat to get rid of some of the snow. As I opened the front door into the entrance hall, Dad's voice called from the living room.

"That you, Andy?"

"It's me, Pops." I shucked off my flight boots.

"Still snowing?"

"Still snowing." I put down my overnight bag and hung my overcoat in the hall closet beside my father's lambskin jacket. The movement disturbed two empty metal hangers and they pinged when they touched, like the last note of the triangle in a kindergarten music concert. I wondered what Dad had done with Mom's winter coats.

When I went into the living room my father was lying on the sofa, propped up with pillows from the bedroom, his right arm in a sling. A folded copy of *The Montreal Gazette* lay in his lap and an empty coffee cup was on the table before him.

"How's the shoulder?" I sat down in the easy chair opposite him.

There was something different about him. He'd lost weight and his colour was poor, but that wasn't it. Then I realized. He wasn't wearing his bow tie. Of course not. With his arm in a sling he wouldn't be able to tie it. Dad without a bow tie just wasn't Dad. And no clip-on for him, thank you very much, he took too much pride in tying his own.

"It was pretty rough yesterday; I'm better today." He stretched his left arm across his body, reaching awkwardly for the lit cigarette in the ashtray. He winced a little from the effort, but his face relaxed once he drew in the smoke. "They'll take the stitches out next week, then I should be back at work within a day or so." He exhaled and settled back on the pillows.

"Can I get you anything?" I pointed to the cup. "A refill? Something to eat?" I wasn't used to this role, looking after my father.

"No, I'm fine. What about you? I'm afraid the coffee's instant. It was all I could manage."

I went into the kitchen and took down a cup from the shelf over the sink. The water in the kettle was still hot so I added it to the powdered coffee. Looking for sugar, I opened the cupboard by the window. There wasn't much there. A box of Shredded Wheat, a can of Campbell's soup, some Ritz crackers and two tins of Brunswick sardines. I found the sugar bowl and spooned a teaspoon into my coffee, then added milk and went back into the living room.

"You don't have much food."

"Well, I wasn't sure how long I'd be in hospital." He put down the newspaper. "I didn't want things going bad."

"No," I agreed, wondering if the operation was as risk-free as I'd been led to believe. Dad always downplayed things like that. It was a habit, I guess, something he'd acquired living with my mother.

"I'm glad you're home. There's something I've been mulling over, something I wanted to talk to you about."

"Shoot." I sipped my coffee. I noticed his cigarette had gone out in the ashtray.

"I've been thinking. This house ... " he gestured with a wave of his hand, "it's too big for us."

I put down my cup and waited. "Too big for us," he'd said. But "we" weren't living here any more. Mom was gone and so was I, except for the occasional weekend. I thought of him alone, wandering from room to room, looking for something to do, finding only memories. Dad was right. This house, until now more than adequate for our needs, was too big for him.

"They're putting up some new apartments on Green Street," he continued. "I thought we might take a look. Two bedrooms ... you'd still have a room of your own." He looked at me expectantly.

"Sounds all right to me. Why not?" A fresh start would be good for him. "What about our lease?"

"That's no problem. We'd have to give three months notice, but the apartments won't be ready until the spring." He watched me.

Thinking it over, I sipped my coffee.

A new setting for the new lease on life?

"Let's do it."

My father smiled. "I thought you might like the idea." He took another cigarette from the open pack on his lap.

I reached for the Ronson lighter on the coffee table. "Let me do that." The flame touched the end of the cigarette and Dad drew the smoke into his lungs.

"I think a move makes sense." I looked around the room, seeing my mother's touch everywhere. She'd selected the paint for the walls, picked curtains and drapes to match, had the final say on which rugs would grace our hardwood floors. It was Trudy who decided when the furniture needed re-upholstering and chose the pattern and fabric. I knew Dad didn't always agree with her choices, but over the years she'd managed to convince him that he lacked the necessary sense of style to have a say in these matters.

"We won't be able to fit all our furniture into the new place. We'll have to get rid of a lot of stuff." For the first time since my mother's death I could detect a hint of enthusiasm in his voice. It was almost as if he couldn't wait to shed the "stuff." "Since you're home for the weekend, maybe you could get started, help me decide what to keep. There are some trunks in the basement that haven't been opened in a while. I'm not even sure what's in them."

ST. LAMBERT, FEBRUARY 1954

ALTHOUGH I'D LEARNED to appreciate the cellar once my darkroom was built, I'd hated it as a child. Those times when I was asked to get jam or jelly from the preserve pantry downstairs required courage, plunging into the windowless dark, groping like a blind man for the string that hung from an overhead light. The creaks I heard whenever the old house adjusted to outside temperature changes were louder in the basement.

Later all that changed. The darkness was an asset in developing film and I learned to tune out the sounds that had previously frightened me. This was one place in the house that had been truly my father's. It was where he had his workshop with its scarred, rough-hewn benches and power tools, the floor littered with wood shavings and sawdust. Good taste was never an issue here. He could lose himself, be completely at home. When I started printing my own pictures, we came to share the space and it became my place too—our place. It was comforting to hear Dad hammering away while I worked in the darkroom. It even had a scent we shared—the unique blend of the aroma of freshly cut wood and the sharp tang of photo chemicals.

By choosing the basement for her final act, my mother had taken away our sanctuary. I knew by the neglected look of the workshop that it hadn't seen much use since Mom's death. The same could be said for my darkroom. I was doing most of my developing and printing at Bishop's. As I pulled down a trunk from the storage area next to the preserve pantry, I noticed the bottles lining the shelves: pickled beets, strawberry jam, stewed tomatoes, all put up the past summer by my mother. Had she known at the time she wouldn't be around to enjoy them?

As I opened the trunk it gave forth the sharp scent of old newsprint, mingled with the inevitable mustiness of containment. I would divide things into three piles. One would be for "keepers," obviously important papers. A second would for things I wasn't sure about—Dad would have to make a decision about these. The third would be a "throwaway" pile.

On the top layer was a small cardboard box. It had once held kitchen matches, but when I opened it I found a collection of coins, medals, and ribbons. The coins were foreign—from Germany, England, and Sweden. I looked at the inscription on the medals. They described some of Mom's athletic achievements, mostly for track and field events. One read, "Gertrude Champion—First Place—100 Yard Dash—1927."

The ribbons were for first, second, and third place finishes with dates ranging from 1921 to 1927, but no indication of what events they represented.

I put these back into the box and laid it on the concrete floor. A keeper.

Next, I removed a dozen or so large unlabelled manila envelopes. They contained what appeared to be old income tax returns. More keepers.

Next was a bundle of letters tied with a red ribbon. I undid it and selected the first envelope. I recognized the handwriting; it was from Aunt Alice to my mother. The Detroit postmarks were clearly stamped; the letters had begun in 1937, after we'd moved to Toronto. Others had been sent to our Ottawa address during the war. The last envelope, mailed to St. Lambert, bore the date 1953. Mom had apparently kept all of Alice's correspondence. I was tempted to read the letters, but I didn't. The fact that my mother was dead made me shrink from the prospect. It would have been more than a simple invasion of privacy; it would be a desecration of her memory. I put them in the "not sure" pile. Dad could decide.

Beneath the letters lay two large scrapbooks. I opened one. A teenage girl's face stared at me from a photograph. It took me a second to realize who it was. My mother, but a mother I'd never known—a picture taken for her high school yearbook when she was sixteen. A stab of sadness struck. I'd forgotten about these scrapbooks. I turned the page. There was the detailed rendering of a daffodil, its watercolours still vibrant. In the corner, my mother had written her initials, "AGC/24"

She had painted this when she was thirteen. AGC stood for Anna Gertrude Champion. I never heard my mother referred to as Gertrude, it was always Trudy. I knew the story. My grandfather, the Reverend J.B. Champion, had insisted that my mother be named Gertrude, after some distant relative. My grandmother, Blanche, had agreed, on condition that the name Gertrude be used only on documents and formal occasions. To Grandma Champion Mom was always Trudy, and you risked incurring her not inconsiderable wrath if you dared to call her daughter Gertrude.

As a teenager my mother had debated between art and music as a career. She'd chosen music, but had continued to paint in her spare time—at least until I was born. One of her early watercolours hung on our living room wall. I hoped Dad planned to put it up in our new apartment.

I flipped through more pages. There was a 1929 diploma from the Royal Conservatory of Music in Toronto. On the program my mother's name appeared twice: once on the list of graduating students and again in the awards section. She had won a prize for the best original composition that year, and I found myself wondering how the piece had sounded, wishing I could hear it. She'd been seventeen then—the same age I was now.

If she turned up in one of my classes today what would I make of her?

Would we hit it off? Would I find her attractive? Would it go any further than that? These thoughts were making me uncomfortable. I reached for the second scrapbook.

On the first page was a yellowed newspaper clipping announcing the debut of her radio program on station CKLW in Windsor. The headline read "Local Star to Shine," and there was a small picture of my mother and an article about her trio, The Chansonettes. The writer noted that Mom "not only leads the group in song, but conducts and arranges all the music as well." It was the story of a small-town girl who'd made good.

I turned the page, and there was the original 8 x 10 glossy photograph from which the newspaper reproduction had been taken. It was a sepia publicity still, a carefully arranged studio portrait that made my mother look like a '30s movie star. On the back was stamped "Van Wyck Studio, Windsor, Ontario, 1933."

I flipped through the remaining pages of the scrapbook. They were filled with other reviews, programs from concerts Trudy had given, invitations to radio station receptions—mementoes of her five-year career as a singer. The last item in the book was a clipping from *The Detroit News*, dated April 26, 1936. It was a column entitled "Air Gossip," and one sentence was underlined:

> Trudy Little, of CRCW and CKLW, is away from the air until the fall ... just now she's mothering a new arrival, an eight-pound boy.

On the next page there were two pictures that startled me. They were of my mother with the Chansonettes again, but this time I hardly recognized her. She wore a haunted look, her face gaunt, her hair chopped short, almost a man's length. Her eyes were unfocused, sad. The pictures had been taken in a radio studio with my mother at a piano and the three singers grouped around her. She looked frail, a painful contrast to the beautiful woman on the earlier page. The back of the picture bore the stamp "1936." My mother told me she'd tried to resume her career a few months after I was born, but had found she was "too nervous" to perform live on the radio.

She did sing for me as child, but the only song I could remember was one about three little fishes who kept leaving home against their mother's wishes. At bedtime I used to ask her to sing it over and over again. I hummed the melody softly to myself now, searching for the words. Then they came to me, and I could almost hear my mother's fine contralto voice joining me for the final refrain:

"They swam and they swam—right over the dam."

There was a time, when I was much younger, when these scrapbooks had been upstairs, on a shelf in the study. Looking at these two pictures I knew why the scrapbooks had been put away. The memories had become too painful for her. They were all she had left from the brief period in the early years of the Depression, when Trudy Champion appeared on her way to stardom.

I closed the scrapbook.

Definitely for the keeper file.

LENNOXVILLE, APRIL 1954

I CALLED HOME from the pay phone in Norton Hall. My father answered on the third ring.

"Happy Birthday." It was the evening of April the fifth and Dad was forty-nine. "Did you blow out all the candles?"

"Oh, sure," he laughed, "but it gets harder each year."

"Big party tonight?"

"Nope. Just a quiet dinner with an old friend."

This was good news. I had visions of him sitting home alone. "Did you get my card?"

"No, when did you mail it?"

"Couple of days ago ... Wednesday, I think."

"Well, it's not here yet. Maybe tomorrow." Dad didn't seem upset. Another good sign. Late mail usually bothered him.

"Let me know what you think." I'd sent a joke card, hoping to lift his spirits.

"All set for the exams?"

My stomach knotted. Tell the truth or lie? I took the easy way out. "I've got another two weeks to study. Ask me then."

Through the phone I heard the sound of a doorbell.

"That'll be my friend. I better go. Don't want to keep her waiting. Keep at it—hit those books."

"Right." I hung up wondering who this "old friend" might be. When he'd said dinner with a friend, I'd assumed he meant a man, someone from work. But he'd said he didn't want to keep "her" waiting. Who was she? I put the thought out of my mind. I had something more important to worry about. Dad's questions about the exams ignited the fear that had been building for the past couple of weeks. Back in my room I found I was restless and unable to concentrate. I sorted through papers, then re-sorted them. I tidied up my desk drawers, rearranged my clothes in the closet, and paced the room.

"What's up?" My roommate was stretched out on his bed, reading.

"I dunno. I've got butterflies. I can't seem to settle down." I realized my fussing was making it hard for him to study.

"Nerves. Just pre-exam jitters." Carl resumed reading.

"Think I'll take a walk." I reached inside the closet for my jacket.

"Good idea," he said without looking up.

As I left the room and descended the stairs a wave of nausea hit. I found myself suddenly gripped in a suffocating cloak of fear. I made it out the door, then vomited on the sodden grass of the quadrangle. I stood there, one hand against the red brick wall of the residence, my head down, my breathing shallow. Three Divines passed me, on their way to the library. One muttered something I couldn't catch and the others laughed. My knees were weak; taking a walk was now out of the question. My bowels begin to churn and I managed to make it back into the residence, into the washroom, just in time. I sat on the toilet, my head between my legs, sweat dripping off my brow onto the bathroom tile.

What was going on? Was I coming down with something? At the sink I rinsed out my mouth and regarded myself in the mirror. Nothing dramatic there: no visible evidence that there was anything wrong. Then it hit me. The boy I saw reflected in that mirror might not be back at Bishop's next year. There was a possibility I might flunk out. A frightening thought. This place had become home. I was in deep trouble.

All year I'd relied on my roommate for help with weekly math assignments. Unfortunately, Carl couldn't write the final exam for me. Chemistry was another problem; it would take an alchemist's magic to distill the term's work into the limited study time I had available before the exam.

I stumbled back to our room. "Jesus, you all right?" Carl asked. "You look terrible."

"Must have been something I ate." I couldn't tell Carl the truth, that the conversation with my father had focused my fears. I was terrified I wasn't going to make it.

I slept very little that night, but I came up with a plan. I knew I had to pass at least five of seven subjects to stay in school. If I could get through those maybe I could shift out of Science and into Arts. At Bishop's the academic year started earlier and ended later than other universities—you could earn a degree in three years. If I switched it would mean a fourth year, but at least I wouldn't flunk out. My father might not like it, but I was going to let math and chemistry slide and concentrate on the courses where I knew I had a chance.

I spent the days studying. But each evening, as the sky darkened, anxiety and nausea would descend. I began skipping supper, but that didn't stop the nausea, the cold sweats, or the fitful sleep.

Finally I called a doctor in Lennoxville.

"First year?" He was leafing through the forms I'd filled out. His office was on the ground floor of a weathered old house, a few doors up the hill from the main street. Dr. Hardaway was middle-aged and casual, his tie loosened at the collar, his tweed jacket frayed at the elbows.

"That's right."

Three framed diplomas hung on the wall behind his desk, slightly askew, as if left that way when someone slammed a door too hard.

He looked up. "What seems to be the problem?" His tone implied he already knew the answer.

I gave him an edited version of what had been one of the most uncomfortable weeks of my life. He listened without interruption, peering at me over wire-rimmed, half-frame reading glasses.

"Ever had this sort of difficulty before?" He rolled a fountain pen between the palms of his hands. "In high school, maybe?"

"No, nothing even close."

"Anything like it in the family?" He looked down at the form again. "What about your brothers? Sisters? They have this kind of trouble?"

"I don't have any brothers or sisters." A chilling thought surfaced. Maybe this wasn't just a simple case of the jitters. Had I somehow inherited my mother's illness?

"Well, we'd better have a look at you." Dr. Hardaway got up from behind his desk and motioned to a half-open door across the room. "Go in there, take off your shirt and pants. You can keep your underwear on. I'll be along in a minute."

The routine physical turned up nothing.

"Nerves." He wrote out a prescription with nicotine-stained fingers. "This will help you sleep." He looked up. "When's your last exam?"

"May eighth."

He finished writing, tore the sheet from the pad, and handed it to me. "That should do it," he said, replacing the top on his fountain pen. "One capsule about a half hour before bedtime." He rose and extended his hand across the desk. "Good luck." We shook hands.

"Thanks." I was embarrassed because my palm was clammy and sweating.

I skipped supper again that night and took the bus into Sherbrooke. The Man With the Golden Arm was playing at the Grenada. Watching Frank Sinatra trying to kick the heroin habit probably wasn't the best way to spend the evening, but at least it distracted me for a couple of hours. On the way out of the theatre I stopped at the water fountain and took one of pills the doctor had prescribed. It was a bright, red-coated tablet and looked more like a candy than a sedative. I caught the bus to Lennoxville, hoping the pill would kick in by the time I reached the campus.

An hour later, in bed, I had my doubts. I gave it another sweaty, frightened forty-five minutes and then took a second pill. By 3:00 a.m. I'd dozed off into a sleep filled with nightmares about writing examinations in the subjects I planned to neglect. I woke feeling guilty about this and decided to call my father again.

"I'm having a problem, Dad." It was shortly before eight; I timed the call to catch him before he left for work.

"What's wrong?" There was concern in his voice.

I explained about the nausea and anxiety, told him about the doctor, the pills. "They don't seem to work very well," I said. "I don't know what to do."

There was a moment of silence on the line. "Do you want to come home for the weekend? Maybe some time away from school would help." He was feeling his way.

"I don't know Dad. I don't think it would change anything. I'd still have the exams to write." I'd decided to tell him the truth. "I've just about given up on math, and the chemistry is iffy at best."

I paused, waiting for the blast.

He surprised me. "What about the other subjects?"

"Well," I said, "if I can hang in there for the next couple of weeks, I think I can scrape by. But if I flunk math and chemistry it will mean an extra year at Bishop's."

"That's okay. We can handle that."

"I don't think Science is my thing," I blurted. This was a touchy subject. Dad, with a degree in electrical engineering, didn't see the merit of a B.A.

"The important thing now is to hang in there." Steel was creeping into my father's voice. "Stick it out." But there was compassion as well. "Pass the five courses. If it means a switch to Arts next year, so be it."

I felt a rush of relief. "Are you sure?"

"I'm sure."

I could feel tears starting to form. "Thanks, Dad." I couldn't think of anything more to say. "Thanks," I repeated.

"That's all right," my father said. "You can do it. I know you can."

We exchanged good-byes and I made my way down the hall to my room, climbed back into bed, and fell into a deep, dreamless sleep for the first time in weeks.

When I awoke, I felt so calm and relaxed that for a moment I wondered if I was making too big a deal about all this. My peace of mind held until evening, when the anxiety unexpectedly returned. It was far more frightening now, because there seemed to be no basis for it. I'd thought it had been brought on by the fear of failure, of disappointing Dad. But my father had been more than understanding, and although I was pretty sure I could manage to pass the five courses I needed to avoid flunking out, no amount of rationalization could dispel the terror I felt. It was as if some foreign body had taken over my emotions and wouldn't listen to reason. I had two weeks; if I couldn't get this under some sort of control, I wasn't sure I could last that long, let alone pass the exams. This was been how my mother must have felt when her anxiety attacks struck.

Faced with the prospect of more nausea, diarrhea, and sweating, I decided I might just as well get drunk. The Georgian Hotel was the only place in town that still tolerated students. Over the years we'd worn out our welcome at the other bars and taverns. It wasn't just the matter of under-age drinking. There'd been too many fights, too much broken furniture, and too many messes to clean up. We were simply more trouble that we were worth. But The Georgian Bar and Grill was different. The decor was impervious to the occasional squabble; there were sturdy metal chairs, heavy-duty tables, and a floor of industrial strength tile that could withstand the worst we had to offer. A corps of beefy waiters policed the place, cutting off the beer when they thought we'd had too much and occasionally declaring a particularly unruly student *persona non grata* for a week or two. So it was to the "G," as it was affectionately known, that I headed that evening.

"Un gros Mol," I said to René, the waiter, and picked a table conveniently close to the washroom. It was touch and go, getting it down, keeping it down. Then a couple of my classmates wandered in and joined me. Distracted by their company, I finished off the Molson's and called for another. An hour or so later, when someone suggested we order a hamburger, I realized to my surprise that my nausea was gone and I was actually hungry. What was more, the beer had relaxed me and the fear had vanished. I felt a faint flicker of hope; maybe I could make it through the term after all.

From that night on I followed the same routine. I spent my mornings and afternoons studying, my evenings at the G. Each night was a balancing act, timing my drinks to keep the anxiety at bay. Too much beer and I risked passing out, too little and I would be swamped with fear. About eleven I would motion René to the table and pay my bill, tipping him generously. Then, on my way out, I'd pick up an unopened quart of Molson, discreetly wrapped in a brown paper bag. Insurance, in case I couldn't sleep.

During the week of the finals, I maintained this self-administered coping program. By day I wrote exams in the same gymnasium where I'd found solitude and comfort shooting the basketball the previous fall. Now there was no solitude and the only comfort I took was knowledge that a release awaited me each night in the Georgian Hotel.

I wrote my last exam on a Friday morning, put most of my things away in storage, bade good-bye to my friends, and boarded the afternoon train for St. Lambert. I hoped the worst was over, that there'd be no more anxiety now that the exams were finished, but I'd bought a pint of rye just in case. It was packed away in my suitcase, and I planned to use it if I couldn't sleep at home that night.

ST. LAMBERT, MAY 1954

OUT THE TRAIN WINDOW everything looked so damned perfect. The sun was shining; the farmers' fields were green with new growth, and at the stations along the way people were going about their business without a care in the world. I envied them the ease with which they seemed to be moving through their lives. Yet even as I did, I realized that among those people there would be some who, watching the train, would envy the college kid heading home. Enough self-pity, I thought to myself, and moved to the club car and ordered a drink.

I tried to think things through. My mother and I shared certain symptoms, that was clear enough, but our circumstances were entirely different. I knew that her attacks seemed to come out of the blue, with no triggering event. My anxiety began when I was confronted with the possibility of flunking out. And there was concern about Dad's health. As the train took me steadily homeward, I began to feel a little better. I wasn't sure if it was the drinks or simply the fact sinking in that the exams were finally finished. I decided to go easy on the booze; a truer test would come that evening when it was time to sleep.

At the train station in St. Lambert I climbed into a cab.

"263 Green Street," I told the driver. It was the first time I'd spoken the new address aloud, and it didn't sound right. But when we pulled up before the new three-storey building my doubts disappeared, and as I climbed the stairs to our apartment I felt excitement begin to build. Dad had moved in the previous weekend, and he stood waiting, framed in the doorway, when I reached the third floor landing.

"Welcome home," he said, reaching for my bag. "Let me take that."

"No, Dad," I said, remembering his surgery. "I can manage."

He ushered me in. "It's a little cramped compared to the old place, but I think you'll like it."

The living room was surprisingly spacious. Light flooded in through a picture window and the overall impression of brightness was enhanced by the pale yellow colour of the walls. Our old sofa and chair had been re-upholstered to match the decor, but Dad's cabinetless radio sat unchanged, its tubes glowing, music playing softly. I was pleased to see my mother's watercolour seascape on the far wall. There was a new Zenith television set in the corner and the familiar copies of the *National Geographic* and *Fortune Magazine* on the coffee table.

"Well," my father said, "what do you think?"

"Amazing." There was just enough of the old mixed in with the right amount of the new. I walked into the living room, noticing for the first time the thick, off-white, wall-to-wall carpet beneath my feet.

Dad smiled. "We have people below us now, the carpet keeps the noise down."

"I can't get over it," I said, sinking into the sofa. "How did you manage?" I gestured to the room.

"Well, I had a little help," Dad admitted modestly. "An old friend of mine turned up at the right time and gave me a hand picking the fabric for the furniture."

"You and your friend should go into the interior decorating business." I wondered if this was the same friend he'd dined with on his birthday.

"Well, I don't know about that," Dad chuckled, a little embarrassed. "Maybe you should have a look at the rest of the rooms before you pass judgment."

I rose and followed him down a hallway. The smell of plaster and fresh paint was still in the air.

"This is my room." He stood back so I could look through the door. It was smaller than I'd expected, but neat and functional. A paperback copy of a Perry Mason mystery lay open on top of a bedside bureau. Dad was a big Erle Stanley Gardner fan.

"Your room is next," Dad said, leading me on down the hall. As I followed I realized that the wall-to-wall carpet extended throughout the apartment.

"Wow!" Somehow he'd managed to squeeze all the furniture from my old room into this much smaller space. It didn't look cramped, just a snug fit. "How'd you do it?" Against one wall was the matching bureau and desk set he'd built for me in the basement workshop of our old house on Merton. The single bed fit neatly into the corner along the opposite wall. On the shelf above the headboard of my bed sat my radio, in its accustomed place. I turned it on. Nat King Cole was singing.

> There was a boy …
> A very strange enchanted boy.

I was indeed enchanted by this new place. My father had been right to move. It was time to put the past in the past.

"What's the word on your shoulder?"

"I was in to see the doctor this week. Just a routine follow-up. Seems I'm in tip-top shape."

At bedtime I brushed my teeth and washed while Dad smoked a final cigarette. My last drink had been aboard the club car; the bottle of rye lay unopened beneath a layer of shirts in my bureau. I hoped I wouldn't need it. I pulled down the sheets and slipped beneath the covers and turned off the light. I could hear my father moving about and taps running; then the door to his room closed and the only sounds were those of the town where I had grown up.

A Montreal and Southern Counties' streetcar rattled by, heading for the terminus in Longueuil. From the harbour across the St. Lawrence River a ship's horn sounded, and I could hear the murmur of a freight train making its way across the Victoria Bridge. I switched on the radio; the illuminated dial cast a diagonal pattern of light across the wall at the foot of the bed. It took a moment for the tubes to warm up. Then, with a little fiddling, I found what I was looking for, the voice of Mel Allen and a Yankee baseball game.

The reception was good and the Yankees were winning. The last thing I remember was Mel Allen's excited voice describing Phil Rizzuto's leaping catch as he took away a sure base hit from some unlucky St. Louis Brown.

When I awoke in the morning it took me a few seconds to get my bearings. I had spent a restless night, tossing and turning, but I realized with growing excitement that I'd managed to get through it without any anxiety and without booze. I lay for a moment in the soft light of the early morning, surrounded by familiar things, savouring the accomplishment.

Maybe the worst was over. Maybe the emotional roller-coaster ride of recent weeks had been simply a normal response to the stress of a rough year.

I swung out of bed and got to my feet, stretching. My radio was still on, but the Plattsburg station faded in and out. Reception was always poorer in the daytime. I switched to a local program. It was going to be a fine day, the announcer predicted, with no rain in the forecast. A burst of static cut him off. Dad was shaving; his electric razor always did that to the radio. I chuckled to myself; being home did have its minor drawbacks.

ST. LAMBERT/NOMININGUE, 1954

I HADN'T LINED UP ANY WORK for the summer, but that weekend a friend called to say he'd broken his arm and wondered if I'd be interested in replacing him as counsellor at Camp Nominingue in the Laurentians, north of Montreal. It seemed I had all the necessary qualifications: I was a certified lifeguard, had coached kids' softball, and could teach tennis. The pay wasn't great, but once again Dad came through.

"Let me worry about the money," he said. "You've been through a lot. It's a perfect summer job. Plenty of fresh air and exercise, all your meals provided. Just what the doctor ordered."

Maybe my luck was changing.

Dad came to Central Station in Montreal to see me off. "When you come home for your weekend break," he said as we waited for the train, "there's someone I'd like you to meet."

I looked at him quizzically.

"You remember I mentioned a friend had helped with the apartment?"

I nodded.

"After Trudy died I wanted to let her old college roommate, Bobbie Vale, know about it. I wasn't sure how to reach her. When I was in Toronto on business I ran into an old Leamington friend, Grace Imeson. She gave me Bobbie's phone number. Grace and I went to the same high school, so we got to talking about old times and I invited her to have lunch with me. We hit it off pretty well and began to see more and more of each other."

I didn't know what to say.

"I've invited her to come to Montreal," he said, then added after a pause, "the weekend of your break."

At this point the conductor called "All Aboard" and blew his warning whistle. I was grateful for the interruption. "I guess I'll see you ... see you both then." I mounted the steps of the passenger car. The train gave a lurch and began moving. I waved to Dad.

He waved back and called out something, but his words were lost in the wind. I turned and made my way to a seat. The lights flickered on; we were in the tunnel that ran deep beneath Mount Royal, heading north for the Laurentians.

I wasn't sure if I'd heard it right, but it certainly sounded as if my father had a girlfriend. I guess I should have been pleased, but Mom had been dead less than a year and I couldn't shake the uncomfortable feeling that this was rushing things a bit.

At Camp Nominingue the six ten-year-olds in my tent were asleep, exhausted by their first full day of activities. Drumbeats of rain on the canvas began as I was reading Hemingway's "The Big Two Hearted River." He was my favourite writer, but even his deceptively simple style was too much for me tonight. A chorus of bullfrogs throbbed in the marsh; a gust of wind blew into the tent and the kerosene lantern flickered, a puff of smoke momentarily clouding the glass. Rubbing my eyes, I reluctantly gave up reading; I marked my place, turned the flame down, and snuffed out the light. Tomorrow I'd have to clean the lantern glass and trim the wick.

I woke to the chatter of my campers, already up, talking excitedly as they dressed. The skies were clearing and for a few sleepy minutes I watched the last of the rain drip off the tent fly to the moist ground below. I was dozing again when the breakfast bell rang and I had to push myself out of bed. It wasn't that hard; I was hungry. I don't know if the meals served at camp were really any better than those at Bishop's, but they certainly seemed to be.

Yesterday had been filled with activity. I'd been on lifeguard duty for both swim periods, taught swimming and tennis in the morning, organized a game of touch football in the afternoon, and improvised a ghost story around a campfire in the evening.

As the days passed, each equally full, there was little time for introspection; I was simply too busy. There'd been no recurrence of the anxiety. Dad had called to say my marks from Bishop's had arrived in the mail; I'd managed to pass the requisite five courses. The problems I'd faced in the past spring seemed less and less important, like the brief squalls that sometimes curtailed our sailing on the lake.

When I boarded the train for the weekend break I was in the best shape I'd been since my mother's death.

ST. LAMBERT/MONTREAL, 1954

IT WAS MID-AFTERNOON when I entered the lobby of our apartment building and headed up the stairs. I opened the door and my father was waiting, standing in the living room. Seated on the sofa was a middle-aged woman wearing a pale yellow summer dress and a pillbox hat. She smiled a nervous smile. The dress was a perfect match for the colour of the walls. So this was the "friend" who had helped Dad decorate the apartment.

"Grace," Dad said simply, "this is Andy."

I felt uncomfortable, unsure of myself. I extended my hand. Her grip was firm. "I'm pleased to meet you." Her voice was soft, with just the faintest suggestion of a lisp.

"Grace and I were in school together," Dad said.

"Your father is stretching the point," she smiled. "He was a senior the year I started high school. I knew about him all right, but I don't think he even knew my name back then." She looked at him questioningly.

He gave an exaggerated palms-up shrug—a mock guilty plea—and laughed. I hadn't heard that laugh in a long time.

It was awkward. My father and I had switched roles. He was the nervous teenager, bringing a girl home for approval. I sat down and lit a cigarette, drew the smoke deeply into my lungs and exhaled slowly in the hope that it might blow away some of the uncertainty I felt.

Grace Imeson had flat, almost Slavic features. Her eyes, magnified by the thick lenses of her glasses, were a pale blue.

"Grace has Monday off," my father explained. "It's a long holiday weekend in Ontario."

"We must be living in the wrong province," I said, laughing.

Grace smiled and seemed to relax a little.

"I can see camp agrees with you," Dad said. "Nice tan. I guess they aren't working you too hard."

"It's a great job."

"How about a beer?" He started for the kitchen. "I'll give you two a chance to get acquainted."

Grace took the cue. "Willis says this was the first time you've worked as a counsellor."

Willis? I wasn't used to hearing my father's name spoken aloud. His friends usually called him Bill.

"Well, I was at scout camp for three years, so I had a pretty good idea what to expect." I was searching for something to like in this woman who had been thrust so unexpectedly into my life.

"Where exactly is Nominingue?" Grace chose her words carefully now that we were alone, dealing them out like cards in a game.

"It's in the Laurentian Mountains, near Mont Laurier. About three hours by train."

"That's a long trip."

"Well, we had a few beers on the way down. That helped pass the time."

"Did I hear the word beer?" Dad reappeared from the kitchen with three bottles of O'Keefe's Old Vienna Lager on a tray. He poured a glass for Grace, tilting it to prevent the beer from foaming to a head. I reached for a bottle and poured my own.

Dad raised his glass. "Let's drink to the future."

"To the future," we murmured in unison.

Grace made dinner that evening. It was a cheese omelette with fresh green beans and new potatoes. "You'll have to forgive the limited menu. With no one to cook for I've always kept things pretty simple."

"Don't apologize." Dad bit into the omelette and looked at me. "This is delicious."

"It's great," I said. "Between college and camp I don't get many home-cooked meals."

We moved into the living room for coffee and an evening of television. Jack Benny's guests that night were George Burns and Bing Crosby. We made small talk during the commercial breaks and I learned that Grace had been raised on a farm outside Leamington and had taken a secretarial course in Toronto after graduation from high school.

When the shows were over I went into the kitchen to make more coffee. I could hear the low murmur of conversation as I spooned the grounds into the percolator. I knew we had some chocolate marshmallow Whippets somewhere and I moved into the hall to check the cupboard there.

"He seems a little young to be drinking, that's all." It was Grace speaking, her voice low.

"He's eighteen, it's the legal age in Quebec," Dad said. "He can handle it."

"Maybe I'm old-fashioned, but I don't think you should be encouraging him at home."

"I'd rather have him drinking here where I can see what's going on than off in a bar somewhere."

"Well, he's your son." There was a pause, then the click of the television set being turned back on. The theme music for the CBC National News filtered into the hall.

When I returned to the living room Larry Henderson, the announcer, was reading the first story about an upcoming federal-provincial conference. He introduced Norman DePoe, reporting from Ottawa. Dad leaned forward to concentrate on the news. I smiled to myself. My father had met DePoe and liked him. "His only problem," he'd once told me, "is that he drinks too much." I wondered if Grace knew this.

When the news was finished Dad turned off the television set and gave an exaggerated yawn. "Time for bed." He got up from his chair. Grace rose and for a moment our eyes met briefly.

"I'm going to stay up a while longer, Dad," I said. "I want to catch some of the late ball scores."

"Suit yourself, Bub." He headed off down the hall into the bedroom.

"It's nice to meet at last," Grace said. "Willis has talked so much about you." She followed Dad into the bedroom, closing the door behind them.

Baseball scores flashed on the television screen, but they didn't register. The next night I made a point of coming home late, after they'd gone to bed.

That weekend I spent most of my time visiting high school friends and getting caught up on the latest gossip. In the smoke-filled poolroom above the Victoria movie theatre I heard all the details about the shotgun marriage of the daughter of a local minister to a promising high school hockey star. Later that afternoon we hitched a ride to Longueuil and slipped into Roy's Tavern for a few beers. To hell with Grace, I thought.

She left for Toronto Monday afternoon. Dad and I saw her off from the CNR station in Montreal. Then we caught a commuter train back to St. Lambert.

As we pulled away from the underground platform, the train picked up speed and headed into the darkened tunnel that ran beneath the city streets. The clack of steel on steel reverberated through the swaying carriage, then we emerged with a sudden whoosh into the bright summer light.

Dad looked at me. "Well ... what do you think?"

I hesitated, seeking something positive to say. "She seems nice."

As the train cut through the flats and factories of Griffintown, the stench of the Goose Village abattoirs slipped aboard along with the penetrating clang of bells at the frequent level crossings.

"I liked her." The words came out easily enough, but they didn't reflect how I really felt. Her comments about my drinking still rankled.

"I'm glad." My father looked down at his hands. "Because I expect to be seeing a lot more of her."

Behind us the Sun Life Building receded, dwarfed by Mount Royal.

"I knew the moment I met Grace that she was special. We have a lot in common."

I nodded. On the Victoria Bridge the last lingering slaughterhouse smells were swept from the train by an off-river breeze.

"She's so different from Trudy." Dad seemed to be talking to himself now. "But I think that's just what I need."

I watched seagulls drift downstream. "Too bad she's in Toronto, you're here in Montreal."

"It is," Dad said as the conductor made his way toward us, calling out stations.

I waited.

"That's why I've asked her to move here." He turned to me, his hazel eyes alive. "I've asked her to marry me." The train was pulling into St. Lambert now. People were getting up from their seats.

"When?" It was all I could manage to say.

"We haven't set the date yet." The train shuddered to a stop. "Sometime this fall."

We rose to join the stream of people crowding the aisle in their hurry to get off the train. I was thankful for the diversion. I was at a loss for words.

NOMININGUE/ST. LAMBERT, 1954

THE MECHANICAL TAP-TAP-TAP of typewriter keys in the deep woods seemed out of place, an odd counterpoint to the chirp of sparrows. It was Quiet Hour, the time after lunch when campers retreated to their tents for a brief rest before beginning the afternoon programs. I was sitting on the edge of a cot with my mother's old portable Underwood balanced on an orange crate, teaching myself to type.

It was a summer project. Camp was the perfect place to make the switch from my slow hunt-and-peck method to touch-typing. There were no essays due, no papers to write. The words I pounded out were just exercises, and mistakes didn't matter. I was getting pretty good. This day I decided to take a break from the exercises and try a letter to my father.

"Dear Dad," I typed, and stopped. I looked at the blank page. Should I tell him about the new kids in my tent? Or about some of the friends I'd made among the counsellors? Or maybe about the canoe trip we were planning.

No. I really wanted to write something else. I wanted to tell him how I felt about Grace, that I was trying to like her but it was going to take time. I didn't understand his need to marry. Why didn't they just live together for a while? But I couldn't bring myself to write these words. The romance had given Dad a boost at a very bad time and I wasn't about to do anything that would take away from his excitement and pleasure. I didn't want to hurt him.

In the months following Mom's death the hostility I'd felt toward my father had all but evaporated. He'd been so damned understanding about my exam difficulties, so accommodating about my switch from Science to Arts. He'd urged me to take the low-paying camp job even though it meant he'd have to come up with more spending money for me at college. What right did I have to question his plans to marry? It was his life, after all. How could Grace be expected to compete with the memories I had of my own mother?

There would be no letter to Dad. I went back to my typing exercises, where mistakes didn't matter. The sound of someone tuning a guitar came down the tent line. A counsellor began to sing.

Somewhere there's music.
How faint the tune ...
Somewhere there's music,
How high the moon?

The tentative, off-key rendition made me smile. My mother had loved that song, the Les Paul and Mary Ford version. They had been two of her favourite musicians. When the record was released it became an immediate hit—a cross between jazz and pop, with intricate guitar riffs and voices that steered the lyrics free of sentimentality. I wondered if we still had the record, or if it had been thrown out in the move.

The second half of the season at camp was a repeat of the first. I gained back all the weight I'd lost the previous spring and wondered if the tan I'd acquired would help me find a steady girlfriend. At the end of August we wrapped things up at Nominingue and I returned to Montreal.

Dad met my train and suggested dinner at McArthur's restaurant on Victoria Avenue, where he'd been a steady customer since Mom's death.

The toothpick in the corner of Wade McArthur's mouth bobbed up and down as he spoke. "What'll it be tonight, gentlemen?" It was almost seven o'clock in the evening and Dad and I were the only people in the restaurant. This was a quiet time; the luncheon trade provided the bulk of Wade's business.

"Steak and kidney pie," I said, and handed him the menu.

"I'll have the liver and onions," my father said, "with mashed potatoes."

Wade took the menu and headed for the kitchen.

Dad lit a cigarette and looked at me across the table. "Grace and I have set the date." He took a deep drag and blew the smoke toward the ceiling. "We're getting married next month."

I hadn't expected this. It was too soon. Mom hadn't been dead a year. He was rushing things. I wanted to protest; instead I reached for my glass of water.

"September the fourteenth."

I put the water down untouched. "But Dad, that's the day I'm due back at school."

"I thought you were starting on the twenty-first." He was clearly surprised.

"No, it's the fourteenth."

"Couldn't you call and explain the situation? I'm sure they'd let you register a day or so late."

"But I have to be there for the start of freshman hazing." It wasn't much of an excuse, but it was the best I could muster.

"Well," Dad said, tapping the ash from his cigarette, "we aren't planning anything big. The wedding is a simple ceremony."

"I thought Grace would want a big church wedding."

"She knows how I feel about organized religion," he said tersely.

I guessed there had been some heated words around this subject.

"What about your honeymoon?"

"Oh, we're not going anywhere. We might take a little trip later in the fall. The ceremony is really just a formality."

"Well, if it's no big deal," I said, "maybe I'll pass on it and come home the following weekend for a visit."

The relief I felt as these words came out surprised me. If Dad and Grace were in such a rush to get married then they could do it without me. I realized I didn't want to go to the wedding and was glad to have an excuse to avoid it.

"I mean ... if that's okay with you?"

"Sure, it's fine with me."

I wasn't sure if he meant it. Was he disappointed or relieved?

The meal arrived and we concentrated on the food. The beefsteak and kidney pie had been a good choice. When we finished supper Wade came to our table, a tray of dishes in one hand and a towel in the other. "What about dessert?"

"Not for me," I said. "Just coffee."

"Coffee it is."

Dad took a sip of his water. He waited until Wade was out of earshot. "I've got some disappointing news."

What now, I wondered?

"I was in to see the doctor." Dad looked down at his place setting. "The tumour on my shoulder is back."

"Shit." My hands began to shake. "I thought they took care of that last winter."

"That's what I thought too," he said, resignation in his voice. "Apparently they didn't get it all ... or they did ... and this is something new. Anyway, they're going to start chemotherapy treatment next week."

"Jesus." I could feel sweat trickling from my armpits down my ribcage. "Chemotherapy?" What did this mean?

"They've done a biopsy," he continued, reading my mind. "It's malignant this time, but it's small and in its early stages and they think with chemo they can bring it under control."

No wonder there was to be no honeymoon.

"Grace is coming down tomorrow to look after things in the apartment." He glanced at me expectantly, as if he thought I might protest.

I remained silent, still trying to sort out things in my head. Perhaps this was why Dad hadn't insisted I attend the wedding.

"Maybe I should delay my registration after all," I suggested, "at least until we see how things are shaping up." I looked at my father across the table. He seemed far away.

"No, you go on to Bishop's. Grace will be here if I need anything."

LENNOXVILLE/ST. LAMBERT, 1955

I DIDN'T RETURN HOME as planned the weekend following my father's wedding. There was an exhibition football game at Bishop's and since I'd been asked to handle the public address announcements for the team that season, it gave me an excuse to postpone the trip.

It was a good thing I did, because at the dance after the game I met Dolce Narizzano. The first time I saw her that evening she was jitterbugging with the captain of the football team. The music was Glenn Miller's "String of Pearls." I remember, because she was wearing pearls over a brown cashmere sweater. She was also wearing a name card, mandatory for new students. Her long skirt flared, showing layers of crinoline as her white saddle shoes moved to the beat of the music. It took me a while to work up the courage to ask her to dance. I waited until the music switched to something slow. As Tony Bennett began "A Stranger in Paradise" I crossed the floor.

"Dolce," I said, "would you like to dance?"

She looked up at me with surprise and smiled. "Sure," she said and as we headed onto the floor she asked, "How did you know how to pronounce my name? Almost no one gets it right the first time."

I shrugged off the compliment. "Just lucky, I guess."

In truth I hadn't been sure and since I wanted to impress her, I'd checked with Ruth Townsend, a student from St. Lambert who was in the same residence as Dolce.

"It's Doll-See," Ruth said, "and for God's sake don't call her Dulse, she hates that."

"What about the last name?"

"It's Narr-itz-sanno and the trick is to run the last two syllables together emphasizing the S rather than the Z."

I tried that a few times. Ruth was right, it was tricky. She listened to me struggle and then shrugged her shoulders. "I don't know why you're bothering," she said, "you haven't a chance with her anyway."

Ruth was wrong. When the music finished after that first dance I held onto Dolce's hand. "How about the next one?"

She smiled. "All right."

The Mills Brothers began their uptempo hit "Glow Worm" and we discovered to our mutual delight that we could jive together without missing a beat. Her anticipation was uncanny; she seemed to know where I was going before I did. For the rest of the evening we danced and talked, getting to know each other. She was the first girl I'd met who'd read most of the books I'd read, liked the same music, enjoyed the same movies.

I learned she was the youngest of five children, that she lived in Westmount, and her father owned a fruit importing company.

"What about you?" she asked.

"Well, I'm from St. Lambert. I don't have any brothers or sisters and my father was married just last weekend."

"What?" She gave me a puzzled frown. "You're kidding."

"No." I held up three fingers. "Scout's Honour. It's true."

I gave her a brief version of the past few months, omitting the specifics of Mom's death and any mention of Dad's illness. As Hoagy Carmichael's "Stardust" signalled the last dance of the night I changed the subject.

"Can I walk you home?" I was holding her closer than I had all evening.

"I don't think so."

"Oh." I tried to hide my disappointment.

"Home is in Westmount," she giggled. "That's a long walk."

We didn't really dance the last dance, just swayed gently to the music, barely moving from our spot on the floor.

It was a warm night and we took the long way back to the Women's Residence.

"What was your mother like?" Dolce asked. "I mean your real mother."

"Well, she was beautiful and talented and she had a great sense of humour." I didn't mention the dark side. "What about your folks?" We were approaching the main entrance to the residence.

"Are you going home for the Thanksgiving weekend?"

"Sure," I said, opening the door for her.

"Then maybe you'll get a chance to judge for yourself," she said as she walked into the residence.

"Good night," I called after her.

She turned and smiled. "Good night."

In the lobby of our apartment in St. Lambert I realized that it was one year ago exactly that Dad had visited me at Bishop's. It had been the Thanksgiving weekend after Mom's death and I'd resented him then, didn't want him there. Now my resentment had shifted to Grace. I didn't want her here, at least not so soon.

I climbed the stairs to the apartment. Grace Imeson—make that Grace Little—opened the door. I stepped inside, put down my bags, and gave her a perfunctory peck on the cheek.

"Congratulations." It was the first time I'd seen her since the wedding. "How does it feel to be Mrs. Little?" The words didn't sound right; I hoped she didn't expect me to call her "mother."

Her cheeks reddened with embarrassment. "It feels ... it feels ... different." She gave a nervous laugh.

"Where's Dad?"

"You just missed him. He's gone to the hardware store. He should be back in an hour or so. Have you eaten breakfast?"

"I had some coffee and a doughnut on the train. I'm fine."

I looked around the apartment. The newness had worn off, and the old furniture, even re-upholstered, still reminded me of the past, of the house where I grew up. I sat down in the easy chair and put my feet up on the coffee table. Grace crossed the room and perched on the edge of the sofa. There was a tightness about her, a closed-off sense of self, and as I watched I was flooded with a new feeling of loss for my mother. I found I actually missed Mom's nervousness, her unpredictability. She'd been fragile, yet at the same time alive. Grace, with her feet firmly on the ground, made me long for the excitement of the tightrope act that had been my mother's existence. Even Grace's way of speaking seemed clipped and lifeless by comparison.

"There's something I'd like to talk to you about while Willis is out."

I looked across the room, alerted not so much by the words she used but by the tone of her voice.

"You know your father hasn't been well." She leaned forward, tense, choosing her words carefully. "He hasn't recovered the way we hoped he would. He had some tests done last week."

I'd never seen anyone less comfortable on our sofa. It was as if Grace was trying to take up the least possible space. "I think it might be a good idea if you dropped in on Dr. Achim, he can explain things so much better than I can." She wasn't looking at me.

"It's a holiday weekend," I said. "Won't he be away?"

"He is in this morning. I called him a few minutes ago. You can drop by any time you like."

I felt the beginnings of fear curdling my stomach, and questions, so many questions, burning to be asked. There were things I needed to know, but her words, the flat, emotionless phrasing, brought me up short. She wasn't going to provide the answers.

"If you go over there now, you can catch him before he goes to lunch."

I felt a sudden sense of urgency. I needed to get away from the apartment before my father returned. I picked up my leather jacket from the back of the chair and headed for the door.

"If Dad does get back before I do, just tell him ... " I paused. I was going to suggest some excuse about seeing a friend, but that would have been lying and it seemed particularly important to me at this point that I tell the truth. "Tell him I've gone for a walk and I'll be back soon." I left without waiting for a reply.

ST. LAMBERT, 1954

OUR FAMILY DOCTOR'S OFFICE was just a few blocks from the apartment. The news had to be bad, because Grace was unwilling to talk about it. I wondered just how bad.

The waiting room was empty and the door to his office was open. "Come in, come in." Dr. Achim reached across the desk and we shook hands formally. "It is good to see you again, Andrew."

He was short, in his early forties, and beginning to put on weight. His suit jacket was draped on the back of his chair, his white doctor's coat hung on its peg on the wall. Clearly this wasn't going to be the usual office visit. There would be no prodding or poking this time, no examination, no temperature to be taken or pills prescribed. I wasn't the patient.

Dr. Achim came quickly to the point. "Your stepmother asked me to explain some things." He toyed with a paperweight, turning it over in his hand. "It's about your father. I'm afraid the news isn't good. When they operated in February, they thought they got everything out, but the tests this week showed something new. I'm afraid the cancer has spread."

That word. Cancer. It hadn't been used before. It had always been there in the background, waiting to be spoken, but until now other words had been used: a growth, a tumour, a lump. Now it was cancer.

"How bad is it?" As I asked the question I realized I'd been holding my breath.

"It is bad ... very bad. It's in the lungs now."

"Can't you operate, cut it out?" Even as I asked, I knew the answer and it filled me with a sickening dread.

"I'm afraid not. It has spread too far."

Numbness overtook me. This wasn't possible; this couldn't really be happening.

"How long does he have?"

"We don't know for sure. These things are very hard to predict. It could be months ... it could be a year. We will give him more chemotherapy, that will slow it down."

"Does he know ... he's ... dying?" Another big word. First cancer, now dying. Each like a punch.

Dr. Achim put the paperweight down on his desk and looked at it as if it might somehow hold the answer. Then he brought his eyes back to mine. "We haven't told him ... not in so many words. We don't want to tell him. If we were to tell him, he might just give up. We need your father to fight this thing. We need his will to live."

I realized now why Grace had asked me to see Dr. Achim. It wasn't just the bad news. She and the doctor had decided it would be better not to tell my father he was dying. They wanted my support, needed me to go along with the deception. Dad had always stressed that honesty was the best policy, but in this case was it the best medicine? I wasn't sure. If this had been Grace's idea I might have protested, but surely Dr. Achim knew what was best. He saw people with terminal illnesses every day.

"All right," I said, hesitantly, "I guess I won't tell him." I didn't have the conviction necessary to challenge the plan.

"I think it's the right decision. Who knows? There is always the chance ... " he shrugged. "Stranger things have happened."

I'd agreed to go along with the plan, but I wasn't sure I could carry it off. I didn't know if I could look my father in the eye and pretend he was going to get better. I rose unsteadily from my chair. Dr. Achim reached across the desk and shook my hand. It was a long time before he let it go.

"I'm sorry, Andrew. First your mother, now this ... " The doctor shook his head sadly.

"Thank you." The words seemed wrong, but I couldn't think of anything else to say.

As I made my way back to the apartment I remembered a game we'd played as little kids. Each of us had to imagine that one of our parents was going to die. We had to decide which one it would be and give the reason for our choice. No one ever suggested the possibility that both parents might be gone.

When I entered the apartment the radio in the living room was on, with music playing softly, but I could hear voices from the kitchen. I took a deep breath. The first few minutes were going to be the most difficult.

"Hello," I called out, hanging my jacket in the hall closet.

"Hello yourself," my father called back. "We're in the kitchen."

Dad was sitting, partially silhouetted, with his back to the window when I entered the room. When my eyes adjusted to the light I could see the changes in him. They weren't dramatic, but they were there. He'd lost more weight, the shadows under his eyes had deepened, and there was a vulnerability about him I hadn't seen before.

"Congratulations," I said, crossing the room, and extended my hand.

"Congratulations?" His grip was firm. It was hard to believe he was dying.

"Your marriage."

"Oh, that," he said, laughing as he released my hand. "Thanks." He looked at Grace. "We're an old married couple now. It will be three weeks tomorrow."

She smiled at Dad and then turned to me. "Are you hungry?" She was playing her part to perfection.

"Starving," I said. It was a lie, of course.

"I've made some lunch." She removed wax paper from a plate of sandwiches and put it on the table. Dad poured himself a glass of buttermilk.

"I guess Grace has told you?"

Jesus, I thought. Has she changed her mind? Has she decided to tell him after all? I resisted the urge to glance at Grace and kept my eyes on my father, chewing my sandwich.

"I have to go back into hospital next week for a few days. More tests." He sipped his buttermilk. I relaxed; he didn't know.

"How are you feeling?"

"Not bad, a little tired, that's all."

So far so good, I thought. If Dad had picked up on anything, sensed any change in my behaviour, he wasn't letting on.

"How's the pain?"

"Nothing I can't handle. They've given me something for it. I usually just take the stuff at night."

"Willis hates pills," Grace said. "But I guess you know that."

For a few minutes we concentrated on our lunch. The pretense wasn't as difficult as I'd expected it to be. Maybe the doctor was right. If we'd told Dad the truth we wouldn't be sitting around calmly eating sandwiches at this point.

"How are things at school?" He pushed his plate away, his sandwich half-eaten.

"Fine. It's so different in second year, now that I know my way around. And having a single room makes a big difference."

"You're not rooming with Carl?" Grace poured Dad his coffee.

"No, they only double up the first-year students." I watched as Dad lit a cigarette.

"What about your courses?" I noticed a slight tremble in his hands.

"Big difference. For the first time I'm studying just the stuff I like. I think you'll be surprised at my marks."

Grace began clearing the table. "Will you be having dinner with us tonight?"

"Nope," I said, and added, with a hint of bravado, "I've got a date."

"Aha," Dad said, "and who is the lucky lady?"

"Oh, just a girl from Bishop's I met at a football dance."

"Does this 'just a girl' have a name?" My father liked teasing me about my dates.

"Dolce ... Dolce Narizzano."

"That's quite a name."

"She's Italian. She lives in Westmount."

"My, my." He turned to Grace. "Westmount is the posh part of town." Then his gaze returned to me. "Is it serious?"

"I'm not sure. Could be."

WESTMOUNT, QUEBEC, 1954

THE NUMBER 14 STREETCAR let me off at the corner of Sydenham Avenue and Westmount Boulevard. It was cool and I caught the whiff of wood smoke as I made my way down the hill to 622 Sydenham.

The house was impressive, a three-storey mansion on a double lot in Upper Westmount. Neo-Georgian in design, its solid, symmetrical look spoke of status and wealth. I'd been warned not to expect an enthusiastic welcome.

"You're not Italian and you don't come from an old Montreal family." Her tone indicated she didn't share her parents' views on the subject.

"What about rest of the family, your brothers and your sister?" I'd asked.

"That test will come later. They're all away this weekend."

So it was with some apprehension that I rang the bell and watched through a leaded glass window in the door as the fragmented image of Dolce materialized. She took my coat and guided me into the living room, introducing me to her mother first, then her father.

"Would you like a drink?" he asked after we shook hands.

"Rye and ginger, if you have it."

"I think we have rye here somewhere." Silvio Narizzano wore a dark blue pin-striped suit, a crisp white shirt, and, bless his heart, a bow tie. I couldn't wait to tell Dad.

He poured a Dubonnet for Dolce, then made my drink and handed it to me. He was older than I'd expected, in his sixties, with greying hair and a thin moustache. His handshake had been firm, his manner seemed relaxed and friendly. He made a drink for his wife, a Cinzano-on-the-rocks, and crossed the room to give it to her.

There was a faint, faded aura of glamour about Dolce's mother. Her hair was ash blonde, cut short and styled to flatter the round face. Makeup was subtle but complete; full lips a delicate shade of pink.

"Dolce tells me your father has been ill," she said, and sipped her drink.

"Yes." I sipped mine. "He'll be going into hospital next week for some tests." I didn't want to get into a discussion about Dad's health; I hadn't had a chance to tell Dolce the news. That would come later, when we were alone. Now, sitting in the spacious living room with her parents, we made polite but stilted small talk. Fortunately, the maid soon intervened and called us to dinner.

In the dining room candles provided the only illumination; the crystal and the polished silverware seemed to glow in the soft light. We sat down and Mr. Narizzano began sharpening a bone-handled carving knife as the maid placed a turkey, ringed with oven-baked potatoes, before him. Steaming dishes of vegetables were already at the opposite end of the table where Mrs. Narizzano sat. I was struck by the contrast between this scene and our dining room at home. We weren't summoned to dinner, there was no oak panelling, no candlelight, and we didn't have a maid. When we had a turkey, the meat was carved in the kitchen.

For the next hour I concentrated on the food and spoke very little, trying to steer clear of controversy. I was feeling my way in unfamiliar territory here. My only contribution came as we were finishing our espresso.

Dolce's mother had been complaining about Montreal's lack of a concert hall. "We will never attract first-rate singers to this city. I can't blame them. Who is going to come to Montreal when they have to perform in a high school auditorium?"

Judging by the lack of response, I concluded this must be a familiar lament.

"If you want decent opera, you have to go all the way to New York," she huffed.

Dolce nudged my foot. She wanted me to join the discussion.

"My aunt was an opera singer." I immediately had Mrs. Narizzano's attention.

"Really? Where did she perform?"

"In Europe. Czechoslovakia and Germany mostly. She won a scholarship to study abroad and eventually became a soloist with the State Opera Company in Breslau."

"You must have been to Europe then, to hear her sing?"

"I'm afraid not. It was before my time. The war put an end to her career."

"What a shame. Is she still in Europe?"

"No. She's back in Canada now. She teaches music and leads a church choir in Windsor."

Since I had her interest, I decided to elaborate.

"My mother studied music too, at the Royal Conservatory in Toronto. She had her own radio program in the thirties."

"Opera?" Dolce's mother was clearly intrigued.

"No, she sang the popular songs ... Irving Berlin, Cole Porter."

"Why, I had no idea your family was so talented."

Later that night as I prepared to leave, Dolce helped me on with my coat in the front hall. "That wasn't so bad, was it?"

"You tell me."

"You were fine. I think Dad quite likes you."

"But not Mom?"

"Don't worry, she'll come around." She laughed. "I've told her if she wants me to date handsome rich Italian boys from old, established families, she'd better produce them. She hasn't had much luck in that department."

I smiled. "I hope her luck doesn't change."

"It won't." She kissed me lightly.

I made my way out the door and down the path to the sidewalk. As I climbed the hill to Westmount Boulevard I was thankful for the evening. Tonight I'd needed the distraction the Thanksgiving dinner at the Narizzanos had provided. I hadn't told Dolce about Dad. There would be plenty of time for that later.

MONTREAL, 1954

AN INSTRUMENTAL VERSION of "White Christmas" wafted through the moist, overheated air of the crowded department store. A week earlier the melody might have provided a soothing balm for customers seeking gifts. Now, with Christmas just a few days off, it seemed too slow, the wrong soundtrack for the scene playing out before me. Many of the shoppers wore the look of dazed desperation so characteristic of this time of the year.

As for me, I wasn't dazed or desperate, just depressed. I was looking for a pair of slippers in Ogilvy's.

"May I help you?" asked a harried young man wearing a blue blazer, grey flannels, and a perpetual smile. The brass nameplate told the world this was "Derek."

"Yes, Derek," I said, handing him a pair of slippers I'd selected. "Do you have these in a size twelve?"

"Just a moment, sir, I'll check on that." He made his way through the crowd of shoppers to the stockroom. The piped music switched from "White Christmas" to "Silent Night," a choral arrangement.

Derek returned, red-faced and out of breath. "You're in luck, sir. We do have them in size twelve, the last pair." He opened the box triumphantly.

"There is one thing ... " I hesitated. "Can I return these after Christmas if they aren't suitable?"

"Of course—as long as they haven't been worn." Derek smiled. I wondered if his cheeks hurt at night from the forced good cheer he was expected to maintain. "We can always exchange them for another pair."

Damn, I thought, I can't very well give Dad the slippers and tell him not to wear them in the hospital.

"No," I said, "I can't guarantee they won't be worn. They're for my father and he'll certainly want to try them out to see if they are comfortable. But if they aren't suitable I'd like a refund, not an exchange."

Derek pointed to the tag on the slippers. "It isn't our policy to offer refunds on items that have been worn." He was trying to be polite, but it came across as patronizing, as if this policy should be so universally understood that only someone from another planet would question it. "Of course if your father tries them and doesn't like them, we might arrange a credit when they're returned ... he could buy something else."

I mulled the problem over. Dad wouldn't be alive to use the credit and I didn't want Grace involved. It was too complicated.

Derek was becoming impatient. "Would that be acceptable?"

"I'm afraid not." I was starting to lose it. The clerk might be tired and overworked, but it was no excuse for his dismissive tone. "You see, Derek," I leaned close to him, keeping my voice low but intense, "I am buying these slippers for a dying man. He is in hospital, confined to his bed. He will never wear these slippers, but he doesn't know that." I could see Derek's eyes widen, his cheeks flush. "He doesn't know he's dying and I don't want him to know." I was almost hissing now. "So on Christmas morning I want my father to be able to open his gifts just like the rest of us. But I want to be able to return those gifts after the holiday for a full refund." I leaned even closer, my face just inches from his. I could smell a hint of mint on his breath, mingled with the sour odour of stale sweat. "Do you understand now?"

"Just a moment, sir," he said, flustered and retreating, "if you'll give me a minute, I'll check with one of my supervisors."

He hurried off and I saw him speak to an older man, also dressed in a blazer and grey flannels, who was in the midst of a sales pitch to a couple on the other side of the department. The supervisor, obviously annoyed at the interruption, started to protest, but Derek persevered and eventually the man looked my way, still listening to Derek. Then he turned back to the clerk, nodded, spoke a few words, and gave him a pat on the shoulder. Derek headed back to me, fending off questions from other harried customers as he crossed the floor.

"I've spoken to the department manager," he said, perspiration beading on his forehead, "and we will be happy to make an exception in your ... your rather unusual case." He smiled and nodded in the direction of his manager. "I'll make a note on the bill and Mr. Prendergast will initial it for you."

I left the store, the bill of sale initialled, the slippers suitably wrapped and tucked safely under my arm. I wondered if I'd ever feel the spirit of Christmas again. There'd been no need to bludgeon the clerk with my personal problems. I knew the anger I felt wasn't with Derek. It was with the elaborate charade I was being forced to play out at the hospital each day. It was poisoning my perspective. Fights with cab drivers, arguments with waiters, impatience with bank tellers—they were all symptoms of my frustration.

As I left the department store and headed up Ste. Catherine Street, it began to snow. The heavy wet flakes vanished when they hit the streets. It was just after four o'clock, but the overcast winter sky had already turned afternoon into evening. Cars hissed by, their windshield wipers sweeping back and forth like so many metronomes keeping time to the canned Christmas music that seemed to be everywhere.

MONTREAL, 1954

IN THE LOBBY OF THE WESTERN General Hospital the carol was "Oh Little Town of Bethlehem." It followed me into the elevator and continued until I got off at the fifth floor and the doors closed behind me. It took me a moment to adjust to the relative hush of the hospital's oncology unit. Then, as if the absence of the Christmas carols had created a vacuum, the smell of the disease swept in to fill it. From the open door of my father's private room came an odour so insidious that no amount of antiseptic scouring would remove it. It had the taint of a badly botched high school biology experiment, as if carbolic acid had been poured on the decomposing remains of some small animal. I swallowed hard and went in.

Dad was propped up in his bed, eyes closed, head resting back on the pillow. In his lap was a folded copy of *The Montreal Gazette.* Around one thin wrist he wore a plastic identification bracelet. His face was gaunt and his breathing shallow and laboured. Although I'd been visiting him for a week now, it was still a shock each day to see how the cancer had changed him. In my mind Dad would always be big, robust, and powerful, but the man in the bed was small, frail, and weak. Each day I had to come to terms with this change anew. I never came to terms with the smell. It was this more than anything else that overwhelmed me; each breath he expelled seemed to add to the corrosive quality of the air in the room. It was the smell of cancer eating away at his lungs. His eyes opened. They were dull, clouded by the painkillers he was taking.

"Hello, Bub," he managed in a voice that was barely more than a whisper.

"Hi, Dad."

"Whatcha got there?" He indicated the package under my arm.

"Oh, that?"

Let the games begin, I thought.

"You know better than to ask about things like that at this time of the year."

The opening lines might be different with each visit, but they weren't going to change anything in the final act. I put the package on a shelf by the window. The wet snowflakes weren't doing any better against glass than they were on the streets below. They dissolved on contact and ran like raindrops down the pane.

"What's it doing out there?"

"A little snow, nothing significant."

"Green Christmas?"

"Could be, but if the temperature drops a degree or so all that can change pretty quick."

"Well," Dad said, "it won't matter much to me in here." There was disappointment in his voice, but no defeat. He'd been hoping to be home for Christmas. "I guess I'll just have to wait until next year." He looked at me, seeking confirmation.

"Yep, next year we will do it up right." I was forcing the enthusiasm. "How's Grace?" She visited him in the morning; afternoons were my shift.

"She's fine. I think she's still getting her bearings. It takes a while to learn your way around a new town."

I sat down in the chair beside the bed. Dad motioned to the paper on his lap. "Want to have a look?" I noticed that the whites around his hazel eyes were a pale yellow. It was jaundice; the cancer had spread to his liver and kidneys.

"Sure." I began browsing through the paper, not really into it, just going through the motions to pass the time. The headline read "Nineteen Feared Lost," and the story speculated on the fate of the crew of a Belgian freighter that had gone down in a fierce winter storm in the North Sea.

A nurse entered the room carrying a tray of pills in one hand and a chart in the other. She put the tray down at the foot of the bed and selected one of the many tiny white paper cups.

"Time for meds," she said, smiling cheerfully. I rose and moved out of the way as she approached the bed. Dad leaned forward slightly and she tipped two capsules from the cup onto his outstretched palm. He popped them into his mouth, and when the nurse lifted a glass of water from the bedside table he sipped from the bent straw and swallowed painfully. The nurse put the glass back down and fluffed Dad's pillows, fussing over him as you would a child. "How's the pain today?"

"It's there," Dad said with a rueful smile. "It's always there, Shelagh."

"Well, if it gets to be too much for you, just ring." She smiled and turned, acknowledging me for the first time. "This must be your son."

"Oh, I'm sorry, I thought you'd met. Shelagh Phillips, this is Andy."

She nodded a polite hello. "I'm usually on the morning shift. Now, with the holidays, everything gets changed around." Shelagh Phillips was small and round, wore her grey-streaked hair in a tight bun. No makeup, just a little lipstick. I guessed she was in her late thirties, but it was hard to be sure. The starched uniforms seemed to rob the nurses of individual characteristics.

"I'll be back in a little while," she said to Dad, "after you've had some dinner."

I sat down again and resumed reading the paper, leafing through to the sports section. Both sports columnists, Dink Carroll and Vern de Geer, were debating how well the Boston Bruins' star centre, Milt Schmidt, would do as coach of the team. A recurring knee injury had put an end to his playing days, so the front office shuffled personnel to move him behind the bench. I didn't think it would make much difference. I liked the Bruins, but it was going to take more than a new coach to improve the team.

"There's something I wanted to ask," Dad said.

"Shoot." I put the newspaper down.

"It's pretty clear I'm not going to be doing any Christmas shopping this year." He smiled wanly. "Could you pick out a few presents for me?" He produced a piece of crumpled paper from beneath his covers and extended it to me. "I've made a list of a few suggestions for Grace. They're just suggestions, mind you. If you see something you think she'd like, go ahead and get it. You were always good at that sort of thing."

I glanced at the list. He hadn't said it, but we'd both felt it. He meant I'd been good at picking out things for Mom. I didn't have the heart to tell him this wasn't a one-size-fits-all quality and that I had no idea what Grace might like.

"I'll do my best." I folded the list and put it in my shirt pocket.

Dad stretched for a package of cigarettes by his pillow and I instinctively reached for matches. He smiled as I lit his cigarette. "One of the perks of a private room." He drew the smoke into what remained of his lungs, then exhaled with a sigh of satisfaction. "And it's one of the few things I can still enjoy."

A few minutes later a candy-striped nurse-in-training brought in Dad's supper. I slipped out of his room and found Shelagh Phillips at the nursing station filling out forms. She looked up from her work. "Does your father need something?"

"No, he's still eating. I just wanted to check with you about his smoking. Are you sure it's okay ... I mean, if the cancer has spread to his lungs ... "

She nodded her head. "I'm sure it's all right." She consulted one of the clipboards on her desk, flipping through the pages. She found the chart she was looking for, read silently for a moment, and then glanced back at me. "Dr. Buchanan feels nicotine withdrawal at this stage of the game would just create more problems. It's too late to make any real difference. We want to make your father as comfortable as possible under the circumstances."

"Under the circumstances," I thought. Like allowing the condemned man to eat whatever he wants for his last meal.

Shelagh Phillips looked at me sympathetically. "Is there anything else?"

I shook my head. "No, I just wanted to check, that's all."

My father had eaten all he was going to eat by the time I'd returned. He'd hardly touched his meal. The trainee finished wiping his face with a wet cloth and removed the tray. "I'm afraid I don't have much appetite," he said apologetically.

I glanced at the unfinished supper. "Can't say I blame you."

"No, the food's fine. I'm just not very hungry these days." He paused. "What about you? Had dinner?"

"No, I'm going to Dolce's for supper."

"The Italian girl?"

I nodded.

"From Westmount?"

"Yes." I reached into my jacket pocket, took out a picture of Dolce, and handed it him.

He took it and tilted it so the light from the lamp illuminated the photo.

"That's Dolce," I said.

He stared at the picture for a long time.

"Nice-looking girl. I'd like to meet her."

"You will, Dad, just as soon as you're feeling better."

"What's she like?"

"She's pretty special."

"Good," he said, with the most enthusiasm he'd shown during the day's visit, "you deserve someone special."

LENNOXVILLE, JANUARY 1955

THE SIGN ON THE DOOR of The Georgian Bar and Grill was simple and to the point. It read "Closed—Religious Holiday."

"Shit," I said to Carl. "This is a surprise." We'd decided to skip lunch at the university and grab a hamburger and a few beers at the G instead. "What religious holiday falls on January the sixth?"

Carl shook his head. "I don't know." As we stood by the entrance to the G the wind whipped the remnants of last night's snowfall into our faces. "What I do know is that if we don't move our asses we're going to freeze." He shivered and pulled his overcoat collar up around his ears.

We reluctantly made our way back down the street that led to Bishop's. We encountered two Divines just before the bridge that humped over the Massawippi River.

"What's the religious holiday today?" Carl asked.

The taller of the two spoke. "It's the Feast of the Epiphany." "Little Christmas," his friend added.

"Of course," Carl's said with just a hint of sarcasm in his voice, "I'd forgotten. Thanks a lot."

"You're welcome." The Divines spoke in unison, and continued past us on the road leading into town.

Carl and I looked at one another. "Jesus Christ," he said. "I'll be damned."

"You're probably right about that," I quipped.

"Fucking Little Christmas. I can't believe it." He shook his head. "The G closed for the Feast of the Epiphany."

The sun was a pale disc in the overcast sky and the wind off the river blew snow onto the freshly ploughed paths as we made our way across the quad and back to Norton Hall. It was the sixth of January; at Grace's insistence I'd returned to Bishop's two days ago.

"Willis will know something's up if you don't go back for the start of classes after the holiday."

I hadn't bothered to argue; the daily visits to the hospital had become torture. It wasn't my father's condition that made them so difficult, but the deceit involved. He must have known by now he was dying, but was probably keeping up appearances for our sake. And to think that we were pretending he was going to get better for his sake. It was all too bizarre!

Carl led the way up the stairs to our floor. Something was tacked to the door of my room.

"Not another Epiphany notice, I hope."

I pulled it free. "No, it's from the principal's office." I opened the envelope and unfolded a single sheet of paper, my hands trembling.

> Andrew,
> Please come to my office as soon as you can.
> I must see you about an urgent personal matter.

It was handwritten and signed by Arthur Jewitt, the principal.

"I guess this is it. It must be Dad."

Carl paused at the door to his room. "Do you want me to come over to the office with you?"

"No," I said. "I've been expecting it. Just not quite so soon."

As I made my way back across the quad to the principal's office I was thankful for Little Christmas. It was a good thing the G was closed. Otherwise it would have been hours before I got the news and I wasn't sure how sober I'd have been.

"Go right in," the principal's secretary said.

Arthur Jewitt was sitting at his desk as I entered. "Ah, Andrew," he said, rising to greet me, "I'm afraid I have some bad news." He shook his head sadly.

"It's Dad, isn't it?"

He nodded. "Your stepmother called." He looked at his watch. "About an hour ago."

"It's all right," I said. "We knew it was coming."

"Is there anything I can do?"

"No, I'll catch the next train home. I'll be away for a few days."

"Of course. Take however much time you need."

"Thanks." I turned to go.

"Andrew?"

I paused at the door.

"You have my sympathy."

Dolce hurried down the stairs in the women's residence. She was holding back the tears. "I thought he had more time," she said as I helped her on with her coat.

"So did I." We opened the door and walked outside.

"If I'd known he was going to go this soon," I said, with a flash of anger, "I'd have stayed home. I just got here, for Christ's sake."

"Are you sure you don't want me to go home with you?" We'd already discussed the question.

"I'm sure." I remembered my mother's funeral. "There's no point really. It's just a formality."

We crossed the bridge in silence. Ice had begun to form along the edges of the river. In another month it would be frozen solid. Today the wind dimpled the surface of the cold, black water.

"You seem so calm," Dolce said.

"I know it sounds awful, but in a way I'm glad it's finally over. It's a relief." We walked on, my arm around her shoulders, hers circling my waist. "At least we don't have to play that silly game any more, pretending he's going to get better. I hated that."

"How is your stepmother taking it?"

"She sounded okay when I phoned. I guess it is a relief for her too."

"You keep using that word. Relief. What about the sadness, the loss?"

"That'll come later. For now I just want to go home, get the funeral over with and get back here." I remembered how I'd grieved my mother. Would it be the same this time? Would I be shooting baskets again, alone in the gym?

"When's your train?" We'd reached the main street and were heading for the station.

I looked at my watch. "It's only three o'clock. We have almost an hour."

"You're sure you don't want me to come with you?" she asked again.

I looked at her. "I'm sure." There was no way I wanted to put Dolce through the funeral. It was going to be difficult enough for me, alone.

"Let's get a cup of coffee," I said. "I don't know about you, but I'm cold."

ST. LAMBERT/MONTREAL, 1955

ON THE TRAIN TO ST. LAMBERT I leaned back, closed my eyes, and invited grief in. It didn't work; I didn't feel anything. Not grief, not sorrow, not even relief. I was numb. I tried reading the paper, but couldn't concentrate. My eyes scanned a single ad over and over. Trans-Canada Airlines was offering a return trip to Europe by Super Constellation for only ninety-nine dollars. I wished I could take them up on it. I'd give anything to avoid the next few days. It was definitely time for a drink. I headed for the club car.

The taxi dropped me at the apartment. Although I'd had several rye-and-gingers on the train, I was stone cold sober as I climbed the stairs. Grace was waiting for me on the third floor landing. We held each other awkwardly and I could feel her shoulders shake as she sobbed, but when the embrace ended there were no tears in her eyes. I noticed she was already in mourning, wearing a tailored black suit and white silk blouse. A simple gold cross hung from a tiny chain around her neck.

"Come in." She motioned me into the apartment and closed the door quickly, as if she feared some unwanted intruder might slip by. I shrugged off my overcoat. "Have you eaten?"

"I had supper on the train, but I could use a cup of coffee."

In my room I unpacked my suitcase, hung up my blazer, and slipped two freshly laundered white shirts into the top drawer of my bureau.

"Coffee's ready," Grace called from the kitchen.

We sat down at a table in the breakfast nook. "I'm glad you're here," she said. "We have so many things to decide."

"Things?"

"You know ... funeral arrangements. I'd like the service to be what Willis would have wanted."

I thought back to my mother's funeral. Dad had arranged that. "I guess he'd want it simple ... nothing fancy. Not a church funeral, he didn't believe in all that stuff."

Grace winced. "I'm not so sure," she said defensively. "There were times at the end when he seemed to want to believe in something."

Who wouldn't, I thought, with death lurking just outside the door? "When Mom died we had a simple service, just relatives ... " I was testing the waters. I could sense trouble ahead.

"But that was different. Her death was so sudden and ... " She searched for the right word. "And circumstances were different."

So Grace had an agenda. That came as no surprise.

"What sort of funeral do you think Dad would have liked?" I took out my package of cigarettes and placed them beside my cup of coffee.

"Well, he was an important person here in St. Lambert. Past-president of the Sports Association, very involved in community activities." She looked at me.

"Go on." I removed one of the cigarettes and tapped it lightly on the tabletop.

"And his job with the CBC was important. He was the Supervising Engineer for the Corporation, that has to count for something."

So that was his title, I thought. I'd never asked. I lit the cigarette.

"And he received a medal from the Queen for the part he played in the television broadcast of her coronation."

I'd forgotten that. "So you want a big funeral?" I made it clear from the tone of my voice that I didn't.

"Not big, no. Just ... " Again she searched for the right word, then found it. "Appropriate. I think your father deserves an appropriate funeral."

"I agree." I exhaled and flicked an ash from my cigarette into the glass ashtray. "I'm just not sure we agree on what an appropriate funeral is, that's all."

"Well," she said, apparently sensing a stalemate, "why don't we sleep on it?" She wasn't conceding anything. "We have a meeting with the executor tomorrow morning. We can talk about it then."

"Okay."

"Then I'll see you in the morning," she said, and walked out of the kitchen.

"Goodnight," I called, and ground out my cigarette.

I heard her bedroom door close softly.

As it turned out, I had very little say about the funeral arrangements. In his will my father had left it all up to Grace. The executor, Charles Wilson, a friend of Dad's, explained this to us next morning in his offices in Old Montreal.

"What it boils down to is this," he said, summing up twenty minutes of discussion, "Grace will look after the funeral and pay off all of the hospital expenses from the insurance money."

Watching Charles, I was aware for the first time that he could have passed for Dad's older brother. He was roughly the same height and build, even had a moustache similar to Dad's. But he wasn't wearing a bow tie.

"When that's done you'll split what is left of the money down the middle, fifty-fifty. There should be about fifteen thousand dollars each. How does that sound?"

He glanced at me expectantly. I wished I'd had the chance to talk this over with my father. "If that's what the will says," I mumbled, "then it's fine with me."

Charles looked down at some papers on his desk. "That should be enough to see you through university if you are careful. We can set up a regular monthly allowance. Send the tuition bills to me and I'll see they're paid." He rose and extended his arm across the desk. He shook Grace's hand, then mine. "I've had extra copies of the will made up. You can pick them up on your way out." He walked us to the door of his office.

At the reception desk each of us was given an envelope bearing the gold embossed crest of the General Trust Company. Until now I hadn't given much thought to Dad's will, but I was suddenly sure, as we left, that the same couldn't be said for my stepmother.

ST. LAMBERT, 1955

THE VISITATION was at MacGillivray's Funeral Home on Riverside Drive in St. Lambert. Grace had insisted on an open coffin. My mother's had been closed, understandably given the nature of her death. But the moment I entered the viewing room and saw the body of what had once been my father lying in the casket, I knew the open coffin was a mistake.

The undertaker apparently didn't know that Dad parted his hair on the left side. He had combed it straight back, pompadour style, without a part. The face was pale and the cheeks were hollow, the lips had too much colour, and the folded hands seemed carved from beeswax. Thank God for the moustache and bow tie. They were the only authentic touches remaining.

In the men's room, locked in a cubicle, I took the silver flask from my jacket pocket and raised it to my lips. A Bach fugue filtered into the room through a recessed speaker in the ceiling. I drank the rye, shuddering as it went down. Then I took a deep breath, opened the door to the cubicle, checked myself out in the bathroom mirror, and rejoined the mourners.

The next few hours were a blur of murmured condolences, handshakes, and embraces. Many of the people who approached me mentioned my mother, and I realized that these were mourners who had not had the chance to offer their sympathy in person to me at the time of her death.

The Kerrs, Janet and Al, had been my parents' best friends. Janet, a trim little woman with carefully coiffed hair, gave me a long embrace. She wore a simple black dress of knitted wool with a single strand of pearls. The scent of her perfume lingered as we disengaged, and she held me at arm's length.

"How are you doing?" Her eyes were filled with tears.

"I'm all right."

"Last year it was Trudy, now Willis." She glanced at the coffin and shook her head, eyes closed as if to dispel the truth. "I'm sure you've heard this a thousand times," she said, "but if you need anything ... I mean anything at all ... just ask."

"Thanks, Mrs. Kerr." I knew the offer was genuine. "I'll be fine."

"I mean it," she said, her hands still clasping mine. "If you ever need somewhere to sleep or even someone to talk to, our door is always open." She smiled a sad smile.

At this point Al, Janet's husband, joined us. He was a tall man, balding and slightly stooped. Something was missing today—I realized it was the first time I'd seen him without a cigar. "My condolences," he said, and shook my hand, patted my shoulder. "He had so much to live for." He paused as if trying to remember something. "How old was Willis?"

"Forty-nine. He'd have been fifty in April."

"So young." He shook his head sadly.

They moved off to pay their respects to Grace. I watched them go and found myself thinking that forty-nine wasn't that bad; Dad had a pretty good run. Mom was only forty-two when she died.

The funeral, the next day, was not held in a church. I don't know if this was a victory for me, or if Grace simply couldn't find a minister who knew my father well enough to sanction the service. She did find one willing to preside over the ritual in the chapel of MacGillivray's Funeral Home. That Reverend Canon G.B. Stevens had never met my father was clear from his platitude-filled eulogy.

The crowded, overheated chapel smelled of damp clothing. I tried to avert my eyes from the open casket, but the more determined I was to look elsewhere the more often my eyes found the coffin and the profile of my father's face. Midway through the service a thin trickle of liquid escaped from the corner of his mouth. Then, as I sat transfixed by this, a fly landed on his nose and, drawn to the liquid, crawled down his cheek to explore. It was all I could do to contain myself. Surely others could see what I could see. Why didn't someone deal with it? Why not just close the coffin?

It was at this moment, when it was clear that no one was going to do anything, that my body filled with rage. It was directed at the woman sitting next to me, my stepmother. Grace Imeson had breezed into our life a little more than a year ago, taken my mother's place with unseemly haste, coerced us into an elaborate sham in the hospital, inherited half of the estate, and was now forcing us to submit to a ritualistic hocus pocus that my father would never, not in a million years, have condoned if he'd had any say in it.

When the last note of the last hymn reverberated through the chapel, I was on my feet pushing my way through the crowd to get away from Grace. I burst through the doors and stood for a moment on the steps of the funeral home drinking in the chilled winter air. Across the St. Lawrence River on Mount Royal the lights on the cross were on. To the west of the cross a television antenna reached for the sky, a single red light atop it winking. I noted with satisfaction that the antenna was a good deal higher than the cross. That was Dad's memorial.

My friends John Foulkes and Bryce Weir came out of the funeral home and we took our places in the lead car.

"Isn't your stepmother joining us?" Bryce asked.

"No." I turned and looked through the back window of our limousine. "She's in the car behind us." I wasn't sure I could have endured the ride to the cemetery in the same car with Grace. As the procession moved off, I took out the flask.

"Want a hit?"

Bryce shook his head. "No thanks."

John took a pull and so did I. The last time we'd been together like this we'd been on our way to celebrate our high school graduation.

As we crossed the Victoria Bridge the rage subsided. The worst was over. The cremation was going to be a simple ceremony. By tomorrow I'd be back at Bishop's.

LENNOXVILLE, 1955

THREE WEEKS AFTER Dad's funeral, with things beginning to settle down, we were in the midst of a January thaw that had worn away the blanket of snow covering the campus. All that remained now was a tattered grey coverlet with patches of grass poking through like the stubble of a day-old beard. It matched my mood this morning, walking across the quad, hung over from too many beers the previous night. My stomach was registering uncertainty about the scrambled eggs I'd eaten for breakfast and the canned grapefruit juice had left behind a faintly metallic taste in my mouth.

The porter's office was on the ground floor of the university's oldest building, McGreer Hall. It had a vague musty smell, not unpleasant, a subtle something left behind by generations of students who'd passed this way. A stooped, grey-haired man smiled as I approached.

"Any mail?" I asked.

"You're in luck today, my boy." Mr. Tribble took an envelope from one of the boxes that lined the wall behind him. "A letter from home."

The man we called "Trib" didn't miss much. He'd noted the postmark on the envelope. As he handed it to me he was seized by a racking cough, a legacy from an encounter with mustard gas in the First World War.

I waited for the coughing fit to subside. "Are you all right?"

"Fine. I'll be fine." He took a handkerchief from the pocket of his cardigan and with a trembling hand wiped his mouth. Then he waited, eyes still watering, hoping I'd open the letter right there, perhaps reveal a little about the contents and add something to Trib's most treasured commodity—information. He gathered snippets of news the way some people collect coins, trading them only when he was sure of something really juicy in exchange. As porter, he issued the exeat forms you were supposed to fill out if you were planning to be off campus overnight. He probably had a better idea of what the students were up to than anyone on the faculty.

I didn't recognize the handwriting on this envelope, but since I'd been receiving almost daily condolences in the mail I didn't give it much thought. I was aware of Tribble hovering as I tore it open. I leaned on the counter and began to read silently to myself.

> Dear Andy,
> This is a difficult letter for me to write. I am doing it because I feel it is my duty. It is about your father and your stepmother, Grace Imeson.

There was a tightening in my scrotum.

"Good news, I hope?" asked Trib, seeking substance.

I knew as I read on that there was nothing in this letter I wanted to share with the college porter.

I made my way out the door, leaving a disappointed Mr. Tribble wondering in my wake. I read on as I crossed the campus, ignoring murmured greetings from other students.

> I want you to know that Grace Imeson is the reason your mother took her own life. She was carrying on with your father and Trudy found out. It was simply too much for her. Your mother was a wonderful woman and didn't deserve this.

My father and Grace? The reason for my mother's suicide? The shock was like an unexpected punch in the stomach. My knees sagged. I had to swallow hard to keep my breakfast down.

> I thought a lot about you before writing this letter. Your father managed to hide things from your mother for a time, but she eventually found out. I think you should know the truth too.

I was shaking. My body felt as if it had survived some massive jolt of electricity. Nothing had prepared me for this.

> Grace Imeson has always been a greedy woman and will try to take everything she can from you. Be warned. She may pretend to care for you, but all she really wants is your father's money.
>
> A friend.

A friend? Who?

The letter implied that Dad and Grace had been involved for some time before Mom's death. If this was true then their decision to marry had not been the sudden impulse it seemed, and the overly generous division of the estate money in Grace's favour was no accident.

I reached Norton Hall, climbed the stairs to my room, and threw myself down on the bed. I was nauseous, my mind spinning with disjointed thoughts, each fighting for recognition. My mother had been sick a long time. I knew she'd told my father on more than one occasion he should find someone else. Had it actually happened?

As I re-read the letter, written in blue ink on nondescript stationery, I remembered another letter; one I hadn't read. It was my mother's suicide note. And I recalled a moment that put into doubt all of the allegations listed on the piece of paper I held in my hand.

It was the morning after Mom's death and Dad and I had just finished breakfast. "I have to go into town to the coroner's office. A few things to take care of. Do you want to come along, keep me company?"

"Sure." I went into my room to get my leather jacket. The taxi was waiting. I noticed we were heading for the Jacques Cartier Bridge, not our usual route when we went into the city.

Dad seemed to anticipate my question.

"The coroner's office is in Old Montreal. This way we save a little time."

It was mid-morning and from St. Helen's Island I could see that the leaves were beginning to change on Mount Royal. We descended into the city and the colour disappeared.

"Why don't you stay in the car?" Dad suggested as we pulled up to the courthouse. "That way we won't have to hunt down another cab when I'm finished."

"That's fine with me." I had begun to speculate on the nature of the "few things" he had to take care of in the coroner's office.

"I shouldn't be long." He closed the car door.

They wouldn't make him identify the body again, would they? I hoped not. I tried to push those thoughts from my mind. On the sidewalk people hurried by, only a few of them dressed for the unseasonably cold weather. Across the street a wino begged for spare change without much luck. The fare on our meter climbed. It was close to thirty dollars when Dad finally returned, carrying a large manila envelope under his arm. He opened the car door and sat down beside me.

"Just some of her things. And the note she wrote. Would you like to read it?"

"I don't know." A jolt of fear shook me. Reading her last words in her own hand would shatter the wall of protection I'd begun to erect. I was trying to move away from the horror of it all. The note would plunge me back into that darkness.

"It's up to you." Dad spoke softly.

"Is there anything in it I should see?" Safer this way. Let Dad decide what was best for me.

"I don't think so."

"Then I guess I'll pass." Relief, but at the same time a nagging pang of regret. Something lost.

Now, more than a year later, I remembered Dad's offer. If the discovery of an affair had led my mother to take her own life, surely she would have mentioned it in the note she'd left.

Or would she?

Perhaps my mother would have deliberately omitted any reference to it, wanting to spare me in the event I chose to read her note.

There'd been no hesitation on Dad's part when he offered to let me read it. So it was safe to say there'd been nothing thing incriminating in it. But that didn't prove anything, so I was back where I started.

Sick with a mixture of anger, fear, and impotence.

I made my way to the washroom, splashed cold water on my face, towelled it off, and walked down the corridor to the pay phone to call Dolce.

A FEW MINUTES LATER I let her into the Publications Office. This was one of the few places on campus where we could be guaranteed some privacy. I'd a key and had locked the door. Often this privacy served other needs, but not today. I handed her the letter and sat down while she read.

When Dolce finished, she handed it back to me, shaking her head. "What sort of person would write such things?"

"I can't begin to imagine." I slipped the letter back into its envelope.

She moved behind me, put her hands on my shoulders and began to knead gently at the base of my neck with her thumbs. "What an awful thing for you to have to read."

"It was rough." Her touch was light, but I could feel the tension in my neck beginning to respond to the slow, circular movement.

"I don't know how you can stand it." She was close to tears.

I didn't want the massage to stop, but I didn't want tears either, so I pulled her gently down into my lap. "It would be a lot rougher if I didn't have you." I folded her into my arms. I could feel her breath on my neck and the trembling of her shoulders as she sobbed soundlessly. I stroked her hair until the trembling stopped. Then she looked at me.

"You don't have any idea who sent it?"

"Not a clue. It has a St. Lambert postmark, but that's about all I really know."

"What about the handwriting?"

I shook my head. "Probably a woman." I glanced at the letter. "The writing style looks a bit like my mother's. My aunts all write the same way."

"Are you going to show it to Grace?"

"I don't know. I can't decide. I'd hate to hit her with it if there is no truth to it. If I thought it was true ... that would be another matter."

Dolce was silent a while, tracing a finger along the raised letters of the Royal typewriter in a recessed shelf in the desk. "Did you ever wonder about Grace and your father?" She hesitated, then went on, not looking at me. "I mean, you've been pretty critical of her ... you didn't go to their wedding."

"I know, but it wasn't because I suspected anything like this." I indicated the letter. "I didn't go to the wedding because I felt they were rushing things, getting married too soon. But in the weeks after the ceremony I began to come around, to feel that if Grace was what Dad needed, I wasn't going to object. After all, if he had lived, she'd be spending a lot more time with him than I would. Now this." I held up the envelope. "I still can't believe it."

I told Dolce about the trip to the coroner's office and Dad's offer to let me read the note. Wasn't that proof there was no truth to the accusation?

"I don't know. I guess if an affair drove your mother to take her own life, she would mention it."

"But what if my mother deliberately left out any reference to Grace in her note, just in case I might read it. She might have been angry with Dad, but not enough to poison his relationship with me."

"That sounds pretty far-fetched," Dolce said, "but I suppose it is a possibility." Then she got up from my lap and crossed the room to a window. "I think there's something else you should consider." She was staring out.

"What's that?"

"I don't quite know how to put this." She turned from the window, her expression troubled. She picked an imaginary piece of lint from the sleeve of her sweater. "I think maybe there is a part of you that actually wants to believe what's in the letter."

I felt a flare of anger. "That's nuts."

"Don't be so quick. You've often said yourself that your mother might be alive today if you'd stayed home and gone to McGill."

I nodded.

"So you feel some responsibility?"

This was true.

"We know whoever wrote the letter is being malicious." Dolce crossed her arms. "We agree on that?"

"Agreed."

"But that doesn't rule out the possibility that the stuff in the letter is true. And if that's so, it would certainly shift the blame for your mom's death away from you."

"And onto my father."

"And onto your father," she agreed sadly.

The idea was frightening. If the facts in the letter were right, it would certainly change how I felt about my mother's death and how I'd remember my father. Not to mention Grace.

"I guess anything is possible," I conceded reluctantly, and in that moment knew that the only antidote for the uncertainty within me was the truth.

"Isn't there someone you could ask?" Dolce had come back from the window and was sitting on the edge of the desk. "Who would your mother have confided in?"

"Nobody in St. Lambert; that would have just started rumours flying."

"What about her doctor, her psychiatrist?"

"No, anything she told them would be in confidence."

"Relatives?"

"Maybe my aunt in Detroit. She was Mom's favourite sister."

Dolce moved to face me. She put her hands on my shoulders, bent down, and looked into my eyes, as if seeking something within me. "I don't suppose you could just tear up the letter and forget it?"

I rose and took her in my arms. "I wish I could." A bell rang signalling the end of morning classes. I buried my face in the softness of her hair. "I just wish I could."

That afternoon I phoned Detroit.

"Aunt Alice, this is Andy."

"What a nice surprise," she said, but with a note of concern in her voice. "I hope everything is all right? We were talking about you last night, wondering how you were making out."

"I was fine until this morning."

There was silence on the line. I was glad it was my favourite aunt.

"I got a letter I wanted to ask you about."

"A letter?"

"I guess you'd call it a poison-pen letter." No point stalling. "It claimed Dad was having an affair with Grace Imeson and Mom found out."

"Hogwash!" Aunt Alice exploded. "How could anyone say such a thing ... write such lies?" There was a snort of disgust. "And that's what they are Andy, a pack of lies." Her voice was shrill now. "Willis loved your mother and would never have done anything to make her unhappy. You have to believe that."

Suddenly I remembered the conversation I had had with my mother in the kitchen, years ago.

"I wouldn't blame him if he started seeing someone else," she'd said as we sat at the kitchen table. "In fact, I've told him so."

Had Dad taken her advice? Was Grace the "someone else?"

"You know, Aunt Alice, Mom used to tell Dad he'd be better off without her."

"Oh Andy, that was just talk, nothing more. Your Mom was just depressed. There was never a hint of anything like that. And Trudy told me everything. And I mean everything." She sighed with exasperation. "I know what I would do with that letter. I'd put it where it belongs, in the toilet.

Tear it up, flush it, and forget it."

As reassuring as my aunt's remarks were, they didn't dispel the doubts.

"You've got to wipe those thoughts out of your mind," she said.

"I'll try," I promised, but I knew it wasn't going to be that simple.

I reviewed the facts again that evening with Carl MacCallum. We'd retreated to the G after dinner and were on our third round.

"From what you've told me," he said, trying to sum things up, "I think the letter is pure bullshit, just some sick son of a bitch trying to make trouble." He took a swallow of beer. "And I agree with Dolce. I think you should try to forget it."

Someone fed a quarter into the jukebox and a western tune filtered across the dimly lit room. A Tennessee Ernie Ford song.

"But if you can't forget it," Carl continued, "why not ask your stepmother? Show her the letter."

"I couldn't do that," I said, shaking my head, "not without some proof."

"I don't get it. You don't particularly like the woman anyway. What have you got to lose?"

"I'm not sure."

The door to the G opened and a group of students came in, stamping their feet and shivering. The January thaw was over; it had turned bitterly cold.

"Let me put it another way," Carl said. "If someone wrote lies about you in a letter, wouldn't you want to know about it?"

"I guess so ... sure."

"Well then, tell her, for Christ's sake. If it's proof you're looking for, I think she's your best bet."

"What do you mean?"

"Surprise her with it. She won't be expecting it. I guarantee you'll know from her reaction if she was fooling around with your dad or not." Carl drained the last of the beer from his glass. "If it's not true, then at least it will be a warning that someone in St. Lambert has it in for her."

"I'll think about it." A game of darts had begun behind us. It was getting noisy. "Let's get out of here," I said.

On the way back to the campus everything was cold and still; nothing moved. The smoke from chimneys rose in plumes straight and tight, like pillars supporting the sky. We didn't talk much as we walked, our boots crunching on the crusted snow.

LENNOXVILLE/ST. LAMBERT, FEBRUARY/MARCH 1955

IN THE DAYS THAT FOLLOWED I came to accept the fact that I might never know who sent the letter. But the accusations it contained weren't as easy to dismiss. I flip-flopped. One day I'd resolve to bring it up with Grace, the next I'd change my mind. I couldn't do it by phone or letter. I knew if I was going to do it, it would have to be face to face. I made sure, with a flurry of extracurricular activities, that I always had a good excuse ready whenever she suggested I return home for a weekend.

It was early February when I received a call from Arnold Agnew, the editor of *The Sherbrooke Daily Record.*

His voice was casual and matter-of-fact. "I'm looking for a Bishop's stringer for the paper next year. Someone to cover Lennoxville as well."

I held my breath.

"Would you be interested?"

"Would I?" I replied, stunned by the offer. "You bet!"

We met for lunch the next day in Sherbrooke. I guess I was expecting the Hollywood version of an editor: battered fedora, rolled-up sleeves, and ink-stained hands. Arnold Agnew looked more like a bank manager. A slim man in his thirties, he wore an expensive suit and an old school tie. His hair was cut short and slicked back without a part.

"Why me?" I asked after we'd ordered lunch.

"Well, Hugh Doherty has been doing the job, but he graduates this year and he recommended you. He sent me some your columns from the college paper and they seem pretty solid."

I was flattered. "I didn't think anyone off campus bothered with that stuff. What sort of writing did you have in mind?"

"We'd like to have someone actually living on campus to cover the university beat: a weekly column, sport scores, concerts, visiting lecturers, that sort of thing."

The waitress arrived with our food. He examined his lettuce and tomato sandwich. "In Lennoxville we'd expect you to cover council meetings, school board elections, fires ... " His sentence trailed off as he began to eat.

"How much does it pay?" I wondered if he knew that it didn't really matter; I'd have worked for nothing just to get the experience.

"Ten cents an inch." He put the sandwich down and sipped his Coke.

"That sounds fine." I had been expecting a set amount. I had no idea how much money "ten cents an inch" would generate.

Agnew sensed my uncertainty. "I think you can realistically expect to make between twenty and thirty dollars a month."

"Terrific." Maybe my luck was changing.

"Then we have a deal?"

"We have a deal." I reached across the table and we shook hands.

"Welcome to *The Record*," he said, and we touched our glasses of Coca-Cola in a toast.

It was late March before I finally worked up the courage to visit Grace, still uncertain about whether or not to mention the letter. We sat opposite each other in the living room of the apartment. She was perched on the edge of the sofa, her usual position, and I was in the easy chair, feet on the coffee table. The windows were open and the curtains billowed lazily in the early spring breeze. I told her about my job.

"I hope they'll be paying you enough,"

"Well, I won't get rich on ten cents an inch." I smiled. "What about you? Any luck in your job hunt?"

She shook her head. "No, they seem to want bilingual people for most of the secretarial positions." She looked down at her hands. "I'm afraid it's a little late for me to start learning French."

"You wouldn't have that problem in Toronto."

She looked up, "Heavens no. My firm would take me back in a flash."

"Well," I said, "have you thought about moving back to Toronto? It seems silly to stay here for my sake. With my job at *The Record* I won't be able to get home much. There are a couple of the guys from Toronto at Bishop's who have their own cars so I can always get a lift with them for Christmas or the holidays."

Grace looked at me. "I don't know ... I think Willis would have wanted me to stay here."

She was hesitant, but I could see the idea taking hold.

"What about the summers?"

"I won't be home summers. I'll be at Camp Nominingue." Actually, I hadn't decided this yet, but with a part-time job at *The Record* I knew I could afford to work another summer as a counsellor.

"If you're sure ... it certainly would be a lot easier for me."

"I'm sure." A sense of exhilaration flooded through me at the prospect.

It was then that I decided I wouldn't mention the letter. If Grace moved to Toronto I'd be seeing a lot less of her: Christmas holidays and maybe the occasional summer visit. She wasn't part of the life I was planning for myself.

Dad was gone; perhaps in time I'd cease to care about the accusations. The truth, whatever it was, wasn't going to bring him back.

A few weeks later Grace called me with the news that she had sublet the apartment and would be moving back to Toronto in August.

"Did you get work?"

"I start September the first. The firm has given me my old job back." She was clearly happy; this was the most emotion I'd heard her express since Dad's death.

"That's great," I said, and at least part of me meant it. "Where are you going to live?" I was careful to keep the elation I felt from my voice.

"I've made an offer on a duplex. It's just a few minutes walk to the subway and it has two bedrooms. You'll have your own room."

When I hung up the phone I was filled with a profound sense of fatigue. There was no relief. The doubts about the letter resurfaced. I needed answers.

TORONTO/WINDSOR, ONTARIO, MAY 1955

THE SHARP KNOCK on the compartment door woke me from what had been a fitful night's sleep.

"Toronto ... fifteen minutes," the conductor said, and when I grunted an acknowledgement I could hear him move on down the aisle, repeating the ritual at each door.

I struggled into my jeans, tugged on a sweatshirt, and pulled up the blind. The early morning light flooded the compartment and it took my eyes a moment to adjust. Outside, cars and trucks seemed to be racing the train along a highway that ran parallel to the tracks. Small two- and three-storey commercial buildings lined the road, sporting signs as varied as the buildings themselves. TransAm Transmission Repairs, Discount Autoparts, Sam's Office Furniture. Beyond them lay the flat, steel-grey waters of Lake Ontario.

I turned from the window to the tiny metal sink that was wedged into a corner of the compartment next to the toilet. I let the tap water run and examined my face in the mirror. No obvious sign of the hangover I was feeling, but then the headache, the upset stomach, and the thirst never showed. Just, occasionally, the bloodshot eyes. I took one of the tiny paper cups from the dispenser beside the mirror and drank. When the thirst was quenched, I added an Alka Seltzer tablet to the last cup of water and chugalugged the fizzing mixture. Breakfast. I clicked on the electric razor I'd inherited from Dad and gave my face a quick once-over, ran a comb through my hair, and repacked my bag.

Union Station was crowded with people. It was shortly after 7:30 a.m. and the city was already wide awake. I found a tiny restaurant just off the main concourse and sat down to wait. My train to Windsor didn't leave for another forty-five minutes. There were no bars open at this hour so I made do with coffee. I opened a copy of *The Toronto Star.* Local election news took up most of the front page and since none of the faces or issues was familiar, I turned instead to the sports news. The Yankee game against the Red Sox had been rained out.

I wondered what the weather would be like in Detroit. It had been four years since I'd last visited. Although I'd phoned Aunt Alice in January when I received the letter, I still had nagging doubts and wanted to talk things over with her in person. It was now June, I'd just finished my second year at Bishop's, and my summer camp counselling job didn't begin until July. So I had time to kill, and the trip gave me a chance to get away from Grace. I also wanted to spend some time with my grandmothers, who lived close by.

Although Alice was five years older than my mother, the two sisters had always been close. I think that in many ways Alice was more of a mother to Trudy than Blanche had been. I know she was one of the few people who could always make Mom laugh.

On the train to Windsor I dozed and read from the latest Perry Mason mystery, a habit I'd picked up from my father. *The Case of the Missing Matriarch.* I took the paperback with me to the dining car when lunch was called. My hangover had dissipated; I was surprisingly hungry. I sipped tomato juice seasoned with a little Worcestershire sauce, then ordered a hot chicken sandwich and a beer. I'd made this trip half a dozen times as a child, and eating on the train was one of the high points. There were linen tablecloths, polished cutlery, sparkling glass, and better service than you received in a restaurant.

"Dessert?" The black waiter had cleared the table.

"Blueberry pie and coffee."

"Yessir," he said, and disappeared into the galley.

The last time I'd made this trip Mom and Dad had been with me. It wasn't a vacation. Mom was on a mission. In her sessions with Dr. Cameron she'd revealed the depth of her dislike for her father. It was no secret to me. She'd made no attempt to hide her feelings. "He's one mean SOB," she'd often said as I was growing up. Dr. Cameron felt that this loathing might be the cause of her anxiety. He'd urged her to confront her father, tell him how she felt about him. She'd balked at first, but in time she came around. It took courage, but that summer she did it—she had it out with JB.

The train pulled into Windsor just after three o'clock, and through the window of my compartment I could see Aunt Alice standing on the station platform, wearing a brightly coloured sundress and sandals, her hair newly permed and her purse clutched tightly to her side. Alice and my mother looked alike. They had always worn their hair the same way and had the same warm brown eyes, firm mouth, and ready smile, but Alice had the misfortune to inherit my grandfather's hawk-like nose. It didn't look out of place on him, but it robbed her of the fine-featured symmetry that characterized mother's face.

She spotted me the moment I stepped onto the platform and moments later we were hugging, oblivious of the other passengers milling about.

"My goodness," she said, holding me at arm's length and looking me over, tears welling in her eyes, "how are you doing?"

"I'm okay, I guess."

She hugged me again, fiercely.

"We've been so worried about you, especially after you called about that awful letter." She shuddered.

"That's one of the reasons I came."

"Well, let's get you home and we can talk about it there."

We made our way to her car, a new Hudson Hornet, and I put my bag in the back seat while she settled behind the wheel.

"Have you eaten?"

"I'm fine, I had lunch on the train."

We drove out of the station parking lot, through downtown Windsor, and across the Ambassador Bridge.

"How have you been? Are you getting along okay with your stepmother?" My aunt didn't beat around the bush.

"Grace has decided to move back to Toronto. She's been offered her old job."

"I thought she was going to stay in St. Lambert, at least until you finished university." Alice didn't sound pleased.

"I don't get home from Bishop's that much and I'll be away at camp all summer. All her friends are in Toronto—it just makes more sense this way."

Alice concentrated on the road and in a little over forty-five minutes we were pulling into the driveway of her home in a suburb of Detroit.

DETROIT, MAY 1955

AS A CHILD I'D ALWAYS known that my aunt and uncle in Detroit were better off than we were. Their house was bigger and more luxurious than ours; they owned their own summer cottage and traded in their car each year. I saw my first television program in Detroit, went to my first stage show there. Since most of my friends in St. Lambert came from middle-class families like mine, I'd always characterized my aunt's prosperity as somehow American, as if their nationality itself entitled them to more.

Now, for the first time, I realized this wasn't true. My exposure to Dolce's family had put things in a different perspective. My aunt's standard of living no longer seemed quite so impressive.

We sat out on the back patio, next to the swimming pool, and sipped cold Budweisers. I'd forgotten how watered-down American beer was. I brought her up to date on the developments in my life, my switch to Arts at college and the offer of a job at *The Record.*

"Do you have a steady girlfriend?" She smiled. "I bet you do, a good-looking guy like you."

"Oh, sure, I had to beat them off with a stick, there were so many chasing me."

Alice laughed.

"Seriously, I'm seeing someone I like a lot. She lives in Westmount, in Montreal, so if things work out I may have a place to stay once Grace moves."

"That's good." Alice sipped her beer. "I'd hoped you'd find someone."

"About Grace," I said, watching the beads of condensation form on the bottle. "I know you assured me the letter was hokum, but have you any idea who might have sent it?"

"I can't imagine." She looked puzzled. "You didn't ask Grace?"

"No. It didn't seem fair. She has enough to deal with—Dad's death, the move. The timing never seemed right to bring it up."

"Probably just as well. It's something to be put behind you, something best forgotten."

"And you are sure there's no truth to it?"

"Absolutely." She said it with such conviction that I felt my lingering doubts begin to dissipate again.

I changed the subject. "You know Mom tried to end her life a couple of years ago, with sleeping pills."

"Willis told me," she said, shaking her head sadly; "it must have been awful for you."

"It was tough."

"Trudy was always fragile." I could see her mind drifting to the past.

"Tell me about her nervous breakdown, what you remember about it."

"Good God," Alice said with a start, "why would you want to know about that?"

"I don't know, trying to fill in the blanks, I guess."

"You're sure I can't get you something?" She was stalling. "A sandwich? Another beer?"

I shook my head. "I'm fine."

"Well," she said, slowly, reluctantly, "Willis was out of work at the time. It was in the middle of the Depression and jobs were scarce. Trudy had taken time off from her singing career when she learned she was pregnant. She wanted a family, but the timing was bad. Before you were born they had to move back in with your grandparents, your dad's folks in Leamington, and that was hard for her."

"They didn't get along?"

"Oh, nothing serious, your grandfather's diabetes was under control, but he was blind by then and at home. There was no money coming in. We helped as best we could and I think others in the family did too, but Trudy was pretty miserable during the pregnancy."

"Miserable?"

"Well, there was the morning sickness, of course, the nausea." Alice shook her head. "And something else, something I couldn't put my finger on. I figured it was the financial uncertainty, not having their own place."

"The breakdown, it was right after I was born?"

"Let me get us another beer." Alice went back into the house, emerged a few minutes later with two more Budweisers, and sat down. "You're sure you want to hear this?"

"I'm sure. I need to know."

"I'll tell you. But only because I want you to put any doubts you have about what caused Trudy's death behind you. The potential was always there."

"Go on."

"I knew there was something wrong the moment she arrived at the hospital. I was on duty that night, was expecting her, but she seemed ... I don't know ... distracted. And when the contractions got worse she seemed to be fighting them."

I tried to imagine my mother in labour, Alice hovering at her bedside, but I couldn't bring the picture into focus. However, I could see my father, in the waiting room, pacing, chain-smoking.

"She was in labour a long time, almost twenty-four hours, and when the doctor realized he was going to have to use the forceps for the delivery he put her under. I was worried too. It can be risky. But he managed, and within minutes you were there, hollering to beat the band and clearly in good shape."

"My mother told me they had to use forceps."

Alice reached across the table and ruffled my hair. "It was that damned head of yours." She shook her head and smiled. "Big, just like your dad's."

"Still big. I have a hard time finding a hat that's large enough."

"We cleaned you up, and while they were moving Trudy back to her room I went out and told Willis everything was all right, that he had a son. I don't think I've ever seen anyone so relieved. He hadn't slept or eaten during the labour, and must have smoked at least a carton of cigarettes."

"And Mom?"

Alice poured more beer. "When Trudy came out of the anaesthetic, she was pretty groggy. That's normal. But when we brought you into the room she didn't respond the way most mothers do. She seemed confused."

"Confused?"

"Yes, it was as if she was recovering from surgery, not a pregnancy."

"I'm not sure what you mean."

"Well, most new mothers ask about the baby."

"She didn't?"

"No, and it wasn't until we put you into the bed with her that she seemed to realize what had happened. But she still seemed dazed, distant."

"So you knew then that something was wrong?"

"I wasn't sure. It had been a difficult birth and I put it down to that. Eventually she seemed to come around. She wasn't breast-feeding you, but you took to the bottle right away."

"Why the bottle?"

"Not that unusual in those days. And with Willis out of work Trudy had said she wanted to get back to her radio program as soon as possible, so nursing a baby would have made life difficult."

"And the breakdown?"

"Looking back, I think she actually had the breakdown during the labour, the way she fought the contractions. But I wasn't sure at the time."

Alice paused and looked at me as if debating how to continue. Eventually she sighed. "It was a couple of days later that I realized there was something seriously wrong. I was finished my shift at the hospital and dropped into her room to see if she needed anything before I went home. She wasn't in the bed."

"Where … "

"She was perched on the windowsill, looking down. Her room was on the fourth floor."

I felt the shock ripple through me. It was how I felt when Dad told me the news of Mom's death, how I felt when I read the poison-pen letter.

"She was going to jump?" It came out as a whisper.

Alice nodded. "I willed myself to stay calm. I closed the door to her room, sat down on the foot of her bed and patted a spot beside me. 'Come here, Tru,' I said."

"Tru?"

"Yes, it was my nickname for her. It was our secret. She had a name for me too. It was Al."

"'Why should I, Al?' she asked me, and I could see she was still poised to jump. I was terrified."

"'Because we need you. Your baby needs you, Willis needs you … ' It was all I could think of to say."

"Jesus." I was reeling.

"After what seemed like a long time—it was probably just a minute or so—she got down off the windowsill, crossed the room, and sat down beside me. I took her in my arms and just held her. I knew then whatever had happened to Trudy it was serious."

I shook my head, trying to absorb these details. Alice shivered. The sun had settled behind the trees and the patio was cooling off. She rose from her chair, put the bottles and empty glasses on a tray, and moved inside the house.

"Postpartum depression," she said in the kitchen. "We didn't know much about it then. In fact we still don't."

It was the first time I'd heard the term. It wouldn't be the last.

DETROIT, 1955

MY CLOSEST COUSIN while I was growing up had been Joan, Alice's daughter. Like me, she was an only child. We were born just a year apart, and although she was older, we seemed to click as friends and confidants from the very beginning. On those summer vacations when our family travelled to the Windsor-Detroit area, we usually stayed with Aunt Alice. My first sexual experience, innocent though it was, came about during a visit when we played "Doctor" together. Joan also introduced me to American cigarettes (Pall Malls) and American beer (Pabst Blue Ribbon). We went everywhere together. One afternoon after a live Spike Jones matinee concert at the Fox Theatre we even ventured into an all-black area of downtown Detroit. Aunt Alice wouldn't have approved. She'd warned Joan to steer clear of Negroes.

During the first day of this visit I didn't see my cousin. She'd married the previous year and was now living in another part of the city. But the next morning she drove over in her brand new Ford convertible, and I was impressed. A few of the older students at Bishop's had cars, but none of my friends did.

Marriage had changed Joan. Before, she'd been plump and, in my mother's words, "rather plain." I could see she'd lost some weight, and with her hair styled and makeup carefully applied she was now an attractive young woman.

I slid into the seat beside her and we hugged briefly. When I'd told her on the phone the previous day that I wanted to visit my grandmothers she had offered to drive me to see them. We would both have lunch with Grandma Champion, who lived in Essex, a small town a few miles northeast of Windsor, then Joan would drop me off at Grandma Little's in Leamington, a larger town on Lake Erie.

It was a warm summer morning as we crossed the Ambassador Bridge. I realized it was three years ago that Dad had borrowed Aunt Alice's car to drive my mother across this same bridge for a meeting with her father, the man everyone called "JB."

"Do you remember that time my mother visited to have it out with Grandpa Champion?" I asked.

"How could I forget?" Joan glanced at me. "Talk about drama, it was right out of a soap opera."

"It was her psychiatrist's idea," I said. "He thought her fear of JB might be at the root of her anxiety."

"I was amazed at your mother," she said. "I don't remember anyone standing up to JB. I always thought of him as scary."

As we moved off the Ambassador Bridge and drove through Windsor Joan fell silent, concentrating on the traffic. My mind took me back to the day of the confrontation.

It had been a coordinated plan. Dad drove Mom to see her father, but that was to be the extent of his involvement. Dr. Cameron had stressed this. Another aunt had taken my grandmother shopping, to get her out of the house so JB would be alone when Mom arrived. Dad parked down the street and waited while my mother had her say. Then, when she was finished, he drove her back to Detroit. It was late afternoon by the time my folks returned from Essex. Mom seemed a little shaky getting out of the car and took Dad's arm as they walked up the path to the house. As she passed me in the hall she whispered, "I did it," and although her voice was soft, it carried an unmistakable note of triumph. "I'll tell you all about it later."

The next morning Dad went downtown to have lunch with an old friend who worked at a Detroit radio station and Aunt Alice left for an appointment with her hairdresser. So I was alone, sipping the last of my coffee and reading the newspaper when my mother came into the kitchen.

"Good morning," she said with a smile.

"Is it a good morning?" I asked.

"You bet your bottom dollar it is." She moved to the stove, poured herself a cup of coffee, and sat down across from me.

"You look like the cat who swallowed the canary," I said and waited.

She laughed. "Well I wouldn't call your grandfather a canary."

"You told him off?" Mom had promised to fill me in on the details.

"For the first time in my life I told JB what I really thought of him."

"Was it hard to do?" I asked and sipped my coffee.

My mother took a deep breath. I knew this wasn't going to be easy for her.

"At first I was terrified. You know my knees were actually shaking as I walked up the path to the house. I rang the doorbell. JB called through the screen door, 'Is that you Trudy?' It wasn't the voice I expected to hear, the voice I remembered as a child. It was the voice of an old man. I think that gave me the courage to continue. I said, 'Yes, it was me,' and went in. He didn't come to the door to greet me and when I went into the living room he didn't get up from his chair. He just sat there glaring at me. That was so typical and it made me angry. 'Who'd you expect,' I said, 'the King of England?' I was surprised at how normal my own voice sounded.

"'No need to be rude,' he said to me in that huffy manner of his.

"'If you think that's rude,' I said, 'just wait—you haven't heard anything yet.'

"'I don't know what you're talking about,' he said.

"There was a cup of tea on the table beside his chair and when he took a sip I could see his hand tremble. I was a little surprised at how much he'd changed. He looked so much older. I had expected him to be bigger, more formidable.

"'I had to see you,' I told him.

"He asked me why, when we hadn't spoken in the Lord knows how long. Why now, so 'out of the blue' were the words he used. What was so important I couldn't tell him on the phone? And why alone? Why did Blanche have to be out of the house?

"It was strange. As he spoke he seemed to be gaining strength. It was as if his own words were somehow changing him. He was no longer a frail old man, but something else, something closer to the father I knew as a child. It's crazy, I know, but somehow I was glad this was happening. It would have been impossible to say the things I'd come to say if I felt sorry for him."

Mom paused and I waited, not wanting to interrupt. She sighed, shook her head, and continued.

"I told him I didn't want Blanche here ... didn't want her to hear what I'd come to say. There was a quiver in my voice and I was fighting back panic, but I gulped a breath and plunged on. 'Things about other women, my own friends,' I said.

"It was then that he got out of the chair, pushed himself up, and stood facing me. When he did this I had the urge to run, but I fought it, stood my ground.

"He said, 'It's not right,' picked up the cup and saucer, turned his back on me, and started for the kitchen. I followed him. 'Dad,' I said, 'it is right—you've always been such a hypocrite. You stand up there in the pulpit every Sunday and preach one thing, but when it comes right down to it, you do another.'

"He ignored me at first, washed out his cup at the sink and put in the rack to dry. Then he turned to look at me. He said he didn't have to take this kind of talk from his own daughter in his own house. I said he did because a lot of it happened in his own house."

I sat listening to my mother, mesmerized. She'd confided in me in the past, but something about this time was different. She stared down at her hands. She was reliving the confrontation.

"I told him it was time someone stood up to him, that he was a disgusting old man. 'Do you know,' I said, 'that all the years I was in high school I was afraid to bring girlfriends home because I knew you'd be after them, running your hands over them, feeling them up, your peppermint breath on their necks? You were the laughing stock of the school. All the kids knew about you, told jokes about you behind your back. The Randy Reverend, that's what they called you. Do you have any idea how it feels when your father is a joke?'"

She paused again, then looked up from her hands and spoke directly to me.

"That's when JB started in on your dad," she said. "All that business about how Willis wasn't good enough for me, that I could have done a lot better. He said he was ashamed that his daughter married a man whose father ran a pool hall. I'd heard all this before, but I wasn't ready for what came next. He shook his finger at me and said, 'Don't think we didn't know what you two were up to those nights you said you were staying over with friends.'"

For the first time my mother seemed embarrassed to be telling me this.

"I wasn't expecting that ... about the sex," she said. "But I told him he was a fine one to talk about us carrying on before we were married. 'You carried on after you were married with anything that moved and wore a skirt.' When I said that I could see him tremble with rage. He pushed past me and went out onto the front porch. I followed him. 'You, married and a minister, in the beds of other men's wives.' This time when he spoke it was through clenched teeth. 'You keep your voice down, missy,' he said. 'Bad enough you come here, but you keep your lies to yourself. I wouldn't want anyone to hear you making a fool of yourself.' That made me doubly furious. He wasn't worried about what I had to say, he was worried about what the neighbours might think."

My mother was holding a napkin in her hands, twisting it as she talked.

"I started to shout. I said it was no wonder we'd moved so many times, that we'd probably have been run out of town if we'd stayed any longer. I didn't know if this was true—I just blurted it out. There must have been something to it, though, because he actually flinched. Then he took off down the steps and around the side of the house. As I watched, he disappeared along the path that led to the back garden. I was still furious. I followed him. When I reached the garden, he was nowhere in sight. Then I sniffed the air. I could smell cigarette smoke. It was coming from the shed. The old bastard was in the shed, smoking.

"'Dad, I know you're in there,' I called. 'Hiding. That's great. Hiding and sneaking a smoke. You think we didn't know about that too? You preaching about the evils of tobacco while all the time you were secretly puffing away.'"

My mother put her head in her hands.

"That's when something from the past tugged at me ... something about the smell of his cigarettes. I could picture him in there smoking, laughing at me. I could feel anxiety beginning to take hold ... I had to get away. I ran back to the front of the house and fortunately your dad was there, waiting in Alice's car. I opened the door, jumped in, and told him to drive. I'd done what I'd come to do. I had to get away."

"The confrontation didn't work, did it?" Joan's words brought me back to the present.

We were out of Windsor now, on the open highway. Ahead was a truck, loaded with hay. Joan passed it easily, the Ford's big V-8 engine kicking in with a surge of power.

"No. Mom did say she was no longer afraid of JB, but when we got back to St. Lambert she still suffered from anxiety attacks. It was disappointing. Her doctor was expecting more. We all were."

Joan shook her head. "It's such a shame."

I watched out the window as flat farmland rolled by. Tractors tilled the fields and along the side of the road there were stands with fruit and vegetables for sale.

Joan turned on the radio, fiddled with the dial and found a station playing music. Judy Garland was singing "Over the Rainbow." It had been one of my mother's favourite songs. If things had been different—if JB hadn't been such a bastard, if Dad hadn't lost his job during the Depression, if I hadn't come along at the wrong time—it could have been my mother singing on the radio.

ESSEX, 1955

IN ESSEX, JOAN DROVE along Centre Street, then turned into the driveway of a modest bungalow. She parked the car, switched off the ignition, and put on the emergency brake. I looked at the house. This was where Mom had come for her showdown with JB.

The old boy was gone now, died on the fourth of September, almost a year after my mother's death. Dad told me at the time that JB had been ill and in the hospital, but no details beyond that. A long-distance call had come from Aunt Alice as I was getting ready for my return to Bishop's.

"Your grandfather died last night." Dad's voice was flat, emotionless.

"JB's dead?" I wasn't sure how to take the news.

"How did it happen?"

"A stroke, apparently."

"Are we going to the funeral?" I held my breath. It was the last thing I wanted to do.

"I don't think so," Dad said. Still no emotion.

I wished my mother was still alive. She'd have probably danced a jig.

My father muttered something I didn't quite catch. It sounded like "good riddance."

"What?"

"Oh, nothing," he said, and picked up a newspaper.

"How is Grandma holding up?" I asked Joan.

"Oh, she's fine. Relieved, I think."

"Had JB been sick long?"

Joan laughed. "I guess you could say he was sick."

"Well, he was in a hospital, wasn't he?"

"If you can call St. Thomas a hospital."

"What do you mean?" I was confused.

"St. Thomas is a mental hospital. The family had JB committed."

I was stunned. "You mean he was crazy?"

"Crazy? Maybe—all I know is we got this panic call from Grandma in the middle of the night. The next day Mom drove here and signed some papers and they put him away. Apparently he threatened Blanche."

"Your mother never mentioned it to me."

Joan laughed again. "Of course not. She's embarrassed. The whole family is embarrassed. The idea of the Reverend J.B. Champion in the loonie bin isn't something they want advertised."

"When did all this happen?"

"I'm not sure exactly. It was just after your mom died, because my mother had just come back from her funeral."

We got out of the car. "Now don't let on I told you. It's supposed to be a big secret."

Joan pushed the doorbell and we could hear the echo of chimes inside the house. It was a long time before the door opened.

Blanche Colpitts Champion was a tiny, birdlike woman, with rimless glasses perched on a fine-featured face. "Come in, come in." She led us down a hall, walking with the aid of a cane. She was wearing a bright print dress and had her silver hair tied back in a bun. I sat down in the living room while Joan and Blanche went into the kitchen to get our lunch ready.

This was where it happened, where Mom "had it out" with her father. The sun filtered into the room, illuminating a matched sofa and chair on a worn oriental rug. Over the mantle a watercolour painting hung in a gilt frame. I rose for a closer look. It was a summer landscape—a country scene with billowy clouds. Neatly written in the bottom right-hand corner was the inscription "Gertrude Champion, 1926."

"Your mother did that when she was just fifteen." Grandma Champion had re-entered the room. "I had it put up after she died."

"It's beautiful."

"So was Trudy," Blanche said, and shook her head sadly.

Joan brought a plate of sandwiches to the dining room table and we sat down to eat.

"I was sorry to hear about Grandpa," I said as my grandmother poured tea.

"Oh," she said. She paused and glanced at Joan. "It's not easy you know. Old age just creeps up on us." She looked back at me. "Cream and sugar?"

"No, I'll take it straight, thanks."

When she'd finished pouring I reached for a sandwich.

"You look well," my grandmother said. "University seems to agree with you."

I told her about my switch to arts, my part-time job at the newspaper, and my stepmother's plan to move back to Toronto.

"Do you know Grace?" I asked.

"I'm afraid not." She shook her head. "How old is she?"

"I'm not sure ... forty-four or forty-five."

"Trudy might have known her. They'd have been about the same age."

I wondered about this. Was it possible? "But Grace is from Leamington," I said. "Mom grew up here in Essex, didn't she?"

My grandmother sipped her tea. "Yes, but the schools in the area sometimes got together for field trips, athletic events ... that sort of thing."

This was something I'd have to ask Grace about. Hard to think of my mother and stepmother together. I needed some time to sort out these new possibilities.

The rest of the lunch passed with polite small talk. After dessert we got up from the table. Joan cleared away the plates and took them into the kitchen.

"You leave those for me to wash," my grandmother called to her.

"You sure?" Joan's voice came from the kitchen. "It's no trouble."

"I'm sure. The one thing I do have these days is plenty of time on my hands. It will give me something to do."

Joan came out and at the door my grandmother gave me a parting kiss on the cheek and held my face in her hands for the briefest of moments.

She smiled sadly. "You have your mother's eyes."

We got into the car and my grandmother waved to us as we pulled away from the house. When we were outside Essex, on the road to Leamington, Joan turned to me. "I just remembered something about Grandpa Champion."

"What's that?"

"When I was little, maybe seven or eight, my mother warned me about JB. She said I had to be careful when we visited. She didn't want me alone in the same room with him."

"Did she say why?"

"Nope, and it's funny, I never asked her the reason."

"Maybe he was a little loonie, even back then?"

"I guess." Joan shrugged.

LEAMINGTON, 1955

WHEN WE WERE APPROACHING Leamington I asked Joan to drop me off on Talbot Street, outside the pool hall. I'd walk the rest of the way to my grandmother's. As she drove off, the top of her convertible still down, she waved goodbye and beeped her horn twice. I waved back.

The last time I'd been here, in 1952, I'd unwisely beaten my father in a game of snooker. Dad could see from the way I played that I was no novice.

"If you put that much effort into your homework," he'd grumbled, "maybe your grades would be better."

The hall where we played had once belonged to my grandfather. For more than twenty years Clyde Little's Billiard Academy had been a sanctuary for the sporting men of this sleepy southern Ontario town. Then, during the Depression, Clyde developed diabetes and lost not only the business, but his eyesight as well.

Each summer vacation when we visited, Dad would take my grandfather's hand and place it on the top of my head. "The boy's growing like a weed, Willis," Grandpa Little would say, his eyes blank. At five-four, Grandpa always felt his size deprived him of the chance to be a major league ballplayer.

After Clyde's business and health failed, he spent his last years in darkness, sitting in his rocking chair on the front porch, smoking locally grown tobacco in his briar pipe and listening to baseball games on the radio. He died in that chair in the summer of 1947 with the radio tuned to a game between the Detroit Tigers and the Boston Red Sox. It had been eight years since his death, but Anna Maria hadn't moved the chair. It still occupied the place of honour on the porch.

I turned the handle of the mechanical doorbell. There was a movement behind the lace curtain in the front room and a moment later the door opened.

"Land-a-Goshen," my grandmother said, and I was enveloped in a powerful, bony embrace. Her scent was musty and her accent still carried a trace of her Swedish ancestry. "Let me look at you," she said, standing back. She was wearing a dark blue housedress patterned with white flowers. Her silver hair was closely cropped, displaying the solitary diamonds she wore in her pierced ears. "My, my ... " She shook her head, at a loss for words. "There's so much of Willis in you ... and Trudy too."

The sound of a Lawrence Welk polka greeted us as we entered the parlour. It came from a floor model Stromberg-Carlson radio that stood against the far wall. My grandmother turned the volume down, but not off.

"Would you like something to eat?" she asked, innocently. The rich, sweet unmistakable smell of fresh doughnuts beckoned from the kitchen.

I nodded and she led the way. I sat down at the kitchen table while she lifted a wire basket of doughnuts from an iron pot on the stove. She held it there for a moment, letting the excess oil drip off. Then she swung the basket to some folded newspapers spread out on a shelf by the sink. I knew they had to sit a bit, to cool off and let the newspaper absorb more of the oil. It was hard to wait, but as a child I'd burned my mouth more than once biting into a doughnut too soon.

"Don't let him at them until they've cooled," my mother pleaded with Anna Maria, exasperation in her voice.

"He's got to learn these things for himself," Anna replied tartly. "I won't mollycoddle the boy."

"I think these are almost ready." My grandmother tested one of the doughnuts with a finger. "Why don't we sit outside where it's more comfortable? I'll get us some buttermilk."

It was late afternoon and the veranda was in the shade. A locomotive shunted a dozen empty freight cars along the spur line that ran past the house to the Heinz canning factory down by the lake. My grandmother waved to the engineer. He waved back and gave a quick toot on the train whistle.

She smiled and sat down in one of the rockers. "How are things at university?"

"It was hard last year, but since I switched from Science to Arts I've been doing pretty well."

"And how's your stepmother?"

"Grace is fine. She's going to move back to Toronto."

"Oh?" My grandmother's eyes arched. "I thought she'd be staying on in St. Lambert, at least till you finished school."

"No, she doesn't speak French and hasn't had any luck finding work."

"Well that's a surprise. She was always bright, that one. Not much to look at, mind you, but smart as a whip."

"You knew her then?" I was feeling my way, not sure where the conversation was going.

"Not very well, really. The Imesons were dirt poor, farm people. But Grace did well in school, took a secretarial course when she graduated, and landed a job here at the Heinz plant."

"Dad said he met her in Toronto." I tried to sound casual.

"Yes, she didn't stay here long. I guess there were more opportunities in a bigger city."

I continued to probe. "Did Dad know Grace when they were at school here in Leamington?"

"Oh, he probably did, but he was a good deal older—five or six years. I don't think he ever mentioned her."

I decided to move back onto safer ground. I told my grandmother that I'd be working part-time for *The Sherbrooke Record* when I returned to Bishop's. "I won't be home that much, so I think Grace will be better off in Toronto. They've promised her she can have her old job back."

"I guess that makes sense," she said, but I detected a note of disapproval in her tone.

Another locomotive shunted to a stop on the siding. The engineer waved something from the window of his cab.

She rose from her chair. "'Scuse me, Jack, there," she said, motioning to the train, "needs a refill." She went into the kitchen and emerged with a white enamelled pitcher filled with water. The engineer got down from his locomotive and approached the fence that separated the tracks from my grandmother's yard. He took the full pitcher from her and handed back an empty one, thanked her and made his way back to the train.

"The boys get dry shunting freight cars back and forth all day." She put the empty pitcher down on the porch steps. "Do you remember the time when you were little and one of the engineers offered to show you the inside of his locomotive?"

I said I wasn't sure.

"You must have been four or five."

"Tell me about it."

"I arranged it, but you weren't having any of it. You screamed bloody murder."

Fragments from the past floated into my mind. As my grandmother filled in the details, I closed my eyes and the memory of that day returned.

Dad is sitting in the kitchen, eating a ham sandwich. He'd been out most of the afternoon, helping a friend repair a faulty radio. I am on my grandmother's lap, nibbling a doughnut. From the floor above we can hear the sound of my mother's footsteps as she moves about.

"How's Trudy been today?" Dad asks.

"Not much change," my grandmother says. "I tried to get her to eat

something this morning, but without any luck." She shakes her head sadly. "But this little guy has been having a great time."

Dad smiles at me. "It's a nice day. I guess I should take him for a walk."

My grandmother shifts me a little, relieving the pain in her arthritis. "I spoke to Vernon this morning," she says. "Vernon McGwire ... one of the engineers who works the Heinz siding. He said things are pretty quiet these days. He wondered if you wanted to show Andy the train."

"That'd be great," my father says. "Do you think he'd let us up in the cab?"

"I'm sure he would."

Dad has me all ready to go when Vernon shunts the big locomotive onto the siding. The noise of the trains had frightened me at first, but I'd always been a safe distance from them and over time that fear had disappeared. I'd even learned to wave at the engineers and was usually rewarded by a wave back.

Dad picks me up and heads down the steps. Vernon descends from the cab of the locomotive. My grandmother is watching on the porch; Clyde is listening, beside her in his rocking chair.

As we approach the train I grow apprehensive. The locomotive seems gigantic, with steam hissing from beneath its black body. I start to cry. My father, embarrassed, seeks to reassure me.

"It's okay, Andy, there's nothing to fuss about. We're going to meet Vernon. You know Vernon ... he waves to you." Dad is trying to ignore my crying.

I bury my head in his shoulder, but I can't hide from the sound. I begin to struggle, kicking my feet.

"There, there, you're not going to let a train scare you, are you?" my father asks, trying to contain me.

Vernon, not quite sure how to handle this, approaches awkwardly.

"Hello, little fella," he says tentatively.

By now I am sobbing non-stop. I can feel the engine's heat ... it seems almost alive.

"Maybe he'll calm down if we get him in the cab," Vernon suggests. He turns and mounts the ladder.

My father extends his arms, pushing me up to the engineer. At this point I'm hysterical, kicking and screaming. One of my kicks lands on my father's cheek and he staggers, almost dropping me. He recovers his balance and clasps me close to his chest, restraining me, trying to stop my struggling.

"Maybe today isn't the day," Vernon says from the cab above us.

"I guess not," Dad says, still trying to control me. "Perhaps another time, Vernon. Thanks anyway."

As we turn and start back to the house my father is angry. "I'm surprised at you, a big boy like you, frightened by a train."

By now my crying has subsided into sobs. My mother has heard me and has come down from the bedroom. She crosses the lawn and takes me from my father's arms.

"There, there now ... it's all right ... it's all right. You're with Mummy now ... it's going to be okay."

She looks at Willis. "That was a damn fool idea ... anyone with half a brain could see a child his age would be frightened by something like that."

Dad shrugs his shoulders. "I think that's part of his problem," he says. "You're being too protective." He mounts the stairs and goes into the kitchen, slamming the screen door behind him.

It was a long time before I waved at passing trains again.

LEAMINGTON, 1955

THE SOUND OF A TRAIN rumbling by my grandmother's house woke me from a fitful sleep. It was a moment or two before I remembered where I was. Then I smelled bacon cooking and realized I was hungry. I got out of bed and slipped into my clothes.

"It's about time, sleepyhead," my grandmother chided me with a wink as I sat down at the kitchen table. "Any later and I'd be getting you your lunch." She filled my cup with coffee.

"I suppose you've been up for hours," I said with a grin.

"You don't need much sleep when you're my age." She put a plate of fried eggs, toast, and bacon before me and sat down herself.

"You've eaten?"

"I had some toast earlier while I was getting things ready." She poured herself a cup of coffee, added cream and sugar, and watched me eat. "The eggs okay?"

"Just right."

"Sunny side up." She smiled to herself. "Your grandpa liked them that way. I remember the first time we met. I was working in a restaurant in a hotel in Wilcox, Pennsylvania. It was the summer of 1897 and Clyde was playing baseball for a team from Ontario that was touring the state."

My grandmother sipped her coffee.

"He came into the hotel dining room and I was so shy I was almost afraid to serve him. But when I did he was so down-to-earth and friendly, I liked him right away."

"I guess those barnstorming ballplayers lived a pretty wild life?"

"I suppose some of them did." She smiled to herself. "I know my father wasn't thrilled when your grandpa asked me out. He was from the old country, Sweden, and things were different there."

"What did he say?"

"He didn't think much of ballplayers. He might have refused to let me go, but Clyde came around to the house and introduced himself. It turned out they were both Masons so that was a big plus."

"What happened?"

"Well, we went to the regular Saturday night dance in Wilcox."

"And Clyde behaved himself?"

"A perfect gentleman."

"Didn't drink too much?"

"Goodness no, he was never much of a drinker. The only bad habit he had was chewing tobacco." She smiled. "Once we were married I convinced him to switch to a pipe."

I remembered my grandfather puffing away on the porch. The drink was usually lemonade or iced tea. I decided to change the subject. "Cousin Joan told me they had Grandpa Champion committed."

"About time, too." There was no love lost between the Champions and the Littles. "The way he was carrying on he should have been put away years ago."

"Carrying on?"

"Oh, so full of himself, always bragging about this and that. He made your mother's life hell, never approved of Willis." My grandmother's voice rose in anger. "He never approved of us. Thought because he was a minister he had some God-given right to Lord it over us. Just because Clyde and I didn't have his education. That was true, but it was no reason to take it out on Willis. Your dad graduated from one of the finest universities in the country."

"Do you remember the summer when we came down and Mom told the old boy off?"

"I knew about it, but only from your father. You stayed with your Aunt Alice in Detroit that time. When it was over Willis called me, said she'd spoken her piece and they were heading back to Montreal."

I realized my grandmother probably knew less than I did about the confrontation. "After I was born, I guess my mother had a pretty difficult time?"

My grandmother sighed. "Well, she was pretty upset when Willis lost his job. A lot of men were out of work in those days, but it bothered Trudy more than it should have. She got really down in the dumps. Then they moved in here with us and you came along. That's when we noticed a big change. Trudy had always been so lively. We tried everything, but she couldn't seem to snap out of it."

I finished breakfast and while my grandmother washed the dishes I dried them. I wondered about her life, living alone in this old house with no family close by. Dad was an only child and wanted her to move into something smaller after Clyde died, but she chose to stay on, stubbornly refusing to make any changes.

"That's it," Anna Maria said, handing me the last dish to dry. "Finish that and we can relax."

"Do you think things would have been different for Mom if Dad had managed to hold onto his job?"

"I don't know." She shook her head. "It was certainly one of the things bothering her, but there must have been more to it than that. I don't think she ever got back to the way she was when they were first married. Too high-strung, I guess. She was never quite the same after you were born."

My feelings were mixed the following day when I bade goodbye to my grandmother and left Leamington. On the bus ride to Windsor and the train trip back to Montreal I went over the things I'd learned on my visit.

I'd filled in some of the blanks in my mother's story. I was gaining a new perspective on the problems that had led to her death. It was clear that my birth triggered the breakdown, but I wasn't sure what else had caused it. Would she be alive if I'd remained at home, gone to McGill instead of Bishop's? Possibly, but that had been her call. She'd urged to me leave, stressed the importance of going away from home for university. She'd done it, Dad had done it, they both wanted me to do it. It was only in hindsight that the doubts had surfaced.

On the question of the poison-pen letter I was almost certain now that my father's version of the facts was the truth. There would be no point mentioning it to Grace. It wouldn't prove anything and would certainly upset her. She didn't need to know she had an enemy in St. Lambert—she was moving back to Toronto. I wanted to smooth over my relationship with my stepmother, because I still needed a place to call home during my final two years at Bishop's. I didn't plan to spend much time with her in Toronto, but I had to have somewhere to go for the Christmas holidays and the weeks when I wasn't at Bishop's or Nominingue.

Ahead lay another summer in the sun at camp. I needed to recharge my batteries.

LENNOXVILLE, 1956-57

IN MY FINAL TWO YEARS at Bishop's things settled down. In the summer of 1956 I convinced my executor, Charles Wilson of General Trust, that I simply had to have a car for my work at *The Record.* My predecessor, Hugh Doherty, had managed to file his stories from the campus without one, but needless to say this wasn't something I mentioned to Mr. Wilson. He forwarded me the money and on the Tuesday after Labour Day in 1956 I bought a used '51 Ford two-door hardtop from a dealer in Toronto for nine hundred dollars. Since I had no driver's licence, a college buddy piloted me back to Montreal. Dolce, who'd learned to drive the family car the previous summer, took over behind the wheel for our trip to Lennoxville. Within a couple of weeks, with her tutoring me at Bishop's, I had my own licence.

By now I knew I wanted to spend the rest of my life with Dolce. I'm not sure she shared this view, at least the long-range part of it, but I had no doubt she loved me. We'd suffered through dozens of arguments and fights, and even broke up and dated others for a few months. But in the end we were always drawn back together.

In my high school days I'd had quite a number of girlfriends and had earned an unwarranted reputation as a ladies' man. It was true that I'd been sexually adventuresome with some of the girls I dated, but I'd never gone "all the way" with any of them. Some of the boldness came from the knowledge that none of these girls had really captured my heart. It was easy for me to push when there was nothing to lose if I was rejected.

With Dolce it was different. It was weeks before I even worked up the courage to kiss her. And when I did, on a cold November night in the dark and sheltered doorway of one the old lecture halls, the connection was electric. The charge that went through me went beyond sex, to a level of connectedness and comfort I'd never experienced before. I knew at that moment that I would proceed slowly and with caution. I had too much respect for this sensitive, intelligent, and incredibly sexy young woman to try anything aggressive. I think Dolce understood this and was relaxed, happy to let me lead the way.

There was a degree of composure about her, an ease with which she handled difficult situations that impressed me. She knew who she was and what she liked and didn't like, and it seemed that nothing could shake that conviction. Her personality was the polar opposite of my mother's. She was calm and resourceful, able to shake off slights and see goodness in people. That's not to say her feelings couldn't easily be hurt, but she was quick to recover and just as quick to forgive. I needed this. It seemed to me that I'd spent most of my life trying to make things right for an unstable, emotionally distraught woman. Her moods shifted on a whim, her vulnerability put her constantly at risk. After a very long time in rough waters, Dolce was an island of tranquility for me and I desperately wanted the safety and shelter she was offering.

I can only guess at what she saw in me. I was certainly different from the boys she'd dated in high school. I wasn't predictable or polished, but a bit of a rebel, an outsider with a sharp tongue. In a way we were opposites. I was a lot less sure of myself than I let on, was quick to take offence, quick to judge, and not nearly as forgiving. Whatever I was—whatever she was—we were a good match. She said she'd never dated anyone who had made her feel as completely at ease as I did. While this may not sound like a particularly passionate endorsement, I took it as the highest form of compliment.

In my third year the students organized the university's first winter carnival. There was a snow sculpturing contest, a figure skating exhibition that Dolce organized, a hockey game with a team from the University of Sherbrooke, and, to wind things up, a formal dance. What made the whole event even more remarkable was the selection of Bishop's first Carnival Queen.

Dolce was a finalist, one of three princesses. Each student had a vote and the name of the winner was to be revealed before the hockey game in Sherbrooke. Since I was doing the public address announcements at the game, it fell to me to tell the assembled crowd that Dolce Narizzano had been chosen Bishop's Carnival Queen for 1956. I think the only one who was surprised was Dolce. She was a popular choice and I watched with pride as she was driven onto the ice in a convertible, flanked by her two princesses. Crowned with a tiara, she waved in true regal fashion from the back seat of the car as it slowly made its way around the rink.

I caught up with her after the game.

"Your majesty," I said with a bow.

"Oh, don't be silly," she said, pushing me away.

"I guess I'll have to behave myself from now on, in such royal company."

"Oh sure," she laughed, "I'll believe that when I see it."

I took her arm and we headed out for Carnival Ball.

The Sherbrooke Daily Record ran her picture the following Monday and the accompanying story earned me a byline.

Work at the newspaper kept me busy. Earlier that year I had received my first journalistic feedback from Arnold Agnew. I was used to critical comments on term papers from professors, but his copy-editing was something new. In books and movies editors are said to "blue pencil" copy—the newspaper term for editing. Arnold was different, he edited with a red pencil. My first stories came back with more red than black on the paper, but in time my copy improved and there were fewer and fewer changes. This was great; I was learning and getting paid for it.

At Bishop's my majors were English and History, and although I loved the subjects and the fear of failure had faded, I still used the Molson solution to pre-empt any potential anxiety problems at exam time. I am not sure I needed the beer, but I wasn't taking any chances. My marks were never exceptional, but they got me through.

I've heard that any student in the journey from grade school to university is lucky if he encounters three truly inspiring teachers. This proved true for me: Miss Graham in grade five, Mr. Rosevear in high school, and at Bishop's, a professor named Arthur Motyer.

"Mooch," as he was affectionately known, was my inspiration. A tall man in his mid-thirties with even features, fair skin, and thinning hair, he had the look of a Romantic poet. He'd been a champion swimmer and a Rhodes Scholar, and he taught English with passion. He seemed to know instinctively how to handle me. He countered my wisecracks in class with wicked repartee of his own. Mooch became the older brother I never had.

He was also the driving force behind the drama program at Bishop's, directing the major plays the university mounted each winter. I'd never had any interest in acting in high school, but two of Dolce's older brothers were in theatre. Silvio was a television producer in England and Dino an actor in New York. So when auditions were held for Jean Anouilh's *The Happy Time* in January of my third year she encouraged me to try out. The fact that Mooch was directing didn't hurt.

The Anouilh play was an English translation of the French original and Mooch wanted the characters to speak with a French accent. This was no problem for me, since I'd been exposed to it growing up in Quebec. In fact I often amused my relatives in Detroit and Windsor with my rendition of French Canadian patois. So I landed the part of Grandpère in *The Happy Time.*

The rehearsals went well, but the prospect of appearing before a live audience was daunting. I wondered if a few pre-performance beers might help—it certainly worked for exams. But I felt I owed it to Mooch to stay away from the booze. So the afternoon before opening night I drove to a hill that overlooked the St. Francis River and rehearsed my lines into the wind. When I took to the stage a few hours later I was stone cold sober.

I'm afraid my performance was stone cold as well. I managed to get through without any major gaffes, but my timing was off and it was clear that stage fright was inhibiting me. So the next afternoon, instead of shouting my lines into the wind, I fortified myself at the G with a couple of tall cold Molson's. It worked. The stage fright disappeared, my timing was back, and I was actually able to enjoy the performance.

This modest achievement prompted me to act again the following year in a more difficult role, that of a mysterious doctor in Jean Giraudoux's *The Enchanted.* Again, with a little help from Dr. Molson, I brought it off.

I guess the warning signals about drinking were there, but I wasn't picking up on them. Booze had become an essential part of my life. It was no longer a social habit, but something I depended upon. Dolce seldom complained, because I held my liquor well and was usually the life of the party when I'd had a few drinks.

She did draw the line one winter night when the university basketball team was playing a game against Johnson College, in Vermont. They'd chartered a bus for the trip and as a reporter for *The Record* I was invited to go along. Another dozen or so students joined us on the bus to lend some fan support at the game. Dolce came too, and as we settled into our seats, waiting to depart, I produced two twenty-six ounce bottles of Manoir St. David wine. She was horrified.

"Two bottles," she said with exasperation. "You need two bottles? One wouldn't have been enough?"

"One for the trip there, the other for the trip back."

"Well," she said, "you can drink by yourself then." She started to get up from her seat.

"All right, all right." I was annoyed with her, but decided to surrender. I slid the window open and pitched one of the bottles out into a snowbank outside the bus. "Satisfied?"

"Yes," she said a trifle huffily, and settled back into her seat. The driver put the bus in gear and we left the campus.

The trip took three hours, the team lost, and on the way home I finished the last of the wine. I dropped Dolce off at the Women's Residence and started back to Norton Hall. It was then that I remembered the second bottle of wine. I hurried to the area where the bus had been parked and searched the snowbank on my hands and knees. It took some time, but I eventually uncovered the bottle intact and nicely chilled. Back in my room I found some students still awake and we finished off the second bottle. The next morning I was so hungover I could barely make it out of bed. It was suppertime before I could even think of food. Even then all I could manage was some dessert. I didn't call Dolce. I was too ashamed to admit she'd been right—two bottles were too much.

In the fall of my final year I was sent a much clearer warning about the danger my drinking posed.

It was the afternoon of the Grey Cup, and we'd watched the football game on television in a bar in Sherbrooke. Back at Bishop's I got into an argument with Dave Campbell, a much bigger student. I was usually a happy drunk, but this time for some reason I turned mean. I've only a vague recollection of what happened next. Apparently the words grew more heated and I put up my fists and challenged Dave to "come and get it." He came—I got it. I woke up in a hospital room in Sherbrooke. In the fight I'd been thrown down and I struck my head on the floor, fracturing my skull.

Those first two days in the hospital were the worst. My headache was unrelenting, and every hour without fail I'd be asked by an intern or a doctor a few simple questions. It didn't matter if it was the middle of the night and I was sound asleep. They would gently waken me. How many fingers did I see? Who was I? Where was I? What was my home address? Telephone number?

Fortunately I was able to answer coherently. There was no internal bleeding. It was a simple fracture, no displacement. But there is no such thing as a "simple" skull fracture. It was two weeks before I was released from hospital. Dolce had my car, so she came to see me every day. A good many of my friends made the trip into Sherbrooke to visit as well. One of those friends was Dave Campbell. I'd given him the fright of his life. Normally good-natured, we'd both lost it after the football game. No one, except Dolce, was happier to see me on the road to recovery.

I was allowed to skip the December exams that year; I took the train home to recover at my stepmother's house in Toronto. By the time I returned to Bishop's in January I was back to normal and suffered no lingering symptoms. I jokingly referred to the incident as my "football injury."

It was a good thing I recovered quickly, because in that final term I was busy. Along with my work at *The Record* and the taxing role in *The Enchanted,* I took over the editing of *The Mitre,* the university's literary magazine. Staid and predictable, it was in desperate need of new blood. Fortunately I had a number of friends with literary aspirations. In fact, the previous year we'd even formed a club. The only qualification for entry into this illustrious body was the willingness to bring something we'd written to each meeting. Calling ourselves Les Nouveaux Pauvres, we hammered out our best imitations of Hemingway, Fitzgerald, and Faulkner. Hugh MacLennan and Morley Callaghan were the only Canadian authors of note in those days, and some of us entertained dreams of joining them. For now we made do with publication in *The Mitre.*

I graduated that spring, and worked in the summer as a timekeeper for Combustion Engineering Superheater, a company that was building a pulp and paper mill in Thurso, just east of Ottawa. We were boilermakers and drank accordingly. Rye straight with a beer chaser. The money was good and I accumulated a nest egg for a planned trip to Europe. While I worked in Thurso I roomed with a neighbour of Carl MacCallum's. His folks lived in Buckingham, a few miles from the construction site. Carl was working in Ottawa but living at home. We'd remained good friends—he'd acted with me in the major plays and was a member of Les Nouveaux Pauvres. So I spent most of my evenings drinking with Carl in the bars of Buckingham, my weekends with Dolce back in Montreal. In the fall I joined a college friend, David McKnight, aboard a tiny tramp freighter, the *Maria Theresa G,* bound for Europe.

EUROPE, 1957

THE MARIA THERESA G, weighing in at twenty-five hundred tons, seemed substantial enough as we sailed out of Montreal and down the St. Lawrence River with a cargo of wheat in the hold. Dolce's father had arranged the booking—he did business with the ship's owners. Our tickets cost seventy-five dollars each and were one-way, something I'm sure appealed to Dolce's mother, who was hoping to find a more suitable suitor for the hand of her daughter in my absence.

David McKnight, my partner on the voyage, was originally from New Brunswick. His father had arranged my summer job as a boilermaker. David was short and wiry, with a dense black beard that gave him the roguish look of a pirate. We'd become instant friends at Bishop's—outsiders who shared a fondness for booze. He was a fearless brawler. In one tavern fight I saw him take on a man who was a good head taller and sixty pounds heavier. He jumped up on a chair and decked his surprised opponent with a stinging left jab to the nose.

We were the only passengers on the *Maria Theresa G.* Our luggage was minimal—everything had to fit into our backpacks. We also took a case of rye apiece—twenty-four twenty-six-ounce bottles. The trip from Montreal to Genoa, with stopovers at a number of ports along the way, was supposed to take two weeks, and neither of us wanted to be caught short in the booze department. The trip also helped us develop a rudimentary knowledge of Italian. Very few of the crew spoke English, but they were quick to appreciate the virtues of Canadian whisky, and were often guests in our tiny cabin.

As we steamed down the ever-widening St. Lawrence River I was filled with a sense of adventure. I was following the path of so many of my favourite writers, whose time Europe had seemed an essential part of their lives. Our first stop was not a port familiar to the likes of William Faulkner or Ernest Hemingway. It was the tiny town of Chandler, on the Gaspé coast. Our ship docked there for three days, taking on some additional cargo of newsprint. David and I found a local tavern and spent our evenings in very familiar surroundings, drinking Molson Export ale and listening to French Canadian folk songs. On our second night in Chandler I convinced one of the local girls to come aboard the *Maria Theresa G* for a "tour" of the ship. Unfortunately the captain spotted us and the tour was cut short. The next day I was summoned to his quarters.

Captain Pinella was a short but solidily built man in his early fifties. His cabin was small and surprisingly modest. He was dressed formally—a crisp white shirt, thin black tie, and blue blazer. The only sailor's touch was his captain's cap, its peak adorned with gold scroll. He rose to greet me as I entered the cabin and his face bore an unmistakable frown of disapproval.

"Mister Little," he said in heavily accented English, "you have made a big mistake."

"Yes." Best to plead guilty.

"You do not bring 'guests' onto the *Theresa*."

"No." I wondered what the punishment would be.

"No," his voice was louder now, "not on my ship. Particularly not ... lady guests."

"I am sorry."

"We ... the *Theresa* ... makes business here. Is bad for our reputation. You understand?"

"Yes," I said, my head bowed like that of a guilty schoolboy.

"What," the captain said, "your father would say I tell him about this?"

"I'm afraid my father is dead."

Captain Pinella flinched at the news. He paused, then continued, "What your mother would say?"

"She's dead too."

Another flinch. "You have older brothers ... sisters?"

"No, I am an only child."

The captain's face softened. "No father ... no mother." He suddenly stepped forward and embraced me in a fierce hug. "All alone ... so young," he murmured, then stood back, his hands still gripping my shoulders. His eyes were moist. "You be a good boy from now on?"

"Yes," I promised.

He released me from his grip, turned to hide his tears, and with a wave of his hand said simply, "You go now."

I did.

As the *Maria Theresa G* sailed into the Gulf of St. Lawrence, I watched the shorelines of the river gradually disappear. The transition to the Atlantic Ocean was different. Choppy waves gave way to long rolling swells, and the ship, seeming so substantial in the port of Montreal, was now just a tiny, inconsequential speck on a vast expanse of grey, pulsing water. Amazingly, neither David nor I suffered any seasickness. Perhaps it was the whisky.

There was very little to do aboard the ship so when weather permitted we tossed oranges back and forth on the deck for recreation. Nights we spent reading and playing cribbage. On the fourth day, at what was supposed to be the halfway point in our trip, things changed. Shortly after 2:00 a.m. David and I found ourselves on the floor of our cabin, pitched there by the advance guard of waves from a fierce North Atlantic storm. As we sat, stunned, a half-full bottle of Seagram's VO rolled from one side of the cabin floor to the other.

The storm lasted three days, and the captain wisely decided to run rather than fight. He changed course, because he was afraid the wheat in the hold wasn't stable enough to withstand any sudden shift of direction. The immense waves crashed against the hull with such power that the shock reverberated through every inch of the *Theresa G.* By the time the storm blew itself out we were halfway down the coast of Africa and almost a week behind schedule.

So it wasn't until our eleventh day at sea that the bluffs of Gibraltar appeared as a tiny blip on the horizon. As we drew closer, an armada of small boats surrounded us. They were selling seafood and fresh produce and members of our crew were lowered to negotiate purchases. That night the ship I ate my first calamari. The squid was tasty, but the salad is what I remember best. Our supply of fresh fruit and vegetables had run out during the unexpectedly long voyage.

The next morning we took a launch into the port, and heard English spoken for the first time in two weeks. The solid ground felt strange beneath my feet. From Gibraltar we sailed on to St-Louis de Rhône, a tiny port on the Mediterranean coast of France, to Marseille, and finally, three weeks after setting sail from Montreal, to our final destination, Genoa. Our supply of whisky had run out and our European adventure was just beginning. We took a cab to the train station, rode overnight to Rome, and booked ourselves a room in a small *pensione* in the Eternal City.

We'd been in Rome less than two weeks when I was hit by a major anxiety attack. It was as bad as my first year at Bishop's, if not worse. And more frightening. There was no reason for it this time—no exams, no fearing of flunking out. Just the unmistakable, paralyzing fear that turned my stomach inside out and had my bowels churning. Booze wasn't the answer, I couldn't keep it down. A local doctor prescribed something, I'm not sure what, but it gave me a temporary respite. I managed to get some sleep. In the morning I found a trattoria and ordered a drink. For the next few days I fought a losing battle with the anxiety. It was no use. I told David I couldn't hack it—I had to return home. He took the news with surprisingly good humour.

"No point staying, if you aren't enjoying yourself."

I booked a flight out of Rome for New Year's Day, 1958. On New Year's

Eve, our last night together, we made the rounds of bars. David had rented a Vespa, and shortly before midnight we decided to head for Bricktop's, a club on the Via Veneto. What we didn't know was that at midnight it was traditional in Rome for revellers to throw wine bottles into the streets. As we hurtled through the night a volley of glass rained down. Fortunately we were able to take cover before suffering any direct hits. We parked the Vespa and slipped into Bricktop's, congratulating ourselves on our escape. The club was owned by a black American jazz singer with brilliant red hair. We sat at the crowded bar listening to the music. My anxiety was gone—I'd be flying out in the morning. We ordered drinks and David left for the men's room. I noticed a dusty bottle of Seagram's Canadian Club on the shelf behind the bar. I beckoned the bartender over and pointed to the bottle.

"Quanto costa?" I asked.

He looked me over, glanced to his left and right, and quoted a price. I did the math. About twenty American dollars. I slid the money across the bar, he slipped the bottle into a brown paper bag, and I stuffed it into the inside pocket of my duffle coat.

We had a few more drinks at Bricktop's then decided to call it a night. At our room in the *pensione* I pulled the bottle from my coat and handed it to David.

"Happy New Year," I said. "A parting gift."

"I'll be damned." He examined the bottle, took two glasses from the sink and handed me one. "This calls for a drink." He unscrewed the top and I extended my empty glass. He tipped the bottle. A clear liquid poured forth. Not the characteristic amber of rye whisky. "What the hell?"

I dipped my finger into the liquid, sniffed it. Nothing. I ventured a taste. It was water. We looked at each other and burst into laughter. I'd been too trusting—a gullible tourist.

The next evening I flew from Rome to Paris on an Air France turboprop. In the fading twilight I could just make out tiny villages nestled in the Alps. Since it was New Year's Day, the stewardess served us fine French champagne.

Two days in Paris, two more in London, then a twenty-four-hour flight from Heathrow to Shannon to Gander, and finally I landed in Montreal. It was good to be home. Now I had to find a job.

PHOTO ESSAY

Josiah Brooks Champion
(1875-1954)

Willis Clayton Little
(1933)

Blanche Colpitts Champion (1875-1972)

Ana Gertrude Champion (1933)

Willis and Andrew
(1936)
Proud father.

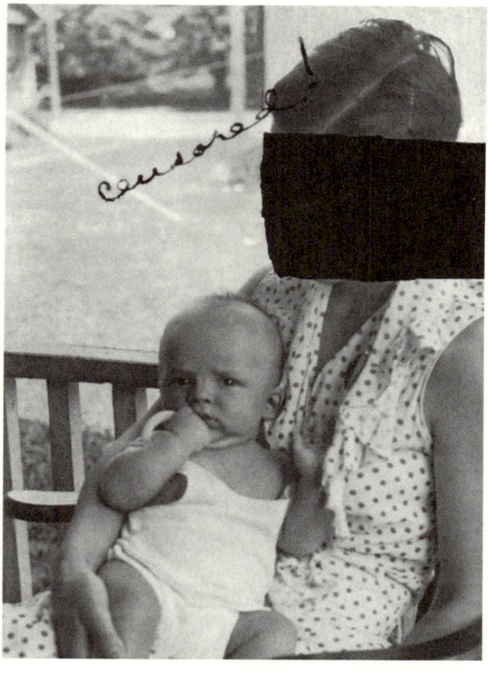

Andrew and Trudy Little
(1936)
As the picture appears in a family photo album. Trudy "censored" this picture herself.

Trudy and Andrew Little
(September 16, 1953)

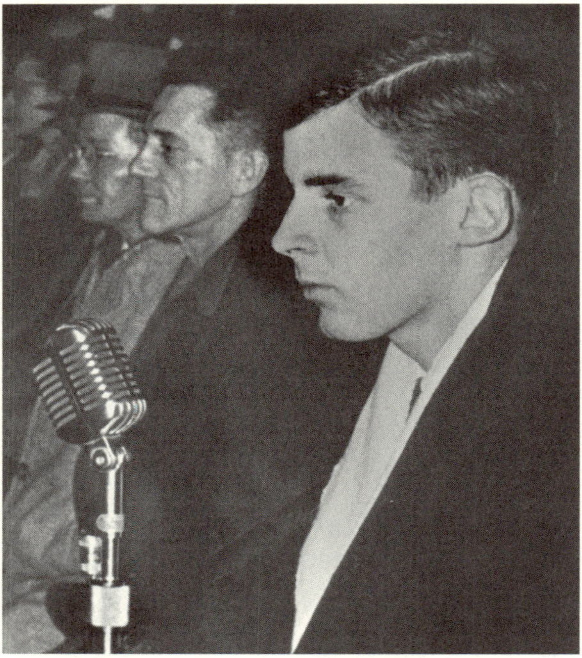

Andrew announcing the name of the Bishop's Carnival Queen.

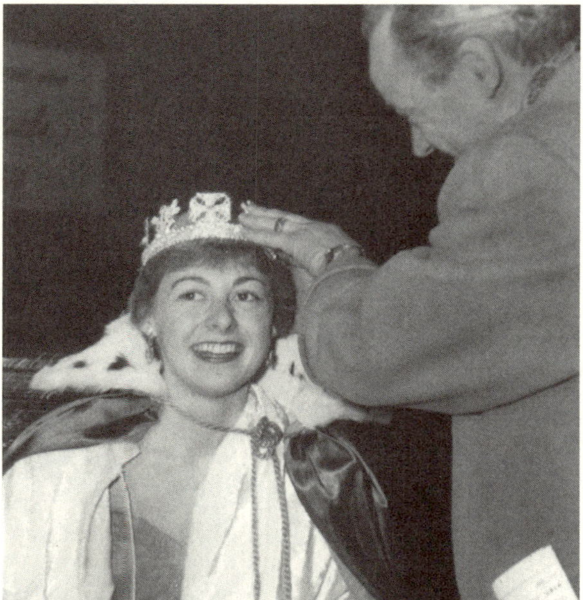

Dolce being crowned Carnival Queen by Armand Nadeau, the Mayor of Sherbrooke.

Dolce and her parents, Dolce and Silvio Narizzano

Joan and Andrew, cousins

Bishop's University, Lennoxville, Quebec

Allan Memorial Institute, Montreal

Andrew's home, 361 Merton Avenue, St. Lambert, Quebec

Dolce's home, 622 Sydenham Avenue, Westmount, Quebec

Andrew reporting (1960)

Dolce Narizzano Little (1960)

Willis Clayton Little (1905-1955)

Grace Imeson Little (1912-2003)

PART 2

"... and their whispers become a silence like
the smoke of a candle being blown out."
—Duane Michals, *Words and Images*

MONTREAL, OCTOBER 1958

BEER FOR BREAKFAST or call in sick?

It was one of those mornings.

The jangle of the alarm clock had shattered my sleep. I'd grabbed for it and missed, sent it crashing to the floor. The ringing persisted, reverberating through my head. I managed to reach down and silence it. My stomach rebelled at the physical effort this required and I gagged, bringing the taste of bile into my mouth. I felt as if someone had turned me inside out; all my senses were raw, exposed. The room was steeped in the smell of stale tobacco smoke and the shaft of light spilling through the drapes hurt my eyes. The sheets chafed at my nude body. I couldn't recall much from the previous night. At least I'd been sober enough to undress, but how did I get home? I couldn't remember. Had someone driven me? It didn't matter. I had to decide what to do now. I'd already called in sick once this week, I didn't want to risk it a second time.

I slid my feet out of the bed onto the cold hardwood floor and managed to sit up, keeping my head down, staring at my feet. When the pounding subsided, I rose slowly and made my way down the hall of the apartment. I took a beer from the half-fridge beside the sink and sat down at the kitchen table. I uncapped the Molson Export and lifted the bottle to my lips. Just a sip. I swallowed and waited. It stayed down. I took another swallow, shivered, and wished I'd worn my robe. For the next few minutes I sat there in the kitchen naked, nursing the bottle. My stomach settled first, no longer threatening to send back its contents. Then my headache began to subside. When the bottle was finished I went into the bathroom. I shuddered; the toilet bowl was spattered with bits of vomit. This was getting out of hand. I had to cut down on the booze. I turned on the shower and got in, wishing the hot water could wash my hangover away. It didn't work, but by the time I towelled off I knew I'd live.

I dressed quickly—the required shirt, tie, grey flannels, and a Harris tweed sports jacket. I slipped on a pair of Clarke's desert boots and headed out the door, pausing to pick up my copy of *The Montreal Gazette*. I hurried down the three flights of stairs from my apartment, checked for mail in the lobby. Just a few flyers, no letters. Outside, the autumn sunlight temporarily blinded me, reviving the hangover. I shielded my eyes with the newspaper and walked across Grand Boulevard to the bus stop.

The ride downtown from Notre Dame de Grace took less than an hour, plenty of time to catch up on the news. It gave me a head start on the day.

The bus let me off in Old Montreal and I walked the few remaining blocks to the offices of Canadian Press on Hospital Street. I'd been hired by CP, my experience with *The Sherbrooke Daily Record* more important than my degree.

I was a junior editor; it was my task to convert carbon copies of stories written by reporters from *The Montreal Star* and *The Gazette* into the more formal wire service style. These were then sent to newspapers across the country. It wasn't a glamorous job, but it paid fifty dollars a week, better than ten cents an inch.

The top local story today was the murder of a six-year-old child, whose body had been dismembered and scattered along a rural road in the Laurentians. I hadn't been at CP long enough to handle the big stuff, the manhunt for the killer, so I set to work on a sidebar, an interview with the parents of the child.

After writing my own stories for two years at *The Sherbrooke Record*, it was frustrating work, operating within the confines of someone else's version of what happened.

That fall CP held a Hallowe'en party at an editor's apartment in the city's east end. I was barely in the door when someone dressed as Superman handed me a cold pint of Molson's Export. It was hot and crowded in the apartment and Bill Haley's "Rock Around the Clock" was blasting from the stereo. The air was thick with smoke that hadn't come from cigarettes. I wasn't into dope, but was willing to bet that if I stayed long enough I could get high just breathing. I had come to the party as Count Dracula and Dolce was supposed to be with me as Queen of the Night, but she had the flu and was at home in Westmount. I wasn't feeling very well myself and resolved to make it an early night. All of the gang from the office was here and as a new boy I was glad I'd at least put in an appearance.

There were murmurs of approval for my Dracula outfit. Not everyone had dressed for the occasion, but there was a Frankenstein, a ghost sporting a rather frayed bedsheet, and two copy clerks who had come as Batman and Robin. I spent an hour or so nursing my beer, listening to office gossip, and looking for a chance to make my apologies. When the bureau chief began to tune his zither I realized it was time to split. "The Third Man Theme" faded in the background as I made my way down the stairs to the street.

Dolce had insisted I take the family car because the party was in Ville d'Anjou. It would save me an hour on the bus so I hadn't objected. I started the Chevy and headed west along Sherbrooke Street. It was raining and the colourful jets of flame from the oil refineries were a blur of orange as I drove by. At the intersection of Pie Neuf I stopped for a red light and felt a sudden chill, the sure sign of a fever. Dammit, I thought, I don't want to be sick. I turned up the heater.

The light changed and I accelerated, shifting the gears. As the car warmed, the windows began to fog and I took my eyes off the road for a moment to switch the setting to defrost. When I looked back up, something was moving through the beam of my headlights. I slammed on the brakes, but it was too late. I felt the tires skid on the wet surface of the road, heard a thump, and knew without question that I'd hit someone. I hesitated for just an instant, debating what to do, then pulled over to the curb, flicked on my emergency flashers, got out of the car, and walked back to check. The man lay in the gutter, motionless. I moved to his side and knelt down. There was no blood. He was an older man, curled up as if asleep, his raincoat a blanket against the rain. I could see he was still breathing.

Then we were no longer alone. I was conscious that a group had formed in a semi-circle around us and I could hear low, hushed words. A man knelt beside me.

"I am a priest," he said. "Father Archambault."

"Can you stay with him?" I asked. "I'll call an ambulance." Without waiting for a reply, I rose and moved quickly through the crowd and up the walk to a nearby house. A woman stood framed in the doorway.

"Can I use your phone?"

The woman motioned me to follow her.

I dialed the operator and was put through to the police. They would send an ambulance.

"Don't leave," cautioned the voice at the other end of the line. "We'll want to talk to you."

"I'll be here," I said, and hung up.

I asked the woman if I might use her bathroom.

"Of course." She indicated a door.

Inside I took a tube of toothpaste from the sink, squeezed some on my finger, ran it over my teeth and rinsed my mouth out. I didn't want alcohol on my breath when the police questioned me. I was thankful for the flu or whatever it was that I was catching; it had certainly curtailed my drinking. In the mirror I noticed I was still wearing the white makeup of Count Dracula. I turned on the hot water and washed off my face.

MONTREAL, OCTOBER 1958

A POLICE CAR was already there when I went back out. Its flashing red light and the crowd of curious onlookers gave the scene the look of an amusement park midway. The unconscious man was still alive, but the priest had given him the last rites. The wail of a siren grew louder and the ambulance arrived while I was answering the questions of the constables. Two attendants in white hurriedly moved the man from the pavement to a stretcher, slid him inside the ambulance, closed the doors, activated the siren, and pulled away.

"How did it happen?" one of the policemen asked. He was holding a clipboard, pen poised to write. The other officer was examining my driver's licence, and the car's registration papers and insurance certificate.

"I don't know." My voice sounded hollow in my ears, as if someone else was speaking. "One minute I was driving normally and suddenly there was something in front of me in the headlights ... a blur. I hit the brakes and I heard a bump."

It had stopped raining but the air was still thick with moisture. I could see beads of moisture on the visor of the policeman's cap.

"I knew I'd hit something, but I wasn't sure what. I pulled the car over," I said, motioning to the Chevrolet parked at the curb, its lights still flashing, "and went back and found ... " I glanced back to where the man had been.

"How fast were you driving?"

"I'm not sure. Not fast. I had stopped for a red light back at the intersection."

"Twenty, twenty-five, thirty miles an hour?" The cop's accent was French, but his English was excellent.

"Maybe twenty-five," I guessed.

The other policeman moved closer. He looked up from the papers in his hand. "Your name?"

"Andrew Little."

He checked the driver's licence, then the registration. "But this isn't your car."

"No, it belongs to my fiancée's father."

"His name?"

"Narizzano. Silvio Narizzano."

"Address?"

"622 Sydenham Avenue, in Westmount."

"And your address?"

"4665 Grand Boulevard, in NDG."

The two policemen exchanged glances. "You'll have to come with us to the station," said the cop with the papers.

I nodded. The enormity of what had happened was taking hold. I had run down an innocent man. I wanted to throw up, but I swallowed hard and managed to keep things down.

The policemen escorted me to their cruiser. "Get in."

"What about my car ... Mr. Narizzano's car?"

"The keys are in the ignition?"

"Yes."

The second cop, the one with the papers, said, "Someone will take care of it."

The rear door of the police car was opened. I felt a hand on my head. They were making sure I didn't bump myself as I slid into the back seat. The door closed. A wire mesh separated me from the driver. I leaned forward, hugging my knees, shivering again.

A moment later the two policemen got into the car. Doors closed, the driver started the engine and we moved out into the traffic. I looked back and could see the Chevrolet parked at the curb, its emergency lights still blinking, reflecting off the slick surface of the pavement.

The radio crackled and I heard French, but couldn't make out what was said. The officer in the passenger seat reached for a mike and acknowledged the call. There was more French and this time I could make it out. The word "*mort*" hit me like a punch. At that moment I knew the man I'd hit was dead.

At the station I was turned over to another policeman, who led me into a small office. I was too numb to notice much. We went over the details of the accident again. He wrote some more and then looked up at me. "Unfortunately the man you hit died on the way to the hospital," he said. "I'm sorry."

"I know," I murmured. "I heard it on the police radio coming in."

"Ah," he nodded, and wrote something more down. "Since the car you were driving isn't registered in your name we will have to contact the owner." He indicated the telephone on his desk. "Do you have his number?"

No, I thought, I didn't want the police calling Dolce's father in the middle of the night with this news. I looked at my watch. It was almost 2:30 a.m. "Can it wait until morning?"

The officer shrugged. "We can't release you until we are sure of the facts. We have to be certain you had permission to drive the car."

"I understand. But I'd rather wait until morning to call him."

"This means we will have to hold you here until then."

I thought about it some more. "That's okay."

He rose from his desk. "Come with me."

I was led along a corridor to a larger room, illuminated in the sickly glow of flickering fluorescent lights. Behind a raised counter another policeman asked for my valuables. He put my money, including loose change, into a manila envelope along with my watch and wallet.

"Your belt?" He held the envelope open.

It was only then I realized I was going to be put in jail. I'd thought my decision meant I'd be spending the night sitting in the station. I didn't know it meant jail. I hesitated.

"And your shoelaces," the cop behind the counter said.

Did I still have a choice? Again, I was brought up short by the thought of the phone ringing at 622 Sydenham, waking the family, the shock and anger that would follow.

I unfastened my belt, bent to untie my shoelaces, and handed them to the man holding the envelope. He wrote something down on a pad, ripped it off, and slipped it in with my things.

"This way," said the cop at my side, and I shuffled off with him down the corridor, past his office, and down a flight of stairs. We entered a vast space in the basement of the building. A row of bars stretched from wall to wall, dividing the room in half. Behind the bars was an assortment of men, perhaps a dozen. Some were sitting on a row of benches, bolted to the floor. Others were asleep or passed out on the floor. The smell was a mixture of sweat, urine, and vomit. A second policeman got up from behind a desk in the open half of the room and moved to a single barred door. He inserted a key into the lock, opened it, and ushered me inside. He closed the door, turned the key, removed it, and went back to his desk. The two cops spoke softly, then my escort left as we had come, up the stairs.

None of the men in the cell spoke, but I felt their eyes tracking me as I moved to one of the benches and sat down. The metal was cold and I shivered again. Somewhere in the city a man was dead and his family was hearing the news. Did he have a wife, children, brothers, sisters? I remembered the shock I'd felt when Dad came to Bishop's to tell me Mom was dead. Others were feeling a similar shock this night and I knew I was the cause of that misery. Sure, it had been an accident, but I knew the law. A driver is supposed to be in control of his car at all times, no matter what the conditions. The rain was a factor, and the man should have crossed at the intersection where there were traffic lights. If he had, he'd be alive. But I knew in my heart that it was my fault, plain and simple. He was dead and I was in jail because I was guilty. That it could have been worse, that I could have been drunk at the time of the accident, was the only consolation I had. It wasn't going be any consolation to the victim or his family.

There were no windows in the cell. What light there was came from bulbs caged in wire in the ceiling above. There was the whisper of a fan on the desk of the cop outside the cell. He was reading a newspaper. I wondered if an account of my accident would be written up in tomorrow's papers. From time to time there would be movement from one of the men on the floor. A groan, a shifting of position, then the quiet would descend. The man sitting beside me rose and walked to the back of the cell. He unzipped his fly and casually pissed into a recessed drain in the floor. He returned to his place and sat.

"What are you in for?" he asked without looking at me. His voice was high-pitched, reedy.

"An accident."

"Sure," he laughed.

"A car accident." I felt a flush trying to explain, trying to make it seem less important than it was. Trying to trivialize it away. It wasn't going to go away and I knew that, but I wanted to keep this conversation going. I needed the distraction.

"You?"

"An accident," he said, "yeah, an accident."

He was mocking me, but I didn't care. "What kind of accident?"

He looked at me for the first time. He was slight, his face thin, hair slicked back with a widow's peak. He had a pencil-thin moustache and a sallow complexion. Without a tie, his dress shirt seemed incomplete, open at the neck. He looked like a bank clerk, relaxing after hours.

"They say I shot someone," he winked.

"They say?"

"Sure. It's what they say. Me, I'm not saying anything. My lawyer will be here in the morning." He rubbed his hands across the stubble of beard on his cheeks. "You got a lawyer?"

"No." I thought about it. "Not yet."

"Some advice?" He leaned forward.

I nodded.

"Get one. Get a good one."

I would remember that advice, much later.

The man I hit was Gaston Belanger, sixty-four years old, a plumber. No criminal charges were laid; Monsieur Belanger was returning home from the local tavern where he went every Saturday night to watch his hockey team, Les Canadiens, on television. Ironic, I thought, that the one night I practise moderation I run down a man who'd probably had too much to drink.

But none of this changed the fact that I had killed someone. The blurred image still haunts me. Something there in the headlights. Just a slight bump, hard to imagine the damage it had done. It was months before I could drive again. It was also time, I realized, to quit drinking.

MONTREAL, 1958

"MY NAME IS NORMAN and I'm an alcoholic."

A middle-aged man wearing a navy blue blazer, button-down shirt, and knitted wool tie spoke the words. Given his conservative clothes, close-cropped hair, and the confident tone in his voice, I thought he might be a successful businessman.

"Until two years ago, I ran my own company."

I silently congratulated myself on the accuracy of my guess.

"But then things started to go sour."

This businessman was the third person to speak. A young mechanic in jeans and a T-shirt went first, followed by a nervous, chain-smoking housewife. I sat well back in the meeting room in the basement of St. Barnabas Anglican Church. The air was thick with cigarette smoke and the smell of coffee left too long on the hot plate. It was the Wednesday meeting of Alcoholics Anonymous. There were fifteen people in the room and none of them fit the stereotype of the drunk. There were no rubbies here, none of the down-and-out derelicts who beg spare change on street corners. If it were not for the topic on the agenda, the meeting could have been the monthly get-together of a local recreation association.

However, these people didn't meet once a month. For most of them this was the second or even third meeting this week. Ed, a friend from work, had been here Monday evening and he'd probably be back on Friday. The story the man in the business suit was telling had a familiar theme. It was the story of a seduction—of the initial infatuation with alcohol, the confidence it provided in the early days, the parties and the good times. The details were different with each person, but the stories all had the same unhappy ending. Heady highs eventually gave way to humiliating lows and the downward spiral began. My own story, if I'd chosen to tell it, wasn't that different.

"What did you think?" The meeting was over and we were driving west along St. Catherine Street.

"I don't know." I lit a cigarette and opened the car window. Ed had offered to sponsor me and I didn't want to disappoint him, but the prospect of a lifetime of meetings frightened me. I'd tried to quit on my own a number of times and had even managed once to go three months without a drink. That experiment ended the night I convinced myself that a little wine with meals wouldn't hurt.

"I'd like to try by myself one more time," I said, then paused. "If it doesn't work, then I'll give AA a shot."

To his credit, Ed didn't push. "Let me know when the time is right." He stopped the car in front of my apartment building and I got out. "There are meetings every night. There's always room for one more."

I watched the lights of his '59 Ford Fairlane disappear around a corner and I vowed I'd be off the sauce by Monday. Over the next few days I cut down little by little. It was tough, but when I felt the need for a drink, I used the memory of the accident to put down the urge. It worked. Sober, I promised myself I'd stay away from booze.

In the apartment lobby I picked up my mail. There were sales fliers, pizza advertisements, and discount coupons. There was also a copy of *Time*, and a letter from Cartier, Feldstein, Lamoureau and Plante, a law firm with a Dorchester Boulevard address. I wondered about this, but couldn't remember any dealings with them. Maybe it had something to do with Grace. We'd been squabbling over a minor detail in Dad's estate.

Upstairs I put the junk mail directly into a wastebasket and absent-mindedly ripped open the lawyer's envelope. I had to read the letter through twice before I understood what it was.

In that instant I was back behind the wheel of the '58 Chevy at the moment of impact, could hear again the sound of the car hitting Gaston Belanger. The letter shook in my hands. Monsieur Belanger's widow was suing me. I sank into a chair by the telephone desk. Madam Belanger wanted forty thousand dollars in damages or she would take the matter to court.

With shaking hands I dialed the number of the Canadian Press lawyer. His secretary asked if it was urgent. I said it was. Within minutes Fred Kaufman was on the line.

"What's the problem?" There was a hint of impatience in his voice.

I told him about the letter. "I thought this was all behind me," I said. "The police didn't lay any charges ... I didn't even get a traffic ticket."

Kaufman sighed. "This is different, this is a civil suit. But it is odd; the insurance company settles most of these cases. Give me their number and I'll check it out."

"I don't have their number. I don't even know the name of the company. The car belonged to my fiancée's father." Panic was creeping into my voice.

"Take it easy," Kaufman said. "This may be just some sort of legal manoeuvring. Find out the company name and phone number and call me back."

It wasn't legal manoeuvring. Mr. Narizzano's insurance policy didn't cover male drivers under the age of twenty-five.

"Fred, what does this mean?"

"It means that unless we reach some sort of settlement with the widow, we go to court."

"Jesus, I'm making less than three thousand dollars a year. How am I supposed to come up with forty thousand?"

"I think the widow's lawyer has done his homework. He knows the Narizzano family has money. He probably figures you can get some of it and settle out of court."

"No way." I turned to face him. "There is no way I'd ask Dolce's father for money. I've already caused them enough grief."

A few months later I found myself in court. My lawyer put forward all the arguments I had used as rationalizations after the accident. It was dark and raining, and Monsieur Belanger had been drinking. These facts hadn't been much consolation at the time and they didn't work at the trial. When Mr. Justice Henri Lambert ruled that a pedestrian, drunk or sober, had rights and I should have seen him in time to stop, I wasn't surprised. It could have been worse; he awarded Gaston Belanger's widow eight thousand dollars and court costs. The tiny woman, dressed in black, stared at me across the courtroom. She wore her dyed blond hair cut short, accenting her sharp features. Her expression didn't change when the verdict was read aloud.

Madame Belanger's lawyer approached me in the corridor outside the courtroom. "Have you changed your mind?" Louis Lapointe was still wearing his robes, which reminded me of the gowns we wore at Bishop's.

"About what?"

"About approaching your fiancée's family for assistance."

"No." I shook my head. "That's still out of the question."

He leaned close to me. There was the faint smell of tobacco on his breath. "You'll be out of town before the first payment is due."

I was shocked.

"I know your type; I'd be willing to bet money on it."

"You are wrong," I said angrily. "You don't know me at all."

He turned and hurried off, his robes flowing behind him.

It was another two months before the automatic deduction for Gaston Belanger's widow showed up on my paycheck. By then I was working for the CBC. I had grown tired of the re-write desk at Canadian Press and when an opening occurred in the newsroom of the CBC's International Service, I applied. The man who hired me, Paul Barrette, remembered my father and liked him.

The CBC work was certainly an improvement over CP. I was editing newscasts for short-wave broadcast to countries all over the world, handling the major stories of the day. And I was making more money. My salary had jumped from fifty dollars a week to sixty-five. It would still take a long time, but I was determined to pay off my debt to Madam Belanger.

MONTREAL, 1959

IN 1958 THE CBC EXPANDED LOCAL TV news operations in Montreal and the following year I transferred from the International Service. I was no longer editing and writing radio copy; I was reporting the news on television. I'd only been on the job a few months when I was asked to cover a story that had personal ramifications.

"I've got something for you, Old Trout." *The Metro Edition* assignment editor held a fistful of papers in the air as if he was auctioning off valuable documents. John Maydue was a forty-year-old Brit, a Second World War veteran with Fleet Street experience who had come to Canada seeking a better life. From his frequent complaints about Montreal I gathered he hadn't found it.

"What's up?" I approached his desk. It was shortly after nine o'clock on a Monday morning and the television newsroom was crowded. A blue haze of cigarette smoke hung in the air; reporters were busy catching up on the weekend gossip and no one had yet thought to open the windows. The chattering wire service teletype machines gave off the smell of hot oil.

"How much do you know about shrinks?" Maydue thrust his florid face forward, his tone belligerent, his question a test.

"A little." I was the new boy on the CBC's local newscast and I was still feeling my way. "Why?"

"Ever heard of Dr. Ewen Cameron?"

The mention of the name brought the past suddenly back. It cut through the wall I'd tried to erect to protect me from memories of that earlier time. "He's at the Allan, isn't he?" I wasn't about to volunteer the information that Dr. Cameron had been my mother's psychiatrist.

"Bravo," Maydue said mockingly. "I'm impressed. There may be hope for you yet, young man." He handed me a news release. "Cameron is meeting reporters at the Allan this morning. He has a new treatment he wants to demonstrate."

I looked down at the release. Maydue had circled the words "Deep Sleep Therapy" with his red marker. The news conference was scheduled for 10:30 a.m. I glanced at my watch. "Want me to check it out?" I was trying to keep the apprehension I felt from my voice.

"No," Maydue said sarcastically, "I thought you might like to volunteer for treatment." His glance swept the newsroom. A couple of the reporters looked up from their desks. "I mean Deep Sleep Therapy should be right up your alley." This produced a chuckle. Maydue had an audience now and was enjoying it. "In fact," he added, "Cameron should probably expand his experiments to this newsroom." He smiled and looked around. "Most of the reporters here are half asleep already." He waited, as if expecting someone to challenge his assessment. When no one did, he turned his attention back to me. "Marcel Deschamps is your cameraman. Meet him in the garage at ten." He dropped his eyes to the papers on his desk and began shuffling through them. I'd been dismissed.

It had been six years since my mother's death, but questions, unanswered at the time, returned with an urgency that surprised me. I hadn't sought out Dr. Cameron then, to ask him about the anonymous letter I'd received. Now I would have that chance. At my desk I read through the press release and realized I didn't really know much about Mom's doctor. In the ten years she'd seen him I'd never heard her utter a single complaint. In fact, she seemed to idolize the man. Dad had shared this confidence, describing him simply as the best in the business.

I took down the copy of *Who's Who* from the reference shelf in the newsroom. Cameron's credentials were impressive. Although he was born and educated in Scotland, it was the work he did in the United States and Canada that made his name. He was appointed Director of the Allan Memorial in 1943, and with the help of generous grants from the Rockefeller Foundations quickly established it as a place where innovation was the rule, not the exception. It was the first mental institution in North America to adopt an open-door policy, with patients free to come and go as they pleased. He was a past president of the World Psychiatric Association and the list of medical research papers he'd presented took up half a column. It seemed my mother had been in good hands.

As we drove up Mountain Street in Marcel Deschamps's 1959 Dodge station wagon my anxiety level grew. Would Dr. Cameron remember my mother? Would he be willing to talk about her case, provide any answers? It was all coming back ... stuff I'd tried so hard to put behind me.

We turned onto Pine Avenue and I forced myself back into my reporter's role. I'd checked out Cameron, but what did I know about the Allan Memorial Institute? Although this was the first time I'd been assigned to cover a story here, I had visited it once before, as a child, when my mother was in for treatment. I must have been nine or ten at the time and all I could remember from that day was learning that the professional wrestler, Sammy Berg, was also a patient. My mother seemed to take pride in this. It was summer and we ate lunch on a picnic bench in the hospital grounds. I hadn't seen her room. Was it true there were no locks on the doors? It didn't fit in with the commonly held perception of treatment for mental illness. No one used the word asylum to describe the Allan.

We passed the Royal Victoria Hospital and made a right turn onto a private road that led up the mountain to the Institute. The building itself was impressive, a converted Italian Renaissance mansion. I knew that Sir Hugh Allan, the wealthy owner of a steamship line, had erected the home a century ago. Then, upon his death, the family bequeathed it to the hospital. I wondered how my mother felt on her first visit here. Was she impressed or intimidated by this aristocratic old home with its panoramic view of the city and the river?

We unloaded the camera gear from the back of the station wagon. I carried the lighting case and the bulky wooden tripod while Marcel followed me with the camera and the sound recording equipment. As we mounted the stairs to the main entrance I saw that the single word "*Spero*" had been carved in the stone arch above the massive wooden door. It was Latin for "I Hope." The credo had worked for Sir Hugh Allan; he'd made his fortune here. It hadn't worked for my mother. Was it working for Ewen Cameron? I was about to find out.

We were ushered into a small, windowless meeting room. Rows of chairs were arranged like those in a classroom, facing a grey metal desk on a low raised platform. Fred Poland from *The Star* and Brian Cahill from *The Gazette* were here and so was Sydney Margoles of radio station CJAD, but there was no one from the French press or radio. This wasn't surprising, since most of the patients at the Allan were English-speaking and Dr. Cameron spoke no French.

While Marcel began setting up his Auricon I introduced myself to Evelyn Morrison, the Institute's public relations representative, a middle-aged woman with an air of quiet efficiency.

"I wonder if you'd ask Dr. Cameron if he could spare me a few minutes after the news conference on a personal matter?" I asked in a low voice. "You see ... he was my mother's doctor."

Mrs. Morrison consulted a clipboard. "I'll have to check with him first, his schedule is always tight." She took a fountain pen from the pocket of her jacket. "What is your mother's name?"

"Gertrude Little."

Mrs. Morrison looked up.

"She died in 1953."

"Oh, I'm sorry." Mrs. Morrison added something to the notes she was writing. She looked up and smiled at me sympathetically. "I'll see what I can do."

The reporters fell silent as a man in a rumpled blue business suit hurried into the room. There was a sense of urgency about his movements, as if he had some deadline to meet. He was carrying a briefcase in one hand and a coffee cup in the other. He put the case down on the desk, turned to face us, took a sip of his coffee, and spoke.

"I'd like to welcome you to the Allan Memorial Institute." His voice was authoritative, with a strong Scottish accent. "I'm Doctor Cameron." He smiled. His teeth were uneven, his smile engaging. He had close-cropped grey hair, wore glasses with clear plastic frames.

"Some of you already know me," he said, nodding to the newspaper reporters. "For others it's a chance for us to meet for the first time."

He reminded me a little of Harry Truman, the former American president. He was bigger than Truman, but had the same blunt face and determined square jaw. He took some papers from his briefcase.

"Do you all have copies of the news release?" His glance swept the room. "Good." Then he added, as an aside, "I'm sure you've all read every word." There was polite laughter.

"I've invited you here today to discuss something we call Psychic Driving, or Deep Sleep Therapy. It's a procedure we've been using at the Allan, on an experimental basis, for a couple of years now. We call it Deep Sleep because patients are sedated while they undergo treatment. The duration of that sleep varies with individual cases. It could be a few days or as long as six weeks."

He paused, giving reporters a chance to take notes in their spiral-ringed steno pads. I glanced back at the cameraman. The tiny red light on his Auricon was glowing red and he gave me the thumbs-up sign. I checked my watch. We had ten more minutes of film in the magazine.

"While the patient is asleep," Cameron continued, "we play a recorded message over and over again through a small speaker in his pillow. It is something the patient has recorded earlier, some positive statement about his condition." The doctor sat on the edge of the desk. "Let me give you a simple example. Let's say the patient is afraid of heights, has a fear of flying. The message might be, 'I like the view from skyscrapers because I can see things from there that I never notice when I'm down at street level. I am looking forward to my plane ride to Toronto this Christmas because I haven't seen my parents in a long time.' These words, recorded, are played over and over again on a loop." He paused again, as if expecting a question. When none was forthcoming he continued. "Notice there isn't anything negative in that statement. We don't mention his fear of flying."

Cameron took a sip of his coffee. "That's the key to Deep Sleep Therapy. The message, played thousands of times while the patient is asleep, is a positive reinforcement. When he awakens, the message is embedded in his consciousness like a pleasant memory." Cameron paused again. "Questions?"

As reporters began to quiz Dr. Cameron I gave Marcel the sign to stop filming. I'd listen to the general question-and-answer session, then decide if more was needed for my report and get that later in a short, one-on-one interview.

I learned that the treatment was still experimental and the duration depended on the seriousness of the symptoms. I beckoned Mrs. Morrison to my side. "Would it be possible," I whispered, "for us to film someone undergoing the treatment?" I knew the answer to this question before I asked it, but I had a back-up plan.

She shook her head. "Oh, I don't think so. That would require a signed release from the patient and since the treatment is still experimental ... " she gave a helpless shrug of her shoulders.

"What about a demonstration?" I had anticipated this objection. "Couldn't we use someone on the staff to pose as a patient? I would make it clear in the report that this wasn't the real thing, but just an example of the procedure."

"I'll have to check that out with the Doctor. It's a possibility," she conceded.

"Remember," I said, "this is television and television without pictures is nothing." I was trying hard to concentrate on the story, putting my personal agenda aside for the moment.

When the press conference ended, Mrs. Morrison conferred briefly with Dr. Cameron at the table as he gathered his papers together. Then she came over to me, smiling.

"You are in luck. The doctor has agreed. While you're interviewing him I'll find someone to act as a patient so you can film the procedure." Then she shook her head apologetically. "I'm afraid I didn't have time to mention your mother. Perhaps you could ask him yourself."

Dr. Cameron had also crossed the room. "Ask him what, Evelyn?"

She turned, embarrassed at being overheard. "Oh, Dr. Cameron, this is Andrew Little of the CBC."

The handshake was firm, the gaze steady. "I believe your mother was a patient of mine." He shook his head sadly. "It's a shame, she was a fine woman."

I couldn't think of a suitable response so I nodded in silent agreement and changed the subject. “I wonder if we might do a brief interview with you, just a minute or two on Deep Sleep Therapy?”

“Of course. Where would you like to set up?”

“Right here is fine.” I indicated the chairs we’d arranged near the camera.

Dr. Cameron sat down. “How do I look?” He directed the question at Marcel, adjusting the knot of his tie and brushing lint from the front of his jacket.

“You’re okay,” Marcel replied, and I smiled to myself because Dr. Cameron had just stretched Marcel’s understanding of English to its limit.

The interview was short; the only time I digressed from the material covered in the news conference was with my last question.

“Do you think, Doctor, that Deep Sleep Therapy could be used to plant negative thoughts?”

He seemed offended at the idea. “It isn’t something we’ve considered.”

We ended the interview on that note and Mrs. Morrison approached again. She spoke to Marcel as he turned off the television lights. “When you are finished here,” she said, “come with me, we’ll arrange a demonstration.”

“There is one more thing … ,” I said, as Dr. Cameron was preparing to leave. “It’s about my mother. I wonder if I could have a moment with you in private?”

“Oh, I think we could manage that.” He glanced at Mrs. Morrison, who checked her clipboard again and nodded. “Why don’t we talk in my office?”

MONTREAL, 1959

DR. CAMERON LED THE WAY along a corridor, ushered me into a room at the front of the building, and motioned to a chair by his desk. He sat down and began to fill a pipe with tobacco. "What can I do for you?" He was tamping down the bowl with a nicotine-stained thumb.

I took a deep breath. "A year after my mother's death my father remarried, someone he had known years ago. Her name is Grace Imeson."

Cameron struck a wooden match and lit his pipe.

"But my father developed lung cancer, and a few months after his second marriage, he was dead."

"I'm sorry. You're an only child, aren't you?"

I nodded, mute for the moment.

"No brothers or sisters." He shook his head sadly.

"I was away at college when my parents died." My hands gripped my knees, but I couldn't stop them from trembling. "A month after Dad's death someone wrote me an anonymous letter. It said my father had been having an affair with Grace, my mother found out, and that was the reason she committed suicide."

Dr. Cameron put his pipe down and leaned across the desk, his hands clasped beneath his chin.

"I am never surprised at the depths to which people sink." His gaze locked on mine. "I suspect the letter is a lot of hooey."

"You don't think it's true?" My hands were no longer shaking.

Cameron shook his head. "I doubt it." He picked up his pipe again. "I can't remember your mother mentioning anything." He lit another match, drew in the smoke and exhaled. "Of course it was some time ago."

"It's important. My stepmother would like to see more of me, but I feel awkward with her. There has always been this nagging doubt."

"You never asked her about it?"

I shook my head.

"Well, let's be sure my memory isn't at fault." He got up from his desk. "Wait here and I'll have my secretary dig up the file. Give me a few minutes." With that, he left the room.

I sat alone, excitement beginning to take hold. If Cameron was right, I could finally put my suspicions about Grace away. I just wished I'd asked him earlier. I rose and looked out the window at the view of the harbour and the St. Lawrence River below. To the south was the Victoria Bridge. My mother had crossed that bridge on her way to this office, seeking a cure. I tried to picture her in this room on the day of her last visit to Dr. Cameron.

The appointment is for two o'clock in the afternoon and, as usual, she arrives a few minutes early. She is still catching her breath from the long walk up Pine Avenue.

She tries to calculate, as she sits in the waiting room outside the doctor's office, how often she has made this trip. It must have been hundreds of times over the years. The short walk from the semi-detached red brick house on Merton Avenue to the streetcar stop. Then the trolley ride across the St. Lawrence River on the Victoria Bridge. She was never comfortable on the bridge, but over the years she'd learned to contain the panic.

I could easily visualize the scene. As I grew older Mom often confided in me, told me about her fears. And I remembered her prejudices as well.

This morning she wonders, as she has so often in the past, why this simple streetcar line was called the Montreal and Southern Counties Railway. It's pretentious, even deceptive. Probably a translation from the French. Well, she thinks, that's Quebec for you. The language is something foreign, something she'd never seen the need to learn, isolated as she was in an English community where French was seldom heard.

Ewen Cameron strode back into his office carrying a manila file folder. I was standing at the window and he motioned me to sit down.

"Let's have a look."

I returned to the chair opposite his desk. He opened the file and began to leaf through it. For a moment I felt I didn't exist, he was so completely absorbed in the material he was reading. It was quiet in the office; the only sound was the papers being shuffled. The aromatic smell of pipe smoke hung in the air, giving the room a professorial feel. I looked around. There was a reel-to-reel Wollensak tape recorder set into the wall behind Dr. Cameron. On the shelves that surrounded it were countless audiotape boxes, each labelled by hand. I looked for a microphone, but couldn't locate it.

"If she'd just held out a little longer ... " his voice was low. It was as if he was speaking to himself. He was still looking down at the papers.

I waited, silent, tense.

He raised his head and fixed his gaze on me. "Your mother was a courageous woman." His eyes were pale blue and penetrating. "We tried just about everything." He shook his head. "Adrenaline desensitization, typhoid fever induction, hormone injections, electroshock, and all of the drugs we had available at the time. She was one of my first patients to try chloropromazine." He tapped the sheet of paper in his hand. "Largactil. It was an experimental drug, an early tranquilizer."

"You said something about holding out a little longer?"

"Another couple of years and we would have had a much better chance of controlling her anxiety. A whole new family of drugs followed Largactil."

I'd often wondered about this. About Miltown. But it had come too late.

"What about Grace?"

A puzzled look crossed Cameron's face.

"My stepmother."

"Oh," he said, closing the file. "There was nothing in my notes about another woman. If your father was seeing someone else, I'm sure it would have come up."

He was saying the words I wanted to hear, but they weren't providing the relief I'd hoped for.

"When was her last appointment with you?"

He re-opened the file. "It was September of fifty-three. September the twenty-first, to be exact."

"A week before she died," I said, almost to myself. "When was she scheduled to see you again?"

Cameron looked at his notes. "The second week in October." He rose from his desk. "You know, if your mother had lived, she might very well have been helped by Deep Sleep Therapy. I'm sorry we lost her."

He extended his hand and I shook it.

As we started for the door, Dr. Cameron stopped. "Why don't you wait here? I'll fetch Mrs. Morrison. I'm not sure where your cameraman has set up, but she'll know." With this he turned and hurried out.

I sat back down and replayed some of Cameron's words in my head. "There was nothing in my files about another woman," he'd said, and I had no reason to doubt him. But it was possible that my mother had learned about Grace after her appointment with Cameron. Would I ever know for sure? I looked around the office and wondered again about that last appointment. I was away at Bishop's by that time. I tried to imagine how that final appointment played out, here at the Allan.

"The doctor will see you now," the receptionist says.

Dr. Cameron is leafing through papers as my mother enters his office and for a moment she stands at the door, watching him. She notices for the first time how untidy his desk is ... a litter of scattered papers, half-empty coffee cups, and an overflowing ashtray.

"Oh," he looks up, noticing her for the first time. "There you are."

She smiles a good morning.

"Well, don't just stand there. Have a seat, have a seat." As usual, he is in a hurry.

Trudy notices the box of Kleenex on the edge of his desk. No tears this morning, she promises herself.

Dr. Cameron looks up from the papers. "Not good." He taps them with his short, stubby fingers. "Not good at all."

"No," she agrees in a whisper.

"Well, we knew from the beginning that the drug hadn't been tried on cases like yours?" He makes a question of the statement.

This part was not hard to imagine. I was aware Dr. Cameron had tried something experimental, a drug called Largactil. Mom had told me about it the summer before I left for university. She was always a willing volunteer for anything new. She was that desperate. She had also mentioned another possibility, an old procedure, something she referred to as a "last resort."

"Yes," she answers with increasing resolve. "And you said we could talk about a lobotomy if it didn't work."

"Lobotomy?" He looks at her across the desk and for the first time that morning she knows she has his full attention. "Lobotomy," he repeats, as if the word has left an unpleasant taste in his mouth. "Yes, I suppose there is always that to consider."

"You promised," Trudy reminds him.

"I said we would consider it, but frankly, it isn't something I'd recommend. There have been too many unfavourable reports surfacing lately. It's not all we hoped it would be."

"We've tried everything else ... " Trudy's voice trails off.

"Not everything, lassie, not everything."

"What else is there? I thought you said the Largactil was the only thing we hadn't tried." Trudy can hear the rising frustration in her voice.

"Now, now ... I said it was the only drug we hadn't tried," Dr. Cameron replies. "There are other forms of treatment, also experimental of course."

Trudy looks down at her hands. "Experimental?"

Dr. Cameron shrugs. "We've been working on something new, a way of wiping out unpleasant memories and replacing them with ... ah ... more positive thoughts."

"When will it be ready?"

"Oh, we're not there yet. It could be a while." He closes her file, an indication that Trudy's time is up. "Make an appointment to see me next month, we can talk about it then."

I couldn't be sure, of course, but it was my guess that my mother gave up on any hope for a cure during that last appointment with Dr. Cameron.

"Mr. Little?" It was Mrs. Morrison. She stood at the doorway. "If you'll come with me, we've arranged a Deep Sleep demonstration for you."

MONTREAL, 1959

THE CLOUDS HAD CLEARED and the noonday sun had taken some of the chill from the late November air by the time we finished filming the Deep Sleep Therapy demonstration. As we were loading the equipment back into the station wagon I told Marcel I'd walk back to the office. I wanted some time alone to think things over.

"Why don't you drop the film off at the lab and have some lunch?" It would be two hours before it was ready for editing. He nodded his agreement, slid behind the wheel, and drove off.

I hurried down Peel, crossed Sherbrooke Street, and made my way into the Berkeley Hotel, an old watering hole, where I still ate occasionally. As I sipped my ginger ale and waited for my sandwich, I reviewed my conversation with Dr. Cameron. The more I thought about it the more I was convinced that it was the failure of the Largactil and not some alleged affair that had finally decided things for my mother. I realized I wasn't far from the downtown store where she bought the rifle she used to take her own life. I finished my lunch, paid my bill, and walked over to Eaton's Department Store. My visit to Dr. Cameron's office had given me an idea. What would surface if I walked where she had walked after that last appointment?

In the store fluorescent lights bathe the sporting goods department with an unhealthy wash of colour. Usually critical of such things, today she doesn't care.

I made my way to the section where they sold rifles. Had it changed much since she made the purchase? It didn't really matter.

She has her story ready. She is buying the gun as a gift for her father. She chose Eaton's because she knew they carried the one she wanted; she'd looked it up in the catalogue.

Her mind is made up. She'd tried pills and they hadn't worked. She dismissed the idea of jumping from a bridge because she had a vision of her body, lying face down in the river, her hair a wreath around bloated features, being taken downstream by the current ... of being found washed up on some Gaspé beach by French Canadians. Children, probably, with their bad teeth and hand-me-down clothes. No, she didn't want that.

I watched as a customer approached a counter displaying camping goods—knives, compasses, and water bottles. Behind the counter, in a locked glass case, was an array of hunting rifles. The clerk waiting there was middle-aged. Was it possible he served my mother after her final appointment at the Allan? Of course he would have been younger then.

"Can I help you?" The clerk's accent is French. No question here about which language to use. He knows an English customer when he sees one. But when in doubt, it is English—Company Policy. He is young, in his early twenties; he wears a nylon drip-dry shirt and fingers a Reynolds' ballpoint pen.

"Yes, I'd like to buy a gun." She is instantly sorry she had used the word gun, afraid the clerk would read her mind. "A rifle," she quickly amends, with what she hopes will come across as conviction. "A .22-calibre, a single-shot Remington." She clasps her purse tightly below the counter to hide her trembling hands.

"Ah, yes," the salesman says, turning to a cabinet mounted on the wall behind him. He twists the key, already in the lock, and opens one of the glass doors. He pauses, scanning the rack of rifles.

"Yes, here it is." He takes down the Remington and turns to Trudy. "Was this what you had in mind?"

Trudy puts her purse on the counter and picks up the rifle. Surprisingly, her hands no longer tremble. It feels familiar and comfortable, like an old friend.

My mother was no stranger to guns. Her father and brothers hunted and as a teenager she'd badgered JB into showing her how to shoot.

At the counter she remembers the day long ago when her father brought home a new rifle and handed it to her.

"A virgin," he'd said. "Never been fired."

She'd learned quickly, became a fair shot, but had refused to hunt, simply couldn't take a life.

JB didn't understand. "Waste of good money," he'd said in disgust, and sold her rifle to a neighbour.

The clerk turns again to the case, taking a second rifle from the rack. I do have other .22s. This is a Mossburg, a better gun ... a little more expensive?"

"No," Trudy says, holding the Remington closer, as if fearing the clerk might take it back. It must be a Remington, her father's favourite. "This will be just fine. And I'd like some ammunition too." There is a quaver in her voice.

"Long or short?"

Trudy hasn't anticipated this question. For a second she is tempted to leave, call the whole thing off. It isn't too late. But the salesman, sensing her confusion, asks, "What are you planning to shoot?"

Trudy draws in her breath sharply at the thought. If he only knew, she thinks, and forces a smile. "It's for my father, he likes to shoot squirrels."

"Long," the clerk decides aloud, opening a drawer beneath the gun cabinet. He puts a box before her. ".22-calibre long, perfect for small game. Now, what about oil, cleaning fluid, polish for the stock?"

"On no," replies Trudy smoothly, confidence returning, the end in sight. "He has those things." She smiles grimly as the clerk begins wrapping the rifle. She can't quite picture anyone cleaning the gun, buffing its wood, after she's finished with it. She wonders idly what Willis will do with it.

"That will be $34.38."

Trudy reaches into her purse for her billfold and hands him a twenty, a ten, and two twos. She opens a change purse and extracts a quarter, a dime, and three pennies, placing them on the counter.

"Thank you, Madam." The clerk deftly deposits the money in the cash drawer and hands her a receipt.

"Thank you." She returns her wallet to her purse and takes the package from the counter. As she turns to leave, the clerk decides to risk a little French.

"Au revoir," he calls to her retreating figure.

At the Eaton's counter today the clerk finished serving the customer, wrote something down, then glanced up at me.

"Can I help you?" No accent.

"No," I shrugged, "I was just looking."

MONTREAL, 1959

A WEEK AFTER the Cameron interview I received a call from Louis Lapointe, Madam Belanger's lawyer. He wanted to meet for lunch. He suggested Delmo's, and the next day we sat opposite each other in the old seafood restaurant in the city's financial district. I had ordered lobster Newburg; Lapointe downed a Malpeque oyster and spoke.

"I was wrong about you."

I looked up, not sure where this was going.

"What I said to you last year, outside the courtroom."

I remembered. "You didn't know me very well then."

"And now I think I know you a little better. At least I know you're an honourable man."

I waited for him to continue.

"And that is why I am going to suggest something I think you will like." He smiled.

The waiter approached with our food. Mr. Lapointe had ordered a mixed grill of seafood. We began to eat.

"It is not my place to judge how well Mr. Kaufman represented you," Mr. Lapointe said, then, after pausing to chew, continued, "but I think he may have missed something you might want to consider. I think the insurance company should have assumed responsibility for the accident."

"But ... " I started to explain about the under-twenty-five clause. He cut me off with a wave of the hand.

"I know all that. But the circumstances aren't the usual ones. Normally your fiancée would have been driving the car. She is insured. The only reason you were at the wheel that night was because she was indisposed. She gave you permission to drive. It is my belief that you should initiate legal action against the insurance company. I think you'd have a fair shot at a settlement."

He sipped some wine and waited for my reply.

"I suppose this is something I should discuss with my lawyer." I picked at my lobster Newburg.

He shook his head. "I have already suggested it to Mr. Kaufman, and I regret he does not share my optimism." He speared a scallop with his fork.

"Then what's the point?"

"The point, Mr. Little, is that I am willing to undertake an action against the company on your behalf," he said, and popped the scallop into his mouth.

"But you know my financial situation. I haven't the money ... "

He chewed, then swallowed. "This is good," he said. "How's your lobster? It's usually very good here."

"It's ... fine. I still don't understand."

"Eat up then, you've hardly touched a thing."

I took a reluctant bite.

"I'm willing to undertake an action on your behalf," he continued, "and at no cost to you."

"Why?" I wasn't sure I had this straight. I put down my fork.

"The main reason is that as honourable as you may be, the money Madam Belanger receives from you each month simply isn't enough. If we could get a lump sum and invest it carefully, that would be another matter." The lawyer finished his meal, pushed back his chair, and looked across the table at me.

"Let me see if I understand you correctly," I said. "You'd be willing to take on the insurance company on my behalf?"

"Your behalf and Madam Belanger's."

"And finance it out of your own pocket?"

He nodded.

I looked at him with new respect. "Then, Mr. Lapointe, it is you who are the honourable man."

He raised his wine glass. "To honour."

I raised mine, filled with water. "To honour," I said, and we drank. He ordered coffee and I finished the rest of my meal. He was right; the lobster Newburg at Delmo's was fine.

A few months later I was typing a story in the TV Newsroom when the telephone rang.

"Can you get that?" I asked Earl Garrety. Earl, feet up on his desk, was smoking a cigarette and reading a copy of *Playboy.*

"Sure thing." He swung his feet to the floor and reached for the phone. "TV News." He listened for a moment and then put his hand over the mouthpiece. "It's for you. Sounds important."

I punched the button and listened.

There was a click and Louis Lapointe came on the line.

"Andrew?"

"It's me."

"Good news."

"Yes?" I was holding my breath.

"Great news, in fact." I could hear him draw in on a cigarette. "The judgment came down a few minutes ago. The insurance company is liable. Madam Belanger will be getting her money within the next couple of days."

"I don't believe it."

"It's true. You'll be getting back everything you paid out, plus interest."

I hadn't realized it might be retroactive. All I'd been hoping for was an end to the salary garnishee.

"I can't begin to thank you ... " I said, trying to do the math in my mind.

"It was my pleasure. I'll call you sometime tomorrow with all the details."

I put down the phone and reached for a piece of paper. I'd been paying out a little more than fifteen dollars a week for almost two years now. That was fifteen times one hundred. With interest it would be close to two thousand dollars.

I phoned Dolce. "Does the idea of a June wedding appeal to you?"

WE SAT IN THE RESTAURANT in Windsor Station, waiting to take the overnight train to New York for our honeymoon. We'd bumped into an old college friend, Jim Ferrabee, and when he heard the news about our marriage he insisted on ordering champagne. I started to protest but thought, what the hell, it's a special occasion.

Jim raised his glass. "To you both."

I sipped. God, it tasted good. It had been almost two years since I'd had my last drink. I promised myself I'd go back on the wagon once the honeymoon was over. On the overnight train to New York I felt that wonderful warm glow and realized how much I'd missed booze.

"Well, Mrs. Little, do you feel any different?" We were crossing the Victoria Bridge and I could see the reflections of the city lights in the St. Lawrence River below.

"Not really, " Dolce smiled. "I guess it will take a while to sink in."

We'd been married that afternoon in a brief ceremony in St. Andrew's Anglican Church on Sherbrooke Street. We were eloping; Dolce's parents would have insisted on a big wedding and she hated all the trappings that went with such events. It hadn't been easy to pull off. In Quebec only a priest, a minister, or a rabbi could marry a couple and neither of us attended church. We approached the elderly minister at St. Andrew's because Dolce liked the Christmas pageant they staged each year. We had to meet with him twice before the wedding to convince him we wanted it this way, without any family present.

The ceremony itself was high comedy. We needed two witnesses, so Dolce invited her best friend, Angela Jackson, and I asked John Foulkes to be my best man. At first, when we arrived, the old minister was confused, thinking Angela was the bride. It took a while to get that straightened out. Then we discovered that Angela couldn't act as a legal witness because she was not yet twenty-one. I made a frantic call to the newsroom, and half an hour later Frank Ward, one of my colleagues, arrived by cab and we were able to complete the ceremony. It was fortunate that neither Dolce nor I attached much importance to the actual wedding. We wanted to be married, but we viewed the wedding itself simply as a ritual that had to be endured to make it legal. I suppose the choice of an Anglican church was fitting, since our alma mater, Bishop's, was founded to prepare Anglican men for service as ministers.

The sound changed as the train moved off the bridge and onto solid ground. It was quieter now, and it slowed down but didn't stop for the station in St. Lambert.

"Home," I said as we passed the deserted platform, "or what used to be home."

Dolce looked out into the night. "I'm sorry I never had the chance to meet your parents."

"They would have loved you."

"How did they meet?"

"It's a long story."

"We have plenty of time," she smiled.

This was a story I knew well. I'd heard it many times.

Willis reaches inside his shirt pocket and takes out a package of Old Kentucky cigarettes. He is the only person he knows who is still smoking this brand. They are a throwback to the old days when everyone rolled their own with locally grown tobacco. He takes the lighter from the console and lights the cigarette, inhaling deeply, feeling the rough texture of the smoke as it passes into his throat, the satisfying click as it fills his lungs.

Through the glass in the control room window he can see Trudy Champion handing out the sheet music to the three Beckett sisters. He wonders how they'd come up with that name for their group, Charmaine and the Chansonettes. Sounded French. Maybe that was it; maybe they felt they needed that extra little touch, something different. Trudy and the Beckett sisters—Genevieve, Marion, and Pauline. Four girls from Wheatley. The French name didn't seem right to Willis. They didn't need the fancy name; they were good enough without it.

Not that they'd asked him, of course. He'd barely been introduced. Just a wave from the producer.

"That's Willis Little in there in the control room behind the glass. You be nice to him ... he'll make sure you sound good." Trudy had held the sheet music above her eyes, shielding the reflection of the studio lights so she could see the man behind the glass.

"Hi, Willis," she'd said, laughing. "Wave to Willis, girls." The Beckett sisters waved.

That was last week, their first day in studio. Since then they'd been oblivious of him, rehearsing each afternoon, going over the songs again and again.

Today he turns off the studio microphones and watches them talking, their lips moving wordlessly on the other side of the glass. They are like tropical fish, all decked out in colourful frocks, swimming silently before him. Even without the sound it is clear who the leader is. Trudy is like that ... she stands out from other people. It isn't just her looks, although Lord knows, she is beautiful. It is something else ... energy maybe ... an aura.

Whatever it is, Willis knows he wants more of it. He just isn't sure how to get it. Trudy always seems surrounded by people, by activity. He'll have to find a way to break through that. There are other guys too—a different one each week it seems. Willis wonders what he will say to her, once he has the chance. What do you say to someone like that, someone so alive, with so many charming, witty friends?

The door to the studio opens. Trudy pokes her head in.

"Hi, Willis," she says, smiling. "I don't suppose you have a cigarette, do you?"

"Sure." He fumbles in his shirt pocket for the pack. Trudy crosses the control room and takes a cigarette, placing it in her lips and leaning forward. When the flame touches the tobacco, she draws in the smoke. She coughs, puts her hand to her mouth.

"These are strong."

"Yes, they're not everyone's cup of tea."

Trudy laughs. "I can see why." She takes another drag and tentatively eases the smoke into her lungs. "They probably go better with tea."

"Or coffee," he smiles. "How 'bout a cup?"

"Sure, we're taking a break. The damn piano is out again. Jack says it will take a few minutes to get it properly tuned."

Trudy watches as Willis shuts down the switches on the console.

She likes this big, quiet man. Even separated as they'd been by the glass partition, she'd sensed his competence. She'd been comfortable with it. He was one of the few men at the station who hadn't tried to impress her, hadn't forced an introduction.

He holds the studio door open for her. "I can't promise the coffee will be fresh," he says as they head down the hall for the cafeteria, "but it will be hot."

In the weeks that follow, Willis sees more and more of Trudy, but they aren't yet thought of as a couple. Just good friends. Then one night Willis is invited to a party at the home of one of the radio announcers. Trudy isn't expected. She is finishing up on some last-minute musical arrangements for her show. Willis is sitting on a sofa drinking his rye and ginger ale, about ready to leave, when the door to the apartment opens and Trudy walks in. There is a round of applause.

"All work and no play ... " she announces and she gives a mock curtsy. The apartment is crowded, but eventually Trudy makes her way to the living room. She looks about, seeking somewhere to sit. One of the sales representatives gets up from his chair and offers it to her. She starts toward him when Willis calls from across the room.

"Why don't you sit here, next to me?" He pats a place beside him. "This is where you belong."

Trudy pauses, then crosses the room and sits down beside him.

"What're you drinking?"

"Rum and Coke."

"I'll get it, you wait right there."

"I promise."

That night, on the way home from the party, Willis asks Trudy to marry him.

"I'll think it over." She teases him and wonders how much he's had to drink.

To her friends, Willis seems an unlikely choice as a boyfriend, but over time Trudy sees more and more of him. Soon she isn't seeing anyone else, and a few months later they announce their engagement.

"So that's their story," I said. The train picked up speed. "I guess they are a little like us—attraction of opposites."

"Not like us," Dolce laughed. "It took us six years to take the plunge."

Our honeymoon in New York is a blur. We stayed with Dolce's cousin, Sandra Scoppetone, in the Village. Sandra liked to drink, so we hit all the New York bars that until then I'd only read about. The White Horse Tavern, where Dylan Thomas once held forth, and the Oak Room in the Algonquin Hotel, where the *New Yorker* writers liked to congregate. We went to a ball game at Yankee Stadium and watched Mickey Mantle hit a towering home run. We listened to the Modern Jazz Quartet at The Village Vanguard and Stan Kenton at Birdland. We took in Broadway plays and generally had a blast. Dolce's aunt and uncle lent us a car, so we drove to Stratford, Connecticut to watch Dolce's brother Dino play Puck in *A Midsummer Night's Dream.*

Finally the honeymoon was over and it was time to return to Montreal and face the music—Dolce's parents. I was certainly not the son-in-law they'd have chosen for their daughter, but I had to give them credit ... they gradually came to accept me. With the birth of our first child, Marcus, a little over a year later the last of their resistance evaporated.

I didn't make good on my promise to get off the sauce when we returned from New York. I fooled myself into thinking I was managing my drinking. I was a reporter and it seemed to go with the job. Virtually everyone in the newsroom drank. For a time I had things under control.

Dolce parent's sold their big Westmount home and moved into the "4300," a new luxury apartment building on de Maisonneuve Boulevard. Our second child, another son, was born when Marcus was two. We called the new arrival Christopher, but Marcus had trouble pronouncing the name. His version of Christopher was Kippofer. A German neighbour turned that into Kipperline, or "Little Kip." So Christopher morphed into Kipper and that was later shortened to Kip. He would remain Kip the rest of his life.

Ironically it took another jail experience to bring my toxic love affair with alcohol to its final conclusion. In the newsroom we had a tradition we called Case Friday. We'd do our best to get most of the work out of the way early, then open and share a case of beer. One cold Friday, after the program and a post-mortem in the Catalongue bar across the street from the CBC, I accepted a friend's offer to stop at his apartment downtown on Rue St. Mark and have a few more drinks. I switched from beer to Manhattans and the rest of the evening is a blank. Details were gleaned later from other players in the drama.

I apparently left the friend's about ten and decided to drop in on Dolce's parents for another drink on my way home. In my drunken state I forgot that they'd moved. I drove to their old house in Westmount. The new owner answered the door and informed me the Narizzanos didn't live there any more. I insisted they did. An argument ensued and he called the police. I woke up the following morning in a jail cell in Westmount with a monumental hangover and no idea how I got there.

It turned out that Dolce, worried when I didn't arrive home, had called the newsroom, and eventually reached the friend who'd provided me with the Manhattans. Concerned and a little guilty, he called the hospitals and then the police, and learned I'd been taken into custody. Fortunately the police picked me up before I could get back behind the wheel of my car, so I was not charged with drunk driving. And since the owner of the house on Sydenham was willing to let the matter go, I was released the following morning.

The cop in charge handed me the envelope containing my wallet, money, and watch, confiscated when I was brought in. Someone had written my name on the envelope and next to it, in brackets, the words "Common Drunk."

That did it. The message was clear.

MONTREAL, 1963

"WHAT SEEMS TO BE the problem?" Dr. Bruce Armstrong asked as I sat in his office on Somerled Avenue. Another journalist had recommended Bruce, a GP, to me. He was young for a doctor, in his early thirties. With his horn-rimmed glasses and lab coat he reminded me of a whiz kid friend I'd known at university who spent most of his time in the science lab and always got great marks.

"I've got to quit drinking." I gave him a brief history of my addiction, including my unsuccessful attempts to stop, details of the fatal accident, and, finally, the story of my Westmount embarrassment.

"Pretty serious," he agreed.

"It used to be fun. In the beginning just a few drinks could produce the buzz I needed. But now I find it's taking more and more booze. It's not fun anymore."

"How much is 'more and more'?"

"I don't know," I shrugged. "Depends on the day."

"What's a typical day?"

"Pint or two for breakfast, if the hangover is bad. A quart or two for lunch. Then more beer at night and sometimes into the hard stuff ... rye, scotch, you name it."

"Every day?"

"Pretty well," I admitted. "You see, it's harder to get to that state where I feel great. And that state doesn't last as long as it used to. It doesn't take much to move me from 'feeling good' to 'feeling no pain' and then to 'feeling nothing at all'."

"And you pass out?" Dr. Armstrong had taken off his glasses and was leaning on his elbows on the desk. "Or end up in jail."

"It's not always that bad. But often I can't remember where I was or what I did. People tell me about it the next day and I just nod. But I have no clue. Not bad stuff necessarily. Just routine things. Details. They might just as well be talking about someone else for all that I can remember."

"Anyone else in the family have a drinking problem?"

"There's nothing on my Dad's side, I'm sure. Or Mom's, for that matter."

"Okay, so we rule that out. You've tried AA?"

"I've been to a meeting and if that's what it takes, I guess that's a possibility. But I'd like to beat it on my own."

"Let me ask you a simple question."

"Shoot."

"If you were on a desert island where there was no booze, could you exist?"

"I guess so. I wouldn't have much choice, would I?"

"Well," he said, "unless you stop, your drinking is going to shipwreck your life and you are going to drown in booze." He let the silence build. "There is an island out there and with luck you might make it." He put his glasses on and closed the file on his desk. "It's called sobriety. It's up to you."

"I'll try this weekend."

"I can prescribe something to ease the withdrawal, but I'd rather not."

"Tranquilizers?"

He nodded. "But the danger with tranquilizers is that you could become dependent on them and just replace one problem with another."

"I don't want that."

"No."

"So it's cold turkey then." I rose and we shook hands.

"Good luck."

I left the doctor's office. It was Wednesday. I had five days to get clean. I wondered if I could make it.

I would taper off. Friday I bought a bottle of rye and a twelve pack of Molson's. By Sunday night the rye was finished and I was down to my last pint of beer. I drank it just before midnight and got into bed. It had been a restless weekend, but I'd managed. Dolce had helped, doing as much as she could to keep my mind off booze. There had been the usual round of shopping Saturday, then a movie. On Sunday we took a long walk on Mount Royal with the kids and had dinner in the evening with her family. I realized, lying there, with Dolce already asleep beside me, that this was the first night in a long time I'd gone to bed this sober.

I slept poorly and was thankful there was no beer left when I woke in the morning. I'm not sure I could have resisted the temptation. By the time I got into the office I was beginning to sense withdrawal symptoms. I was jumpy and irritable. The crackle of the police radio was so jarring I turned the volume down to a point where it could hardly be heard. Fortunately my work kept me pretty busy. It seemed that as long as I was engaged in some sort of activity, or talking to someone, I was all right. The lulls in the day were the hardest. I had the runs and the times alone in the washroom were agony. I'd sit on the toilet, my head down, my nose running, staring at my trembling hands.

I played tricks. I promised myself a drink in an hour's time if I could just hold out that long. Then, when the hour was up, I'd make the same promise again, for the next hour. Lunch was tough; those not working on stories adjourned to a nearby tavern, affectionately known as "Studio T." I turned down the invitation to join them.

"I'm expecting a call," I lied. "I don't want to miss it."

I worked through the lunch break; I wasn't sure I could keep solid food down.

It was odd, but no one seemed to notice the state I was in. The newsroom was like a ship, ploughing on, powered by its own momentum.

The real test came shortly before six, when it was time to join my colleagues in what had become a nightly ritual. The late afternoon sun was bathing Dorchester Boulevard with a golden light as I emerged from the CBC building and crossed the street. Inside the Catalongue Lounge I had no trouble locating the table where the CBMT staffers had assembled. We were always there, at the same spot, every night.

"What'll it be?" André asked. He was polishing glasses behind the bar. "The usual?"

"No thanks," I said, pulling up a chair. "Make it tonic water." The bartender gave me a quizzical look. "With a twist of lemon." I was speaking in a low voice, hoping no one would hear. He shrugged his shoulders and uncapped a bottle of Schweppes.

"You feeling okay?" Earl Garrety, the city hall reporter, sounded as if he'd suddenly come upon someone suffering from some dread disease. So much for my low profile.

"Fine," I said. "Just thought I'd lay off the booze for a while." I didn't want to make a big deal of it, and hoped Garrety would let it pass. He didn't.

"Hey, guys," he announced to the editors and reporters sitting around a long table, "we got a problem here." When he had their attention he looked at me. "Our drinking buddy isn't drinking tonight. Think we should let him sit with us?"

There were some rueful smiles and headshakes, but to my relief no one seemed very interested in Earl's question. André arrived with my drink. He poured the tonic over the ice cubes with a flourish. A slice of lemon bobbed to the surface.

"Keep the change," I said, handing him a one-dollar bill.

"What change?" he asked with a smirk.

"Big spender," Earl said, and tossed a quarter on the table. "This is for my cheap friend." As André picked up the money Earl winked at him, "It's been a long time since he ordered anything non-alcoholic." He downed the last of his beer. "And I'll have another of these," he said, pointing to his empty bottle.

The lounge was filling up. Happy Hour. At our table Al Davis, a sportswriter we called "Jungle," tried to tell a joke. The news director cut him off.

"Not now, Jungle," he said, "it's show time."

We turned to watch the television set that was mounted on the wall.

The theme music for the CBC's local evening newscast began, the black and white animation rolled, and a deep bass voice-over announced, "From Montreal, this is Metro Edition."

An announcer appeared on the screen with the city skyline in the background. "Good evening," he said, "I'm Sheridan Nelson."

I sat there sweating, silent. Each time the waiter arrived with another round of drinks I had to restrain the urge to order something for myself, something to make the misery go away.

When the news was finally over we left the Catalongue and headed up Bishop Street on our way to the Press Club, the second stop in the nightly ritual. "Jungle" Davis finally got to tell his joke and I felt a little better walking. It was as if this simple physical act provided an outlet for the jumpiness I'd been feeling.

The Montreal Men's Press Club, in the basement of the Mount Royal Hotel, was a large, dimly lit room divided into two equal sections. To the right, as you entered, there were six felt-topped card tables. A large television set was positioned in the corner and if the card players didn't object, you could watch programs there. This space became a mini-theatre for the big sporting events, the Grey Cup game, the World Series, the hockey playoffs.

The other half of the room was a collection of leather sofas and chairs in the traditional club setting. A bar ran the length of one wall. It was to this part of the room that the serious drinkers gravitated, closer to the bottles that lined the shelves behind the busy bartenders.

The Press Club was where the stars of the Montreal news business hung out. On this evening Dink Carroll, *The Gazette*'s lead columnist, was in his usual spot. Walter O'Hearne, drama critic for *The Montreal Star*, sat with *Time Canada*'s Bureau Chief, Martin Sullivan.

I found myself at a table, surrounded by colleagues, sipping tonic. If I could just make it through the evening maybe things would improve. By nine-thirty I was aware of a pattern developing that I hadn't noticed when I was drinking. People were repeating themselves, going over the same topics a second or even a third time. It was as if the earlier conversations hadn't taken place; no one was offering anything new. About ten, when Jungle Davis started to retell his joke about the rabbi, the priest, and the parson, I decided it was time to go.

Outside, the change in temperature from the air-conditioned interior to the warm August night made me shiver. I got a cab in front of the hotel and gave the driver my address. It was warm in the taxi, but I continued shivering. I hugged my arms to my chest and bent over.

"Are you all right?" the cabbie asked.

"Fine," I answered. "Coming down with a cold, I guess."

The ride home seemed to take forever. Panicky, I sat up and checked the meter. Would I have enough money for the fare? So far it was just over two dollars and I could see we were at the corner of Decarie Boulevard and Sherbrooke Street. I was halfway home with ten dollars in my pocket. No reason to worry. Yet I had a premonition that something awful was about to happen. The driver lit a cigarette and the smoke jolted me, like smelling salts after a football injury. I hugged myself again, still shivering.

I felt the car's movement stop.

"We're here, buddy," the driver said.

Dolce was waiting in the living room. "How are you feeling?" Curiosity and concern were both present in her question.

"So far, so bad," I said in a weak attempt at humour. "But I'm hanging in there."

"Do you want something to eat?" There was relief in her voice. "I made some soup."

"I guess I should try," I said.

She moved closer, reached up and took my face in her hands and looked into my eyes. "You'll make it," she said in a whisper, and kissed me on the forehead.

I sat down at the dining room table and tried to read a magazine. From the kitchen I could hear Dolce taking down plates from their shelves, removing cutlery from the drawer. These simple sounds made concentration difficult.

She put a steaming bowl of minestrone in front of me. I gagged at the smell. "Let it cool off a bit," she suggested, and sat down opposite me. She pushed a plate of soda crackers across the table. "Try these," she suggested. "I lived on them the first few months I was pregnant."

I reached for one and took a tentative bite. "How are the kids?"

"Fine," she said. "I put them to bed about an hour ago."

I was thankful. As much as I loved them I wasn't sure I could have played the "dad" role tonight, feeling the way I did.

I forced myself to try some of the soup and managed to keep it down.

"Shall we watch the news?" Dolce was looking at her watch.

"I guess so." Anything to take my mind off my thirst.

We sat side by side on the sofa watching Earl Cameron read *The National*. I only caught bits and pieces: the Non-Operating Railway Unions were threatening a nationwide rail strike; in Quebec, the Liberal government of Jean Lesage wanted control over hydroelectric development in the province. The minister in charge, a former Radio-Canada broadcaster named René Lévesque, was threatening to resign if the takeover failed.

As the newscast ended I began to shake and Dolce put her arms around me. When the shaking stopped, she rose and turned off the TV. The guest politician on *Viewpoint* faded to black.

"Are you coming to bed?"

"I think I'll wait here a while," I said. "You go on ahead, I'll be there in a few minutes."

"I can stay with you if you like," Dolce offered.

"No." I shook my head. "I'll be okay."

"You're sure?"

"I'm sure."

I never did make it to bed that night. I paced the living room, and at one point, although it was still summer, made a fire in the fireplace. The crumpling up of old newspapers and the adding of kindling gave me something to do. I washed the dishes, re-arranged the books in our brick-shelf bookcase. It was as if physical activity, in any form, eased the anxiety. I'm still not sure how I made it. I remember turning off the lamps when the first light of the false dawn filtered into the living room.

Then I must have fallen asleep on the sofa, because the next thing I knew the high piping voice of Marcus woke me. He seemed confused to find me fully dressed, asleep in the living room.

"Daddy get up early?"

"Sort of ... how about some breakfast?"

"Capan Crunch?"

"Sure." I stumbled after him into the kitchen.

My second day without a drink was pretty much a repeat of the first. But by evening, the waves of panic began to subside. I passed up the post-mortem in the Catalongue and took the bus home. I was able to eat supper, and realized, after the kids were asleep, that the shaking had finally stopped.

That night I showered and got into bed about midnight. I held Dolce in my arms. We didn't talk; we just held each other. In time her breathing grew deeper, and when I was sure she was asleep, I rolled onto my back and stared at the ceiling.

About an hour later I woke with a start. Something was different. It took me a minute to realize what it was. Then my eyes filled with tears of gratitude. I felt weak, as if I'd just recovered from the flu. My head still ached, but it didn't matter. I no longer needed a drink. And I knew that I never wanted to go through withdrawal again. Maybe that fear would be enough to keep me sober.

TORONTO, 1963

THE CESSNA FLEW PAST the sprawling safety of the illuminated city, out over the cold waters of Lake Ontario, and into the darkness. For the first time since we left Windsor there were no lights ahead on the horizon, no points of reference. Then Herbie Foxcroft banked the plane and the glittering skyline of Toronto re-appeared. Fear flooded into the tiny cabin; soon I'd be talking to half a million people on live television. As we began our descent to the Toronto Island Airport, I remembered to breathe again and the fear let up.

The story had potential. The previous night someone had erected a crude wooden cross on the front lawn of a black union leader in Windsor and set it ablaze. Had the Klan come across the border from Detroit into Canada? No one seemed to know. I'd recently transferred from Montreal and was working out of Toronto now as a reporter for *The National*, the CBC's flagship network television newscast. By the time I arrived in Windsor, police had pretty well ruled out the Klan connection and were convinced the incident was the product of political infighting among striking members of the United Autoworkers Union. Not a lead item anymore, but a good story nonetheless. This was the first major story I'd been handed since the move and I wasn't sure how well I could handle live television at the network level.

There was a pay phone in the tiny airport terminal. My hand trembled as I dialed the number for *The National.* "What's the word?" I asked Bill Johnson, the lineup editor.

"Sorry, old chum," he said. "We've got bigger fish to fry. The PM's just called parliament back into emergency session. We've dropped your live report—we'll let the announcer read the story. "

As I drove north along the Don Valley Parkway I wondered if I was in the right job. The mere thought of a live network television appearance made me queasy. Until now almost all my work had been at the local level, with as many drinks as I needed to get me through it.

The lights were on in the townhouse we'd rented on the outskirts of Scarborough. Dolce was waiting up for me.

"Everything okay?" I asked.

"Fine," she said. "I put the boys to bed after you called. They were a little disappointed they weren't going to see you on television, but I told them there would be plenty of other times."

"I don't know about that."

"What do you mean?"

"Driving home tonight I realized I was actually glad I didn't have to report on the story." I paced the floor. "That's a little nuts, you know. I mean a good reporter lives for these situations. Without the booze, I'm not sure I can hack it." I flopped down on the chair across from her.

"You forget," she said, "even when you were drinking you were nervous when you had a live report to do. But no one would guess, watching you."

"I know, I know. Maybe it doesn't show, but that doesn't change how I feel. I thought it was something I'd get over. You know, like stage fright. But it's been three years now and I still hate it every time I have to go on camera."

Dolce crossed the room and sat down gently on my lap, put her hands on my shoulders and looked into my eyes. "Isn't there something else you can do?" She brushed her lips to mine. "Something that doesn't require on-camera work?"

"Well, I don't know. I guess I could try line-up or assignment. They're both desk jobs, at least the hours would be a little more regular."

Dolce smiled. "We wouldn't mind that."

"Let me think it over ... see how I feel in the morning."

Our lovemaking that night had an intensity that had been missing in the six months we'd been in Toronto.

A week or so later I received a phone call in *The National* newsroom. It was from Bobbie Vale, my mother's old college roommate, who was living in Toronto. She's seen me on television and called the CBC. When I heard from her, the whole ugly business of the poison-pen letter surfaced. But here at last was a chance to find out the truth, to lay to rest the fears that an affair with Grace had led Mom to take her own life. I suggested lunch and she recommended a little restaurant on Yonge Street.

A tiny woman with the face of a mischievous elf rose to greet me. "Bobbie?"

"Andy Little!" She gave me a teary hug, we sat down, and she reached into her purse for a hankie, dabbed her eyes. "I'd know you anywhere—you have Trudy's eyes.

"It's good to meet you at last," I said. "Mom used to talk about you all the time."

"Ah yes. We had some wonderful moments together, your mother and I. Wonderful times. You know, when we roomed together in Toronto she was such fun. She worked hard at her studies, mind you, but we'd often sneak out after curfew in the evenings and double date. She was so full of life."

We ordered lunch and I waited until we were served—a hamburger for me, a chicken salad sandwich for Bobbie—to broach the subject that had been haunting me since her call.

"How well do you know my stepmother?"

"Grace? Grace Imeson?"

I nodded.

"Well ... let me see ... I guess we first met in Leamington. I'd finished school in Toronto, and with some help from your Mom I got a job at the Heinz Company in Leamington. That's when I met Grace. She worked there too. Then, a few months later she moved to Toronto. We stayed in touch and a few years later I married and moved here too."

"Do you remember Dad calling you after Mom died?"

"Yes, I'm afraid I'd lost touch with your mom." Bobbie took a bite out of her sandwich, chewed it thoughtfully and swallowed. "I always felt badly about that." She sipped some water. "I wondered if we'd stayed closer if I might have helped her ... you know ... get through her troubles?" She shook her head sadly.

"Oh, I don't think so." I wanted to move the subject away from Mom's death. "There wasn't much anyone could do."

"I guess not."

I took a deep breath. "Dad said he didn't know how to reach you until he met Grace, by accident, in Toronto."

This was the moment of truth.

"I remember his call," Bobbie said. "It was a shock, I can tell you. I had no idea. I'd have certainly come for the funeral if I'd known at the time."

"Do you remember Dad mentioning Grace when he called?"

Bobbie closed her eyes, going back in time. "Yes, he must have." Then she looked across the table at me. "In fact I'm sure he did. That's how he got my phone number ... from Grace."

I let out a breath, and with it, the last of the doubts I had about Dad and Grace.

We spent the rest of the lunch catching up on our respective families. Bobbie was divorced, had three grown children, and was working for Bell Telephone.

"Are you in a hurry?" Bobbie asked as we were at the cash, waiting to pay our bill.

"No," I said. "My shift doesn't begin until four."

"How would you like to see the house where you used to live?"

"Here in Toronto?"

"It's just down the block. That's why I suggested this restaurant."

"I'd like that."

TORONTO, 1963

AS WE PASSED a grey stucco bungalow it started to come back to me. I recalled that there'd been a death in the family in that house ... a child, I thought. I looked for the vacant lot that had been next to it, where we'd played hide-and-seek, but found a new townhouse there instead. And then, across the street, a duplex that I recognized instantly.

"That's it, isn't it?"

Bobbie smiled. "That's it. I visited you here in 1937, a few months after Willis started work with the CBC. You were still a baby. I guess it was three or four years later when your Dad was transferred to Ottawa."

The house had originally been a single family home but had been converted during the Depression. We'd lived downstairs and although I couldn't remember the interior very well, I knew there was a fake fireplace in the living room. My father had taken pictures of me one Christmas, peering up the chimney, waiting for Santa.

"When your folks moved here I thought things might change for your Mom," Bobbie said. "Living with your grandmother hadn't been easy for Trudy. But at least while she was in Leamington she had someone to help look after you. When you moved to Toronto she didn't know anyone and was pretty lonely. I guess it got to her."

As I stared at the house it suddenly came back to me. It had happened when I was five years old.

The wind whipped the lightly falling snow along Cranbrooke Avenue, filling in the walks that had been cleared that morning. I don't know how long I'd been outside, tethered to a length of rope. It was tied to one of the banister railings on the porch; my only company was a snowman standing on guard in the front yard with a carrot nose, eyes of coal, and a smiling pipe-cleaner mouth. Dad and I had made him on the previous weekend, and as a finishing touch we had crowned our creation with an old grey fedora. Now a sudden gust of wind blew the hat off the snowman and onto the sidewalk. By stretching, I could almost make it, but the hat was still just beyond my reach. The bite of the leather straps on the halter brought me up short. I walked back up the steps and banged on the front door. I wanted my mother. The house remained silent. No one came to the door. I couldn't reach the doorbell so I banged again. Still there was no response. I turned, went down the steps, and tried for the fedora again without any luck. I was worried now, worried that the wind would carry it off.

I searched for a stick, for something that would extend my reach and let me recover the hat. The tether rope limited me to a half circle in the front yard and I couldn't find anything there. Maybe on the porch. I went back up the stairs and checked. There was a sled leaning against the brick wall, but that wasn't going to help. Dad had shovelled the walk that morning; I'd watched him from my upstairs window. What had he done with the shovel? I banged again on the door but the result was the same. No luck. I went down the steps and peered through the lattice into the area beneath the porch. There was nothing there. The area was sheltered, but the exposed earth was frozen hard. The wind moved the spider webs that stretched across the beams supporting the porch. I shivered. It was getting colder.

A streetlight came on, the snow slanting through its illuminated cone. It fell on the fedora, a light dusting like icing sugar on a cake. I had to pee. I banged again on the door, harder now. I wasn't worried about the hat any more; I didn't want to wet my pants. I hadn't wet my pants in a long time. I sat on the steps and shivered. I went back up the stairs and banged again, calling out this time. There was a mail slot halfway up the door. I pushed it open with my mittened hand.

"Mom," I called, and waited. Nothing. I stood on my toes and looked in. The light was on in the front hall but the ceiling fixture was above my line of sight. Overcoats, jackets, and scarves hung from pegs on one wall, on the other hung my mother's framed watercolour painting of ships in a harbour.

"Mommy," I shouted, "I have to pee." I waited, but when there was no sound from the interior of the house I let the mail flap close and went back to a spot at the top of the stairs to wait. I noticed lights had come on in the houses across the street. It was getting darker. I began to sob, hugging my arms to my chest. The sobbing made the need to pee worse, but I couldn't stop. I finally gave up and let go. I felt the warm urine flow into my underpants, down inside my snowsuit. I don't know how long I waited after this, but I know that by the time my father came home from work the pee was no longer warm and I was ashamed. I'd even forgotten about the fedora.

A few days later Dad hired a full-time housekeeper and I was never tethered outside again.

"I've got to get to work." Bobbie's words brought me back to the present. "Can I give you a lift?"

"If it's not too much trouble."

"It's the least I can do."

TORONTO, 1963

I HURRIED THE FEW BLOCKS from the Eglinton Avenue subway station to my stepmother's duplex; the evening was cool, a reminder that summer was winding down. In the past I had always approached any contact with Grace with a sense of dread, whether it was a telephone call or a face-to-face meeting. I'd never told her about the letter, never confronted her with the accusation. But the temptation to do so had always been there, and that had frightened me. Tonight that fear was gone. Bobbie's news had removed the doubt, but I still hadn't decided if I'd mention the letter or let matters rest.

I paused before the home that Grace had bought with her share of my father's estate. I'd spent Christmas holidays in this house when I was in university, but hadn't been back since my graduation. I walked up the stairs and rang the doorbell.

"Well, hello there." She was wearing tan slacks and a cotton summer blouse. "It's good to see you again." Her hair seemed a little greyer and she had new glasses. The only makeup she used was lipstick in a muted pink shade.

"Hi, Grace," I said as I stood in the doorway.

"Come in, come in." She ushered me into the hall. "How about some coffee? I have some freshly brewed."

"Sounds good." I followed her into the kitchen.

"What do you hear from St. Lambert these days?" she asked, removing the coffee from the stove. "How are your friends ... Bryce and John?"

"I don't see much of Bryce," I said. "He's married now and interning at the Royal Vic, wants to be a neurosurgeon."

"I'm not surprised." Grace poured coffee into two cups. "And John?"

"He's teaching high school in St. Lambert. We've sort of lost touch since I moved here."

"Why don't we go back into the living room?" Grace said. "We can be more comfortable there."

I sat down on the sofa, balancing the cup and saucer on my lap.

"Goodness me, I've forgotten the napkins." She hurried back into the kitchen.

The room had a familiar feel; half of the furniture was new, but half had been ours in St. Lambert.

"Here we are." Grace handed me a napkin. She sat down opposite me, sipping her coffee, her eyes magnified by the thick lenses in her glasses. "How are things at work?"

"Fine." I wasn't going to get into the uncertainty I was feeling about reporting.

"I see you on television from time to time. Your dad would have been proud."

"I often think of that. He was there for the beginning of television at the CBC. I've made a career of it."

"Like father, like son."

I laughed. "Oh, I don't know about that." I put my cup and saucer on the coffee table. "Do you know who I met the other day?"

Grace shook her head.

"Bobbie Vale." I waited for a reaction.

"Bobbie Vale ... "

"Mom's old college roommate. She saw me on television and called the newsroom. We had lunch."

"Oh, I know Bobbie. We worked together in Leamington. I'm afraid it's been a while since I last talked to her. How is she?"

"She fine. Divorced, three kids ... working at Bell."

"I remember now," Grace said, thinking back. "Willis was trying to reach her after your mother died. We'd just met and he asked me if I knew her phone number."

My doubts about Grace and Dad were gone, but nonetheless it was comforting to hear the account validated without any real prompting on my part.

Grace stirred her coffee. "Did you know your mother and I knew each other?"

"I think my grandmother mentioned it."

"She was a year ahead of me in school so we were never friends. But we were rivals."

"Rivals?" The old fear resurfaced.

"Your mom was a good athlete."

I knew this. I remembered the medals I'd recovered from the trunk in the basement of our home on Merton Avenue.

"Track and field?"

Grace nodded. "I was a pretty fair runner too. We used to compete in the hundred-yard dash." A note of bitterness crept into her voice. "In fact there was some controversy about the last race we ran."

I looked at her questioningly.

"It wasn't your mother's doing. It was her father's."

"JB?"

"J.B. Champion," she said with note of derision. "Local ministers often acted as judges. For this meet they'd invited J.B. I didn't think he should be judging the race when his daughter was one of the contestants."

"What happened?"

As Grace told her story I let my mind provide the pictures. I'd seen the field in question. It was at Leamington High School, across the railway tracks from my grandmother's house.

The day is crisp and clear, perfect for the annual track and field meet. Grace sits on the bottom bench of the stands that line one side of the track. She is getting ready for the dash, running against her old rival. It will be the third year they'd competed. Trudy won the first time, Grace the second. Sitting across from the stands, Trudy bends to tighten the laces on her running shoes. It has been a good morning for her. She won the broad jump and now, in the early afternoon, she is waiting to compete in the hundred-yard dash, her specialty. She is not happy her father is judging the event. In fact she wishes he wasn't even at the meet.

I imagine a different JB—a younger version of my grandfather—like the one I'd seen in family portraits. He wears a three-piece suit, dress shirt, and tie. A homburg hides the bald patch on the back of his head. He is strolling about between events, his posture erect, his chin thrust forward, his eyes probing.

For the Reverend J.B. Champion judging is more than an honour, it is a pleasure. He loves watching the firm bodies of the young women as they run, jump, hurdle, or throw the javelin. There are boys competing as well, of course, but JB's eyes are on the girls. It is a pity, he thinks, that they have to wear their school gym uniforms for these events. The bloomers, the long stockings pulled up to just below the knees, the full blouses—they hide so much. If only the girls had the freedom the boys enjoyed, with shorts and singlets.

"My older brother Joe was there that day," Grace said, bringing me back to the present. "I told him I didn't think it was right that your mother's dad was going to judge our race. Joe just laughed and assured me I'd be so far ahead at the finish line it wouldn't matter. But it nagged at me, just the same."

Grace paused to sip some coffee and I try to imagine how my mother must have felt that day.

Trudy sees JB across the field, at the official scorer's table, talking to Miss Standish, a pretty young history teacher. He laughs at something she has said and places his hand on her arm. The old bugger, Trudy thinks, he never lets up. Well, at least it isn't one of my friends he's after, and wonders for the thousandth time how a man like that gets to be a minister.

"It was mid-afternoon by the time our event was called. I hated that, the waiting around." Grace frowned. "But we were seniors that year and the younger kids got to race first. It just gave me more time to get nervous."

The official starter puts the megaphone to his lips and announces the race.

"Senior girls, one-hundred-yard dash, stand by."

Grace approaches the starting line, dangling her arms loosely at her sides, trying to shake out the butterflies in her stomach.

"On your mark," the starter shouts. The girls line up.

"Get set." They tense, in a half-crouch.

At the crack of the pistol, they're off.

There are seven girls running, but it is clear after the first few yards that it is going to be a race between Grace and Trudy. The rest of the field is falling behind.

From the finish line, JB peers down the track as the young women head toward him, their muscles straining, their bodies pushing as hard as they can. He sees his daughter, Trudy, running stride for stride with another girl.

It is close, so close that those watching can't be sure who won. Grace's classmates think she did, Trudy's friends are just as sure it was her win. It is going to be up to JB to decide. All eyes are upon him except those of the runners, who are bent over, breathing hard.

"It was more than thirty years ago, but I remember it as if it was yesterday. Your grandfather knew that the decision was his to make. I could see he liked that, liked being the centre of attention."

JB, aware he is centre stage, clears his throat and announces, as if he is back in the pulpit, "A very close race ... very close indeed ... but the winner is ... Trudy Champion."

Grace was lost in the memory of the moment. Her hands trembled and she put her cup and saucer down.

"But you won?"

"You bet," she says angrily.

"Did Mom realize it?"

"I don't know. I never asked her."

If Grace did win and my mother knew it, I bet she must have been mortified. "Did you ever ask Dad?"

"Willis didn't like to talk about Trudy. It was too painful for him."

I looked at my stepmother and realized that, as different as she was from my mother, they had one thing in common. They both hated J.B. Champion.

ST. LAMBERT, 1964

IN THE FALL OF 1964 a local assignment editor's job opened up in Montreal. Since I was the only candidate who knew the city, had lived and worked there, I got the position. The people in the national newsroom were surprised. The career path was usually to the network centre, not away from it. But I didn't doubt the wisdom of my decision. It meant I'd no longer be reporting on camera and our kids would be seeing a lot more of their grandparents.

Dolce and I listened to the Grey Cup game on the car radio as we drove from Toronto back to Montreal. My already good mood improved as the game wore on. The Ottawa Roughriders were winning, riding the passing arm of Russ Jackson, a Canadian quarterback. They were playing the Calgary Stampeders. It was a crisp November afternoon and while the autumn foliage had long since fallen to the ground, the bare landscape now glowed with a soft gold radiance as the sun dipped behind us. Marcus and Kip were a little too young to appreciate the game, but they'd been good on the trip, dozing off and on in the back seat. The Rough Riders triumphed 28-21. It was a good omen. I turned off the radio.

"Excited?" I asked Dolce.

In the distance we could make out Brother André's Shrine basking in the twilight on the side of the mountain.

"Yes," she said. "It feels so right."

We'd hoped to find a house to rent in Lower Westmount, close to Dolce's parents, but couldn't find anything in our price range so had taken a semi-detached house in St. Lambert instead.

Living where I grew up would be a challenge. A lot of people in the south shore suburb would remember my parents and the nature of my mother's death. It was a small town and suicide wasn't an everyday occurrence. I'd never had to deal with these people, because I'd been away at college at the time, and when Grace moved back to Toronto after Dad's death I'd pretty well cut all ties with my hometown. Choosing St. Lambert now meant raking up memories I'd tried to bury. Maybe the time was right. There were advantages. I was familiar with the town, comfortable in a way that only comes when the streets you walk as an adult are the same streets you walked as a kid.

The house we rented was on Sanford Avenue, just a couple of blocks away from our old place at 361 Merton. As we came off the Victoria Bridge I decided to show Dolce another house, the one where we'd lived for a brief time in 1943, after Dad's transfer from Ottawa. It was a short detour and I wondered as I drove how much had changed in the years I'd been away.

It was twilight when I turned onto Upper Edison. The street lights had yet to come one. The old house was still there. The wood trim had been repainted, but the stucco exterior remained as I remembered it. There was a single light on, in an upstairs bedroom.

"It's big," Dolce said, looking up.

She was right. It had been too big for us, but there was a war on and houses were in short supply.

"And frankly, a little scary."

"Well, I was seven at the time, and it sure scared the hell out of me our first night here."

Dad held my hand as we walked up the flagstone path. He put the key into the lock, turned it, and the front door swung open. I followed my mother inside. My father closed the door behind us. To our right was a large, open living room with curved glass windows. To our left was a flight of carpeted stairs leading to the second floor. The ceilings were high and the oak trim was dark, almost black, in the fashion of the day. This was much bigger than our house in Ottawa. We'd rented it furnished, putting our own things into storage. Everything here was formal and unfamiliar. There were too many nooks and crannies; I feared what might be lurking in them.

"We're lucky to get it," my father said.

To me the gloom and fear that had been in the air since the start of the war seemed to have followed us here. My bedroom was on the second floor in the back. It was small, with faded floral wallpaper. That first night I went to bed with the uncomfortable feeling that we didn't belong here. Dad kissed me goodnight and Mom sang my favourite bedtime song about the three little fishies, but when she closed the door I was afraid.

"Leave it open, Mummy, please?"

"All right, honey, but just a crack."

As her footsteps receded down the stairs they were replaced by another sound, a tapping at my window.

"Mom," I called out, more frightened now.

"What is it?" Her voice was distant, tired.

"Mom, there's a noise."

"Don't be silly, honey, it's just the wind."

It wasn't just the wind, I was sure.

"Mom, it's not the wind."

My father's voice carried up the stairs. "It's his imagination, Trudy." Then louder, "Go to sleep now, Andy."

In the silence that followed, I was aware my mother had paused halfway down the stairs. I could also picture my father, seated in the living room. Maybe they were right, perhaps it was only my imagination.

Then the tapping resumed.

"Mom, it's not the wind." I could hear the stairs creak as she turned, poised to come back up.

"You're babying him, you know." It was my father's voice again.

"I'll just settle him down," she said as she started back up. "After all, it's his first night here." The sliver of light that marked my door widened and Mom came into the bedroom and sat at the foot of the bed.

"Now what's this all about?" she asked, her hand resting lightly on my leg.

"Listen, Mom." We both listened in the half-light of the bedroom. For what seemed like the longest time there was silence. Then, to my immense relief, it came again. A faint tapping.

"There," I said. "Did you hear that, Mom?" It was strange; what had previously frightened me now provided vindication.

My mother moved to the window and looked out. The tapping resumed. She turned back to the bed.

"It's only the wind, Andy. It's blowing the branches of the tree against the side of the house." She crossed back to my bed and leaned over to kiss me. "You go to sleep now, it's nothing to worry about."

As I listened to her departing steps on the stairs and the occasional tapping at the window I wished I were back in my own bed in our old house in Ottawa. These thoughts comforted me and I relaxed a little, slipping into a restless sleep.

Much later I awoke, roused this time by a faint hum. The house was dark and there was no other sound, the wind having died down. No tapping, but the hum was louder. It was coming from the window—the windowpane was vibrating. Then another sound, at first just a low rumble, but gradually building. Then the two sounds, the rumble and the hum, blended into one. The room began to shake as the noise level rose. This wasn't my imagination. As the sounds and vibration filled the space around me, the whole house shook, and I screamed, but my voice was drowned out by another louder sound—the high-pitched whistle of a steam locomotive.

Then Mom was with me, holding me in her arms, rocking me gently. "There, there, it's all right. It's only a train, that's all. It's just a train going by."

I trembled and she held me closer. It was a long train and the house continued to vibrate, as freight car after freight car rumbled by. My trembling continued long after the sound of the last car had faded into the night.

The next morning I looked out my bedroom widow. Below, I could see the gentle curve of the railway track. It ran alongside the backyard and very close to the house. Too close, I thought.

My parents' insistence that it was nothing to worry about vanished a few weeks later when a freight train jumped the tracks just a hundred yards up the line from our house. The locomotive ploughed up a stretch of rail bed before rolling over into a ditch. Freight cars telescoped past it, splitting open, sending their cargo of Florida oranges cascading out onto the frozen ground. The engineer and the fireman were killed, pinned in the wreckage. The area was quickly cordoned off, but not before we had helped ourselves to some of the oranges. It was wartime and they were a luxury, but they didn't have much taste. My mother said she thought they had been exposed too long to the freezing temperatures. I could only think they'd been exposed too long to death. A few months later we found a more suitable house, far from the nearest railway line.

The street lights flickered on and I realized it was time to leave. When the children were older and could understand more, I'd show them another home, the one where I grew up, and tell them about the woman who once lived there. I wondered what sort of a grandmother my mother would have been.

We drove to our new home on Sanford Avenue. I vowed that nothing would frighten my boys that first night. It helped that we were a long way from the nearest railway line.

ST. LAMBERT, 1964

ONE SATURDAY MORNING a few weeks after our move to Sanford, I walked over to the main street, Victoria Avenue. The town had changed; the empty lots I'd cut across on my way to school were now filled in with new homes. I heard more French spoken during my fifteen-minute stroll than I'd heard in the entire time I'd spent here as a child. A bus rumbled by on Desaulniers Boulevard, a reminder that our streetcar link to the city had been terminated. The exclusive homes along Riverside Drive no longer looked out on the river. Tons of earth had converted the area into parkland and, in the distance, beyond the park, lay the St. Lawrence Seaway. Great Lakes ships now plied the waters where we once swam as children. The ponds where we'd hunted frogs in the summer and skated in the winter were also gone, gobbled up by new residential housing.

The late November sun provided the illusion of warmth without the substance. I wondered, as I hurried home, if Mrs. King was still teaching piano. I passed the duplex where she'd lived and remembered my first lesson with her when I was eight years old.

I rang the bell, was buzzed in, and walked up a long flight of stairs. The inner door opened. Before me was a busty, middle-aged woman dressed in a silk blouse and a simple black skirt.

"Hello, young man."

"I'm Andy Little."

"Yes, yes," she said, and impatiently ushered me into the house. Her words came out in a rush, as if she feared interruption. She wore horn-rimmed reading glasses suspended around her neck by a tiny silver chain.

"Let me see your hands."

Surprised, I held them out, palms up. We were standing in the hall.

"Turn them over."

I did.

"Into the bathroom, young man," she said, "and wash them." She pointed to a door down the hall.

When I returned, she was sitting in the living room. An upright piano was against the far wall. The afternoon light filtered into the room through lace curtains drawn across three windows facing the street. The house smelled of cooked cabbage.

Mrs. King got up from her chair and crossed the room to the piano. "In future, I want you to make sure you wash your hands before you come here for your lesson."

My hands hadn't seemed to need washing, but maybe Mrs. King saw something I didn't. She sat down at the piano bench.

"Sit here," she said, patting a place beside her.

I did as I was told, aware for the first time that she smelled faintly of lavender.

"Put your hands on the keys, like this." She spread her fingers on the keyboard to my right. I followed suit. "You have good hands," she said matter-of-factly. "Spread your fingers as wide as you can." I stretched them. "You can almost reach an octave." She explained what an octave was and I noticed that my eight-year-old hands were almost the same size as hers.

Mrs. King spent the rest of the hour explaining the importance of posture at the piano and demonstrating how the foot pedals worked; she went over flats, sharps, and simple chords. She opened a book of music and had me follow along as she played a simple tune. I learned I'd be assigned a piece and would be expected to play it, reading from the music, the following week. "If you can manage that," she said, "I'll put a little silver star on that page in your book. Then, if you can play the same piece from memory, without looking at the music, you get a gold star." Her smile seemed to indicate she thought this prospect unlikely.

With that, she closed the music book and rose from the bench. I could hear the soft swish of her nylons rubbing together as she walked across the living room to the hall. She opened the door and I started down the steps, clutching my new book of music.

"See you next week," she called after me.

I never liked Mrs. King. She had this habit of rapping my knuckles with a pointer if she didn't approve of the way my hands were positioned above the keyboard. I'm not sure if it was that or her lack of any apparent sense of humour, or simply my indifference to music. Whatever it was, I didn't look forward to my weekly lessons, but was sufficiently intimidated to make sure I knew my assignments. In this I had help.

Our piano at home was in a little alcove beside the dining room, and I usually practised my piece in the late afternoon when my mother was preparing supper. Whenever she heard me struggling with anything, she would come to my rescue. Patiently, and with humour, she'd coach me through the week's assignment.

On Tuesday afternoon I would turn up at Mrs. King's flat, hands clean, and play my piece twice: first with the music, then without. By year's end most of the pages in my music book were adorned with silver and gold stars.

Each spring, friends and parents of Mrs. King's pupils were invited to a recital, held in the recreation hall of the United Church. Students were assigned a piece appropriate to their skill level. I practised mine for more than a month and the night before the recital I played it in my sleep.

I'd always passed up school plays, public-speaking contests, and just about anything else that required performance before an audience, because of stage fright. I had no trouble playing the fool in a classroom, but the prospect of playing the piano in front of close to a hundred people filled me with dread. My mother assured me she had the same problem and that the fear always melted away once the first note was struck.

The night of the concert the hall was full, and my mother and father were sitting proudly in the second row. My turn came about halfway through the recital after the younger pupils had finished their performances. I could feel the sweat soaking my white dress shirt as Mrs. King introduced me. I shakily made my way onto the stage, bowed, and sat down at the stool before the piano. I waited while the audience settled, then, on Mrs. King's cue, began to play my piece.

My mother was wrong about stage fright. It didn't diminish with the first note. It grew. I was about thirty seconds into the selection when I hit a wrong note.

"If that should happen," Mrs. King had advised me again and again, "don't stop, keep playing." It was a sentiment my mother echoed.

I stopped, and started again from the beginning. And promptly made another mistake. And started all over again. By this time I was so rattled that even hitting the first note correctly was a challenge.

Mrs. King appeared from the wings and smiled apologetically to the audience. She was carrying the sheet music for my piece. She put her hand on my shoulder.

"Relax," she said, and spread the music before me. "Take a deep breath, and when I give the signal, begin again." She smiled at the audience and moved off the stage.

What no one realized was that my mother's constant coaching had left me without the ability to read music. I'd always been shown which notes to hit and never had to consult the pages. No wonder my book was filled with gold stars. Every piece I played for Mrs. King was from memory.

So on this night placing the music before me just made things worse. Bad enough that I couldn't remember the piece. Now it would be clear to everyone that I couldn't even read it. From the wings Mrs. King cued me with her golden pointer and I began again.

I blundered into another mistake. I tried from the beginning one more time, but when I heard the jarring sound of another wrong note, I got up from the piano, vaulted off the stage, and ran down the aisle, past the people in the audience and out the back door of the hall. I ran all the way home, into our house, and up the stairs; I threw myself down on my bed, sobbing with humiliation.

I don't know how long it was before my parents returned. I don't know if they stayed for the rest of the recital or left after my debacle. I'd lost all sense of time.

My mother rapped softly on my door. I didn't respond. She pushed into the room. I buried my face in the pillow. She sat down on the edge of my bed and ran a hand gently up and down my back. For a time, she didn't say anything.

"I feel like such a jerk," I said into the pillow. "I'm never going back to Mrs. King. She's horrible. I hate her."

My mother remained silent; she moved her hand to the base of my neck and continued the massage.

"My friends don't take piano lessons." I was no longer crying. "I don't see why I have to."

My mother stopped the massage. "We won't make you," she said softly. "Lessons are finished for the year anyway. If you don't want to go back in the fall you won't have to."

With these words my body relaxed for the first time in days. My mother rose from the bed and went downstairs. I could hear her in deep conversation with my father. I couldn't make out what they were saying at first but as the voices grew louder the words became clear.

"We can't let him walk away from something like this," my father said.

"But it was my fault, Willis. I thought I was helping him. I didn't realize he wasn't learning to read the music."

"Dammit, Trudy, this isn't about you. We can't let him quit. You have to get back on a horse once you've been thrown. It's the only way. Otherwise you never get over the fear."

The argument went on a long time, some of the words lost to me as they paced from room to room downstairs. Then there was a moment of silence and I hoped the discussion was over. But it began again, and this time I could hear clearly every word that was spoken.

"He goes back to Mrs. King in the fall and that's final." It was my father.

"He does not," my mother hissed. "I've promised him and I'm not going back on my word."

"You'll do as I say."

"I will not."

The next sound was unmistakable.

A slap.

Then my mother's footsteps as she ran up the stairs and into the bedroom. Her door slammed. A moment later the door downstairs slammed. The only other sound I remember after that was the chirp of the crickets in the warm spring night.

My mother didn't come down from her room the next morning. Dad had left for work by the time I got up. I made my own breakfast and went off to school. I hadn't exaggerated when I said none of my friends took piano lessons. No one mentioned the incident at school. It was as if it hadn't happened.

At home, although it wasn't discussed, the ramifications were hard to miss. For the next two weeks my parents barely spoke to each other. Routines were followed, but they were silent and sullen. Dad slept in the guest bedroom. I didn't know what to do, what to say.

Then, suddenly, one morning it was over. I'd wakened during the night to the sound of my parents in conversation. Their voices were low, the words impossible to make out, but I knew they weren't arguing. I drifted back to sleep.

"Good morning," my mother said cheerfully as she put a glass of freshly squeezed orange juice in front of me.

I washed down a cod liver oil capsule with the juice. A bowl of porridge appeared. I poured molasses over it, added cream, and ate, waiting for my mother to speak.

"Your father apologized last night," she said. "He has promised it won't happen again."

So they knew I'd heard the slap.

She smiled at me. "We've made up."

ST. LAMBERT/MONTREAL, 1964-65

WHY HAD I BEEN SENT to Mrs. King in the first place? My mother was a trained piano teacher. Why hadn't she taught me? For that matter why hadn't Mom taught piano in St. Lambert? She could have done it at home; Mrs. King did. It was a question I never asked. Three years later, when my mother wanted to earn some money to help pay part of her medical bills, she organized a nursery school in our home. The only use she made of her musical training was playing the piano at the beginning of each day as the children marched around the room. In all the time I knew my mother, those years when she was running a morning nursery school were her best.

This morning it was something by John Phillip Sousa and I was glad when it finished. I had convinced my mother that I should stay home from school, because I still had the remains of a winter cold. I actually sounded worse than I felt, but I was using every excuse I could to avoid school that year. My grade six teacher and I couldn't seem to agree on what constituted appropriate classroom behaviour.

With the march over, things were quieter, and I reached for a Captain Marvel comic book to read. A full bottle of Canada Dry ginger ale and a plate of home-made oatmeal cookies were on a tray at the foot of my bed. Mom didn't want me venturing down, spreading my cold germs, so she had made sure I had everything I needed. On the table beside the bed was a box of Kleenex and a package of Smith Brothers' Wild Cherry cough drops.

I came across the word "sanctuary" in the comic I was reading and had to look up its meaning in the dictionary. "A sacred place where one finds refuge." That seemed a perfect definition for my room. Maybe it wasn't sacred, but it certainly was special. The furniture had been custom-made by my dad. I'd helped with the design and had the final say on the red-and-blue colours. The desk, bureau, bed, and bookshelves fit snugly, like pieces of a puzzle, using up all the available space. It made the place mine in a way no other room had ever been.

The other thing that made it special, a refuge, was the sound of my mother's voice as she taught the children. It filtered into my room and told me all was well, that I didn't have to worry about her. That was another reason why I skipped school whenever I could. Her words had a soothing quality and when she laughed, as she did a lot in those years, it was a bonus. She was fine and I didn't have to do or be anything for her. I could be myself. I could be anyone I wanted to be. I went back to my Captain Marvel comic.

In St. Lambert I kept meeting folks who remembered my mother and her nursery school. Parents whose children had attended were unanimous in their praise for the school. I'm sure they were sincere. Unspoken were questions about my mother's death. What people never understood was that there were actually two Trudy Littles. In private she was often anxious and depressed. In public she was always a friendly, outgoing woman who charmed just about everyone she met. It was confusing, growing up with someone like that, but she could produce moments of sheer delight. I remembered one of those moments as I drove by the local softball field.

I decided to park the car. I climbed into the bleachers. Floodlights had been added—they weren't there when I was a kid. In fact, in the late summer when the days grew shorter and it got dark earlier, starting time for our games was moved from seven to six o'clock in the evening. This meant that family dinner schedules had to be altered. Mothers fed their sons early. Fathers who worked until five usually ate after the game. They often sat with empty stomachs, cheering their sons on. Today the field was deserted, but my mind provided a game.

In the summer of 1951 our team made it to the finals. Mom and Dad were in the third base stands for the opening game, diplomatically applauding good plays by both sides, but clearly pulling for my team to win.

The game was scoreless when a walk, a bunt single, and an error loaded the bases for the bottom of the seventh inning. It was our first real chance. The clean-up hitter was up and, with visions of a grand slam home run in his head, he was swinging for the fences. He struck out on three pitches. I moved to the on-deck circle as the next batter headed for the plate. Excitement and fear began to build in my stomach. If he didn't deliver, it would be up to me.

He swung and made good contact, but the sharply hit ground ball was fielded cleanly by the pitcher, who threw home for the easy force-out.

I was queasy as I headed for the plate. The game was on the line and I was a glove man, known for my fielding, not my hitting.

The first pitch was low and away. I took it and a deep breath. Ball one. A little of the fear subsided. The pitcher had lost something off his fastball. The next pitch was inside, and I swung too soon, pulling it foul by several feet. But the swing had been a good one and I relaxed some more. The pitcher looked in, past me to the catcher. He nodded at the sign, checked the runners, and fired the ball down the heart of the plate. I guessed fastball and timed my swing to meet it.

The contact was solid, and as I sprinted to first I saw the ball skip between the second baseman and the shortstop.

Base hit!

The outfield grass was heavy with evening dew; it slowed down the ball, allowing two runs to score. The first base coach patted me on the butt.

"Good hit, Andy. Good hit."

Standing on first base I felt an immense surge of relief and light-headedness. The cheering slowly subsided. The next batter started for the plate. The pitcher moved to the rubber. Then, with the game about to resume, a high, excited voice broke through the still evening air.

"That's my boy!"

It was my mother.

Fans turned their heads in surprise. The pitcher hesitated and looked to the stands. A ripple of laughter went through the crowd. The focus shifted to me and I dropped my head and looked at my feet, waiting for the embarrassment to take hold. To my surprise, it didn't. In its place were feelings of pride and pleasure—pride at the hit, pleasure that Mom had so publicly acknowledged it. I raised my head and looked across the diamond. I smiled. So did she.

It was good to be back in St. Lambert. We'd been there almost six months and had no regrets. The kids were able to see their grandparents a couple of times a week in Westmount. I was on much better terms with Dolce's folks now that I'd stopped drinking. They'd never been openly critical of my habit, but I knew it had worried them. My decision to get out of reporting meant I was leading a less hectic life, with regular hours. If I had any doubts about the wisdom of the move, they were dispelled forever on the night of April 7, 1965.

Earl Garrety sucked in the smoke from his cigarette and pondered his cards.

"Hit me again," he said.

It was just after ten o'clock in the evening, and in the Montreal newsroom of the CBC we had the late local news edited and ready to go.

I dealt him an eight of clubs.

"I'll stick."

It had been a routine evening. Most of the newscast was a repeat of the supper hour show, with some late sports scores and an updated weather forecast.

Across the desk Earl was showing the eight and a six of diamonds. I turned my card over. Queen of hearts. I dealt myself another, the Jack of diamonds.

"I'll stick," I said. "What have you got?"

He smiled. "Twenty-one." He flipped over a seven of spades and swept the pot of small change to his side of the desk. He'd beaten me again.

"Want to play another?" he asked, shuffling the cards.

"No," I said, disgusted. "I'd better check the wires."

The bell that signalled breaking news began to ring as I pushed open the door to the teletype room. It was the Canadian Press machine and the story was datelined Toronto.

> Two men, a CBC television reporter and a cameraman, were killed tonight when their light plane crashed in dense fog at Malton Airport. Herb Foxcroft, 42, the cameraman, was piloting the single engine Cessna. Robert Sciafino, 28, a reporter, was the only passenger. Witnesses said as the plane approached the runway it apparently clipped a high-tension hydro line and plunged to the ground. There was no explosion and rescue workers were able to recover the bodies. A formal inquiry into the accident has been ordered. The victims were returning from Windsor where they'd been on assignment for The National, the television network's main news program.

I stood by the teletype machine, unable to move.

Bob Sciafino had been the man they hired to replace me. If I'd stayed on in Toronto, there was a pretty good chance I'd have been aboard that plane. I don't know how long I stood there, staring at the copy, but eventually Earl appeared at the door.

"What's up?" he asked.

I ripped the copy from the machine and handed it to him. The bell had stopped ringing and it was quieter now with just the low clatter of machines churning out routine news.

Earl read the story, then shook his head. "Jesus," he said, and handed it back to me. He knew its significance.

I called *The National* newsroom in Toronto. I learned that Bob and Herbie had been working on a series about automobile safety in Windsor. The weather had been clear when they took off, but a bank of fog moved in from Lake Ontario and by the time they reached Toronto visibility had been reduced to a few hundred yards.

My hand was shaking as I put the phone back in its cradle.

"Why don't you go home?" Earl suggested. "The show is all wrapped up. I can handle things here."

As I drove across the Victoria Bridge, the lights of St. Lambert beckoned. I was going home to a wife and two children. The relief I felt was so powerful that for the moment I forgot about Bob Sciafino and Herbie Foxcroft. And when I did, a sense of guilt accompanied the horror and sorrow I felt for my colleagues.

NOTRE-DAME-DE-GRACE, 1969

DOLCE LOVED BEING a stay-at-home mom. More and more women were choosing to return to work in those days, but Dolce delighted in looking after Marcus and Kip, and since I was making good money at the CBC there was no need for a second income. In 1968 we decided to try for another child. I'd always wanted a daughter, so a year later, when we learned that a baby was on the way, I crossed my fingers. I also realized we'd need more room. My father-in-law had a friend who owned some rental houses in Notre-Dame-de-Grace, a Montreal suburb. We checked them out and found a semi-detached home we liked on Patricia Avenue. The rent was reasonable and it meant we'd be closer to Dolce's folks. So we moved. There were other children on the street and Marcus and Kip soon had a new group of friends. Dolce's due date was September.

It had been seven years since the birth of our last child and things had changed. It was all so organized this time. When Dolce's due date passed, the doctor decided to induce labour. We dropped Marcus and Kip off at their grandparents for a sleepover, had a leisurely dinner, and drove to the hospital, where she was admitted and shown to her room. It was like checking into a hotel.

The next morning the telephone roused me from a light sleep.

I grabbed for the receiver. It was a nurse calling from the Catherine Booth Hospital.

"Yes?" I was wide awake, rolling out of bed.

"Dr. Patrick asked me to let you know they've given your wife her epidural."

"I'll be right there." I reached for my pants.

"Oh, there's no need to hurry." There was a chuckle on the line. "It will be a couple of hours yet. Take your time."

The words were wasted on me. I backed the car out of the driveway, slammed it into first, and floored it. At Sherbrooke Street a red light and heavy traffic forced me to a reluctant stop; I drummed my fingers nervously on the padded steering wheel.

The light changed and I accelerated past a city bus. I made it from our home to the hospital in just under ten minutes, not bad for the peak of the morning rush hour. Skipping the elevator, I took the steps two at a time to the third floor and pushed my way into Dolce's room, sweating and out of breath.

She was sitting up in bed, reading *The Gazette*. "Good morning." She smiled and put the paper down. I approached the bed and kissed her lightly on the lips. She was so composed. It was as if she'd just recently awakened from a refreshing night's sleep.

"Everything all right?"

"Great," she said. "The nurse says the contractions are strong, but so far I haven't felt a thing. I wish it had been this easy for the first two."

"I came as quickly as I could ... "

"Relax," she said, and motioned me to the chair beside the bed. "Did you have any breakfast?"

I shook my head.

"There's a cafeteria downstairs." She glanced at her watch. "They'll be back for me in a few minutes. You can grab a bite, then wait for me here."

Feeling both foolish and useless, I took the stairs to the main floor. After a stale Danish and a cup of questionable coffee I took the elevator back to the third floor. The public address system crackled, paging a Doctor Solomon. The matter-of-fact tone of the amplified voice reminded me that the Catherine Booth was for pregnant mothers only; there wasn't the same degree of tension you find in a full service hospital.

Upstairs, I sat alone in Dolce's room, waiting. I found *The Gazette* she'd been reading. There'd been another terrorist bomb explosion in a mailbox in Westmount. Militant separatists seeking an independent Quebec. No one hurt. The deadline for a settlement in the contract dispute between the city and its police force had passed with no agreement. The cops could now legally walk off the job any time they wanted.

"Mr. Little?" A nurse stood in the doorway, smiling.

I jumped to my feet, the newspaper falling to the floor. "Is everything okay?"

"Just fine," she said reassuringly. "Your wife is in the recovery room."

"And the baby?"

She smiled and beckoned me to follow, moving off down the hospital corridor, her crepe-soled shoes making no sound; the only noise was the soft whisper of her starched uniform as she walked.

I knew from the delight on Dolce's face when I entered the room that we had the daughter we both wanted. Our new arrival was tucked into the crook of her arm, a tiny face wrinkled and red, eyes closed, oblivious to the world around her.

"Well," she said, "we did it."

I noted with surprise that our daughter had a full head of hair, still wet from the post-delivery bath. "She's beautiful."

"How do you feel?"

"Wonderful. They said to expect some pain when the epidural wears off, but for now I'm on cloud nine."

Later, as I drove out of the hospital parking lot, I felt some discomfort myself, but I wasn't sure what it was. Elation and pride had given way to a sense of uneasiness. Now it blossomed into full-fledged fear. I was beginning to sweat. This was silly, I told myself. I had the daughter I wanted, Dolce had come through the delivery without any problems. There was no reason for this sense of dread. What was bothering me? I didn't know, but I couldn't shake the feeling that something was wrong.

I parked the car in a lot behind the CBC building and took the elevator to the sixth floor. The sound hit me before I entered the newsroom. It was a sound every journalist loves—the hum of breaking news.

The lineup editor, pecking away on his typewriter, his shoulder cradling the phone, brought me quickly up to speed. "The cops have pulled the plug."

"Bananas?" I asked.

"Bananas," he said.

Every year at least once or twice something happened that revved the newsroom engine to the red line. It might be a prison riot or a crippling snowstorm. Today it was a police strike. When it's something this big, everything else goes out the window. Sports and weather are trimmed, and all of the newsroom resources are focused on the single happening. We call this "going bananas" over a story.

What makes "banana" days so challenging is their unpredictability. They're what journalists crave; reputations can be made overnight. At the assignment desk I tried to catch up on things. Fred Langan, one of our reporters, looked up from the wire copy he was reading.

"Well ... ?" He raised an eyebrow.

"It's a girl."

"Dolce's okay?"

"Fine. They're both in good shape."

"That's great," he smiled. "She picked one helluva day to make her entrance. Some timing. Maybe she'll be a reporter when she grows up."

"Not if she has any sense. One journalist in the family is enough."

"No cigars?"

"Tomorrow," I promised.

It was 2:00 a.m. by the time I got out of the newsroom. Without police, traffic had been a mess all day. There'd been more than a dozen convenience store holdups and some minor break-ins, but no bank robberies and, so far, no looting. Local taxi drivers, locked in a dispute with the airport limousine service, used the occasion to torch the company headquarters.

The parking lot was empty. No sign of my car. A "closed" sign hung in the window of the little booth where the attendant stamped tickets. At first I thought perhaps he'd moved the car, parked it somewhere out of sight, just to be safe. I checked the alley behind the building. Nothing. It was gone. What could I do? I couldn't very well call the cops. I went back into the CBC and called a cab instead. My car had become part of the story we'd been covering.

At home, alone, the anger I felt at the loss of the car gave way to uneasiness again, and the fear I'd noticed that morning after I left the hospital. This, added to the adrenaline left over from the day's events, combined to produce anxiety, something I hadn't felt since I gave up reporting. I checked the medicine cabinet and found something the doctor had prescribed when I had trouble sleeping after the plane crash that killed my Toronto colleagues. I took two tablets, and within an hour managed to doze off.

NOTRE-DAME-DE-GRACE, 1969

BY THE TIME I BROUGHT Dolce and our new baby home from the hospital the police had been legislated back to work and traffic had returned to what might be considered "normal" for Montreal. My Mini Cooper had indeed been stolen, just one of the many cars taken that night. I still hadn't been able to shake the sense of dread that had settled in after my daughter's birth, but the sleeping pills got me through a hectic week.

We told the boys their new sister's name was Holiday.

"It's from a book, *Breakfast at Tiffany's*."

"There's a Tiffany in my class," Kip said, as if that explained everything.

"I've never heard that name before." Marcus was emphatic.

Dolce shifted Holiday from one breast to the other while the boys watched. "Well, we could call her Holly. That's short for Holiday."

"I like that name," Kip said simply.

Marcus gave it some thought. He said the name aloud. "Holly. I like it better than Holiday."

"Then Holly it is," Dolce said. "You all have nicknames. Kip is really Christopher. Everyone calls Marcus Marco. And Holiday will be known as Holly."

"It's neat," Marcus said, "having a sister."

That conversation with the kids reminded me of a time when I was about ten and I was complaining I had no one to play with.

"If you could have a brother or a sister, which would you rather have?" my mother asked me.

"What?" I was ten years old and wasn't sure I'd heard her properly. We were sitting in the living room and I had just bitten into a freshly baked butter tart.

"I said how would you like to have a brother ... someone to keep you company?" My mother wasn't eating, but held a cup of coffee in her lap.

"I dunno." I was going to have to think this over. "I thought you said you didn't want any more babies."

"I don't," my mother said a trifle too cheerfully, "but we could always adopt a child." She sipped her coffee.

I knew about adoption. Some of the kids in my school had been adopted. I always felt a little sorry for them, but I wasn't sure why. I think it was because I knew that at some point in their lives someone had decided they weren't wanted.

"I guess it would be okay." I was feeling my way.

"Which would you rather have? A brother or a sister?" My mother seemed to be turning this into a game.

"A brother," I said without hesitation.

"Older or younger?"

"Younger."

"How much younger?"

I thought some more. "Two years younger, eight years old." I didn't want an older brother, someone who might boss me around.

"Well, your father and I think it might be a good idea. I just wanted to know how you felt." She finished her coffee, rose from the sofa, and started to leave the room.

"How do you do it ... adopt someone?"

"Well," my mother said, pausing at the doorway, "first you let the people who run adoption agencies know that you'd like a child. Then there are all sorts of papers to fill out. And interviews. They don't just give children to anyone who asks. They have to check on the family background, make sure it's going to a good home."

I remembered that the possibility of adoption was discussed, on and off, for several months. The idea of a sister had been ruled out, but I'd been flexible about the age of a brother. A couple of years younger would be perfect, but three or four years would be okay too. Even the same age. Not older though. How would I feel if my new brother was a Negro? It didn't matter. Did I like the idea of bunk beds? I did, as long as I had the top bed.

When would all this happen? Not sure.

"These things take time."

I came home one afternoon after school and found my mother at the kitchen table, crying. She hastily wiped her eyes with a Kleenex.

"What's the matter?" My mother's moods could swing from one extreme to the other, but I rarely saw her cry.

"Oh, it's nothing." She folded a sheet of paper she'd been reading, placing it back in an envelope. "How was your day at school?"

The way she changed the subject I knew she wasn't going to tell me why she'd been crying, at least not that afternoon.

"Fine." I moved to the refrigerator. "We have a new boy in our class. He's from Scotland." I took out a bottle of milk and poured myself a glass. I had to be patient, my mother usually shared her thoughts with me. I grabbed a hand-

ful of Dad's oatmeal cookies from a box and joined her at the table. "His name is Bryce ... Bryce Weir. He lives on Sanford. We walked home together."

My mother reached across the table and took one of my cookies. "What's he like?"

"Seems nice enough. He wore a jacket and tie to school, though, and funny grey shorts. He says that's what they had to wear in Scotland."

"Does he have any brothers or sisters?"

"Oh yes, a big family. Two older sisters, two younger sisters, and two younger brothers. Seven kids." I noticed tears forming again in my mother's eyes. She got up from the table and moved to the sink, looking out the window.

"You should ask him over. I'd like to meet him."

My mother never did tell me why she'd been crying, but I found out that night when I overheard part of a conversation she had with my father.

"We didn't meet the requirements?" Her voice was shrill, loud enough to carry into my bedroom. "What is that supposed to mean?"

I couldn't make out my father's answer, so I slipped out of bed and moved to the hall.

"Keep your voice down, Trudy, shouting won't do any good."

"I don't understand it. What requirements?"

"Maybe if we'd been members of a church," Dad suggested. "I think they put a lot of emphasis on religion."

"You mean if we'd been Catholics we'd have met the requirements?" My mother was angry now and I could picture her pacing back and forth in the living room.

"There's something else." My father spoke quietly.

Silence. The pacing stopped.

"I know they spoke to someone at the Allan."

"At the Allan?" There was a quiver in my mother's voice.

"On the questionnaire, they asked about health, wanted to know if either of us had been hospitalized recently."

I'd heard enough. I moved quietly back into my bedroom. Within seconds my mother came up the stairs, sobbing. Downstairs Dad turned on the radio.

Adoption was never mentioned again. I didn't press for answers. I'd become best friends with Bryce Weir and soon we were inseparable. When we wanted peace and quiet, we hung out at my place. When we wanted company, his brothers and sisters provided it at his house. I felt I was part of two families and so did he. There was no need for an adopted brother.

Although I'd been fortunate to connect with Bryce and his family, I was still an only child. As I grew older I came to the conclusion that being the centre of the universe for my parents wasn't the healthiest way to start life. But then I didn't have any say in the matter. My dad had been an only child too. I was determined to break the pattern with my own family. So when Kip was born, I'd been filled with a profound sense of relief.

Why then were things so different after Holiday's birth? Why did I feel anxious and depressed? I'd wanted a girl, wanted my children to grow up with boys and girls in a family. Yet I couldn't shake the idea that something was wrong.

MONTREAL, OCTOBER 1970

THE DISTINCTIVE WUMP-WUMP-WUMP of the helicopter's rotary blades, the unofficial soundtrack for the real-life drama playing itself out in Montreal, woke me after four hours of restless sleep. I slid out of bed and into my clothes. No time to shave or brush my teeth. We were staffing the newsroom around the clock, most of us working double shifts. Downstairs I poured a coffee and carried it out to the car, the steam rising from the mug in the cool October air. Down the street an armed soldier paced back and forth in front of the home of the local MP. I backed the car out of the driveway and headed for work. The radio was tuned to CJAD, where Rick Leckner was warning early-morning motorists to stay clear of the Decarie Expressway because one lane was closed off for repairs. That was a good sign; if anything had happened while I slept, Rick wouldn't be talking traffic.

It had been one helluva month, I thought, as I gunned the Porsche along Dorchester Boulevard. Two weeks ago James Cross, the British High Commissioner, had been kidnapped by the FLQ, a terrorist group seeking independence for Quebec. Then last weekend the group snatched Pierre Laporte, the provincial Minister of Labour. A few days later his body was found in the trunk of an abandoned car in St. Hubert. He'd been strangled.

Parliament had invoked the War Measures Act, and the army was called in. Hundreds of suspected FLQ sympathizers had been rounded up by police and were being held without charge. Some of them were my friends. When Tim Ralfe, a television reporter, suggested to the Prime Minister that the government might be over-reacting, he was told that the question reflected the sentiment of "weak-kneed bleeding-hearts."

"How far are you willing to go?" Ralfe had asked Pierre Elliot Trudeau.

"Just watch me," the Prime Minister replied.

We'd watched all right, but in the end there was no armed insurrection, no real threat to the status quo, just the bungled attempt by half a dozen separatist extremists to gain support for their cause. They eventually freed the British High Commissioner in exchange for safe passage to Cuba.

When the crisis was over, we went back to normal programming, but I continued to work double shifts. We'd recorded everything broadcast during the previous month, using up our entire supply of two-inch videotape. Most of the material was of little or no value, just talking heads filling time, waiting for something to happen. Since the tapes were needed for other programs, I was assigned to screen them, keeping just the essentials, freeing up the rest. It meant putting in my normal eight-hour shift on the late news, then working overnight to clear up the backlog.

As I screened, my understanding of the crisis deepened. I watched again as the news broke that James Cross had been abducted from his home on Redpath Avenue, listened to the terrorist demands being read on French-language radio stations, was shocked by the death of Pierre Laporte and saddened at his funeral. It took me almost three weeks to go through the tapes, but I managed to reduce them to a few hours, the essence of the crisis, stripped of all ambiguity and confusion. Having done so, I found that my perspective had changed, and it was finally clear to me why events had unfolded the way they did. It wasn't so surprising, after all. Fear had won out over reason and common sense. It was that simple. As I drove home the morning after I screened the last of the videotape, I wondered again about my mother. I wished I'd had tapes of her life to review. I wondered again if my feelings of dread, my fear of travel, had been inherited.

The sign on the door read "Serge Bikadoroff, MD." As upset as I was, I had to laugh. What a perfect name for a shrink. If I'd been writing a movie script I couldn't have come up with anything better. I wondered if the doctor had the requisite goatee and Viennese accent.

His waiting room was small, but tastefully decorated with framed prints by Kandinsky and Chagall. I sat down on a comfortable two-seat sofa. On a table to my right was a small radio playing classical music, its volume low. On another table, in front of the sofa, was a scattering of newspapers and magazines. To my surprise, they were current: *The Star* and *The Gazette*, the latest copy of *Maclean's* and *Chatelaine*, and even *The New Yorker*.

I'd come to see Bikadoroff at the suggestion of my GP, Bruce Armstrong. "He's not everyone's cup of tea," Bruce had said, "but I think you'll like him."

"What's that supposed to mean?" I'd asked.

"Well, for one thing he's young, about your age," Bruce said, then paused; he seemed to be searching for the right word. "And a bit of a free spirit," he added with a smile.

The interior door to the doctor's office opened and the free spirit appeared. He was tall, slim, and wore his hair long, tied back in a ponytail.

"Mr. Little?" No accent, but he did have a beard.

I nodded and he beckoned me into his office. He was wearing a denim work shirt, a knitted wool tie, and khaki slacks. He sat down behind a parson's table that served as a desk while I took the straight-backed chair opposite him. He uncapped his fountain pen, opened a notebook.

"What seems to be the problem?" His eyes, behind rimless glasses, were green, flecked with gold.

I sighed. "I'm not sure. I can't seem to shake this feeling of dread, this occasional panic, as if something awful is about to happen."

"Any reason for this feeling?"

I shook my head. "No. That's what's so confusing. Everything is fine. I have a happy marriage, a good job, and three healthy kids. I don't know why I feel this way."

"I'd better get some family history."

For the next few minutes Bikadoroff took notes as I went through the details of my mother's illness and suicide, Dad's remarriage, and his death. He wrote steadily, without comment. I described the anxiety attacks I'd had at university, my problems with booze, and the struggle I had giving it up.

"When did you stop?"

"Seven years ago."

"Just like that?"

"It wasn't easy. I wouldn't want to go through it again."

"And you say these symptoms, this feeling of dread, surfaced again after your daughter's birth?" Bikadoroff spoke slowly, chose his words with care.

"That's even more confusing. We wanted this child, had been hoping for a daughter. There were no problems during the pregnancy and it was an easy birth. Holiday is a delight. I should be feeling good, not bad."

Bikadoroff stopped writing and leaned back in his chair, his arms folded across his chest. I paused, expecting him to speak, but when he didn't I went on.

"At university there was a good reason for my anxiety. I was afraid I was going to flunk out. When it surfaced again while I was kicking the booze habit, I thought it was just a withdrawal symptom."

"Is there anything different this time? I mean, aside from the lack of an obvious trigger? Any new symptoms?"

I thought for a moment. The window behind the doctor was open a crack. The sound of traffic from Sherbrooke Street filtered into the office. "Well, I noticed I've had a lot of trouble travelling since my daughter's birth. Whenever I go very far, I get anxiety attacks. We don't vacation on Cape Cod any more. It's too far to drive. My limit seems about fifty miles."

"What about planes?"

"Forget it," I said. "I don't fly."

"Aside from travel," he asked, "is there anything else that brings the attacks on?"

I shook my head. "No, but they usually hit in the evening, when I'm at home."

Bikadoroff made a few more notes, then closed the book, rose, and moved to the window.

"And you've been taking Miltown?"

I nodded. "I took it first to help me sleep. Then I found it eased the anxiety. I used to wait for the panic to start before I took any pills, but when I did that I found it took a double dose to bring the attack under control. Now I just take one pill every evening after supper as a precaution."

"I'd like to switch you to something else." He returned to his desk. He scribbled on a pad, then ripped off the paper and handed it to me. "Valium. Take these in the evening instead of Miltown."

"What's the difference?" I was apprehensive. "Why change when Miltown works?"

"Valium does the same thing, with fewer side effects." He reached for his appointment book. "And I'd like to see you again next week." He flipped through the pages. "Same time, Wednesday?"

"Fine." I rose from my chair.

He entered my name in the book and looked up at me. "Have you heard of behaviour modification?"

I shook my head.

"I think it might help you, particularly for the travel problem."

"How does it work?"

He handed me a pamphlet. "This explains it pretty well. Read it and we can talk about it next week. If you're game, I can set something up at the hospital for you."

"You don't do it here?"

"No, it's done in a lab."

"A lab?"

"At the Allan Memorial."

MONTREAL, 1971

THE BEHAVIOUR MODIFICATION lab in the basement of the Allan Memorial Institute had the look of a radio studio. Sandra Tembokem sat on one side of the glass, in the control room. I sat on the other, linked to her by an electrical wire that ran from a small clamp on the index finger of my left hand to a circuit box on the table before me.

I listened to the sound of my own voice, recorded earlier, playing back over recessed speakers. It was describing a trip I'd taken to test a series of relaxation exercises Sandra had taught me. The idea had been to drive out into the country each weekend and, at the first hint of panic, pull over and use the exercises.

On this particular trip I'd been about halfway to my objective when the wave of anxiety hit. In the lab, my account of that moment brought on a similar stab of fear, only this time it was accompanied by a mild electric shock to the finger. I flipped a switch on the box and the current cut off. I forced myself to relax, going through the same exercises I'd tried on the trip, closing my eyes to concentrate.

Inhale.

Tense the toes.

Count to ten.

Exhale and relax.

Then, in sequence, I tensed and relaxed the muscles of my calves, thighs, stomach, chest, hands and arms, jaw, and finally the muscles of my face. When I'd finished, the anxiety was gone. The fear always gave way to relief much more quickly here in the lab than it did out on the road, but I went through the complete set just the same. I could sense Sandra on the other side of the glass, poised, ready to continue. When my breathing was back to normal I nodded and she rolled the tape again.

In the beginning fear had been my constant companion on the trips. And at the Allan, just describing the journey could bring it back again. But as weeks passed my comfort level expanded, first in the lab and then in the car. By the third month of treatment I could usually drive for an hour in any direction, with anxiety under control. It was still with me, but like a nagging back seat driver whom I could ignore.

Crossing bridges was still a problem. The prospect always provoked fear, both on the road and listening to my account on tape in the lab. On a busy bridge I couldn't very well pull over to the side for my relaxation exercises.

On this day at the Allan, the tape described the mounting anxiety I'd felt as I approached the Victoria Bridge. I forced myself to breathe deeply and regularly. I am not quite sure why, but for the first time the narration describing the panic did not produce corresponding feelings of anxiety in the lab. Somehow I'd managed to detach myself, and the words describing the attack went harmlessly by me. The description had failed to trigger anything. There'd been no pulse of electricity. I looked through the window at Sandra. She was smiling. She motioned me to join her.

"Now we're making real progress." Sandra, a slim woman in her late twenties, was usually calm and controlled at the end of a session. Not today. Her features were alive with excitement. "I think the next time you have to actually cross a bridge you may be in for a surprise."

"Why?" I was afraid to hope.

"It's the way you handled it in the lab today. I could be wrong, but why don't you test it out before our next session, see what happens?"

When I left the Allan I crossed my fingers and headed for the Victoria Bridge. No point postponing things. I usually felt dread approaching the river, but not this time. Today hope battled fear to a draw and there was apprehension, not panic, as the vibration of the car's tires signalled the shift from the smooth asphalt of the road to the metal grid of the bridge. I reminded myself to breathe, and as the minutes passed excitement mounted. Suddenly I was halfway across and there'd been no sign of anxiety. I knew then that I was going to make it, and I pounded my fist on the steering wheel in triumph.

Just to make sure it wasn't a fluke I drove back into Montreal over the Jacques Cartier Bridge. Sandra was right. The fear had vanished. I gave a silent thanks to the Allan Memorial for the treatment I'd received. I just wished my mother could have been as fortunate.

I remembered the excitement in her voice one summer when she told us about something new Dr. Cameron wanted her to try, something called adrenaline desensitization. And a few months later the disappointment she felt when it didn't work and she slipped back into the familiar pattern of chronic anxiety. It was then that Dr. Cameron suggested Electroshock Therapy.

Trudy knows she shouldn't hope for too much; she's been disappointed so often in the past. But it's hard not to hope, as she sits in the waiting room, hard not to fantasize about a life free of anxiety. The things she could do, the places she might go—the prospects seem endless. She still has her looks. She might even sing again.

For the past month she's made her way to the Allan three times a week and today is her final session. She waits nervously in the outpatients' lounge, then submissively follows the orderly to the white room, where she is sedated and strapped down with restraints. A tongue depressor is placed between her teeth so she won't bite her tongue when the shocks are administered. She is thankful for the mild sedation.

When she awakes it always comes as a surprise to her that she is in a different, smaller room. She has no memory of being moved. Her mind holds no images of the writhing, twisting contortions she'd been through when the electrical charges were pumped into her brain. She lies there, bathed in sweat, slightly dazed, waiting for the pieces to fall back into place, one by one. When they do, she gets up from the bed, makes her way to the ladies' room, applies fresh lipstick, runs a brush through her hair, and goes back to the reception area. She checks with the receptionist, makes a note of the date for her next appointment with Dr. Cameron, and leaves the Allan. That's when her body reminds her what she's been through. As she walks back down Pine Avenue she feels as if she has just survived an avalanche. Everything aches; she is slightly nauseous and lightheaded. She's never been much of a drinker, but this, she imagines, must be how it feels to be hung over.

When Electroshock Therapy only provided a temporary respite from her anxiety, the disappointment drove her into a deeper depression. My mother blamed herself for this latest failure, as if she somehow hadn't tried hard enough. I'm sure Dr. Cameron did his best to dispel this misconception. I can almost hear him trying to reassure her.

"It isn't your fault, my girl. You did everything we asked. If anyone is responsible, we are. We doctors just haven't found the right answer. But we will." He nods with conviction. "We will."

Trudy listens listlessly. Before the shock treatments she'd felt like a tightrope walker before the big event. If this treatment worked perhaps she'd make it safely to the other side. It didn't, and she feels herself falling. She knows there is no safety net.

On the drive home from the Jacques Cartier Bridge I took Pine Avenue rather than Dorchester Boulevard. I slowed down as I passed the Allan Memorial. There were a few lights on, but most of the building was bathed in darkness. I'd found help in the Allan, but the elation of my own achievement gave way to sadness—my mother hadn't been so fortunate.

NOTRE-DAME-DE-GRACE, 1971

AT MY REGULAR WEEKLY appointment with Dr. Bikadoroff I described the breakthrough I'd experienced in the behaviour modification treatment.

"I couldn't believe it. The fear of bridges just disappeared. It was magic."

The doctor smiled. "Magic?"

"Well, I was getting pretty frustrated. The relaxation exercises were helping, but it was slow going, nothing very dramatic."

"And now?" Bikadoroff's eyebrows arched.

"Now I've seen how quickly things can change. Maybe I can actually beat this travel thing."

"I don't think there's much question about it. Sounds to me as if you're on the way." He opened the file folder on the desk. "Any anxiety this week?"

I shook my head. "Nope. It's been a couple of months now since I had any trouble. I take the Valium each evening. It seems to do the trick."

Bikadoroff made some notes in the file.

"I just wish my mother had held out a little longer. The new drugs, the behaviour modification, I'm sure they would have helped her."

The doctor closed the file and tilted back in his chair. "You were pretty close to your mother. Do you think there's any connection between the way you felt about her and your anxiety?"

I thought for a moment. "Just that I let her down. If I hadn't gone away to university ... " my voice trailed off. This was old territory. "I've already told you about that." I was impatient.

Bikadoroff was silent.

"Do you think that my travel fears might be tied into that guilt? That a part of me still feels that leaving home put my mother at risk?"

Bikadoroff's gaze held mine. "What do you think?"

Something had clicked for me when I made the connection. "It feels right." I was hesitant, not entirely sure yet.

"Do you remember why you came here in the first place?"

"To get rid of the anxiety?"

"Yes ... " He let the word hang in the air for a moment. "But do you remember when?"

"After Holiday was born." I wasn't sure where this was leading. "I came because I didn't understand why I was having the attacks. There didn't seem to be any reason for them."

"But they flared up with the birth of your daughter?"

"Yes," I answered with frustration. We'd been over all this.

"Did any of the feelings you had, after the birth, seem familiar?" He paused, and when I didn't answer, he continued. "Did they remind you of anything?"

It hit me. Yes, of course I'd felt those feelings before. Many times. As a child, whenever my mother failed to respond to my "hello" after school. Or when she was late coming home. I looked at Bikadoroff. "That's it," I said shakily. "The moment I learned the baby was a girl, I felt those feelings again. In a crazy way it was as if my mother had returned, as if I was somehow responsible for her again."

Bikadoroff smiled.

"And the travel phobia. I'm leaving her behind, deserting her. Is that what prompts the fear ... my anxiety?"

As usual, Bikadoroff countered my question with a question of his own. "What do you think?" he asked.

I didn't have to reply. He knew the answer and now so did I.

MONTREAL, 1976-77

IT WAS ALMOST ONE O'CLOCK in the morning by the time we wrapped up our TV coverage of the 1976 Quebec election and headed out into the unseasonably warm November night. The light breeze brought a reminder that just a few miles to the east, oil refineries were working at full capacity. The election coverage had gone smoothly and the program had been without any major snafus, but the results had been a shocker.

"What's that old Chinese proverb," I asked Elly Alboim, "about living in interesting times?"

"It's both a blessing and a curse," he chuckled.

For the first time in history voters in Quebec had elected a separatist government, endorsed a party determined to make the province an independent country. We spoke in subdued voices as we walked across the parking lot in the shadow of the Jacques Cartier Bridge.

As I drove home through the now almost traffic-free streets I pondered my future. With the political situation so uncertain, maybe it was time to get out of Quebec. I wondered if I was emotionally strong enough to handle such a move. Behaviour modification had made travel possible, had extended my comfort zone to the sixty miles it took to reach my summer cottage on Lake Champlain, but that was it. Moving to another city was something else, something that might be quite literally beyond my reach. I was still taking Valium every night to ward off anxiety and occasionally Miltown as well.

We'd tried Toronto in the sixties and that hadn't worked out. Then there were the kids to consider. If the province separated, what kind of future would there be for anglophones in an independent Quebec? It was a tough call: move now or wait and see? Which choice would be better for them? They were all at critical points in their schooling. It would mean uprooting them. Perhaps I was overreacting. Maybe there was no real need to panic; the PQ government had promised a referendum before it undertook any unilateral move to independence. It would be a challenging time for journalists, as exciting as anything I'd covered since the October Crisis. I decided I would hang in, at least for now.

By the following summer the novelty of a separatist government had worn off. The Parti Québécois had been in power ten months and the sky hadn't fallen. It was clear that for now the PQ was determined to provide good government and the referendum on independence could wait.

August was always a slow month in the news business; when a heat wave struck, politicians were among the first to flee the city, seeking relief at cottages and camps in the Laurentians and the Eastern Townships. With the temperatures in the nineties, companies cut back production, and even criminals seemed reluctant to venture out. Except for the weather itself, we were hard up for news stories. It was a time to fall back on "baggers," those timeless human-interest features deliberately shot in advance for days like this one.

The City at Six newsroom was quiet; the lineup for the six o'clock show was already done. A little after two-thirty I scanned the day's copy of *The New York Times.* I wasn't looking for news, just killing time. A headline on page one caught my eye.

PRIVATE INSTITUTIONS USED IN C.I.A.
EFFORT TO CONTROL BEHAVIOR

The story occupied the top right-hand column of page one of *The Times,* the spot the newspaper traditionally reserves for its top exclusives, so I read on.

> Several prominent medical research institutions and government hospitals in the United States and Canada were involved in a secret, 25-year, $25-million effort by the Central Intelligence Agency to learn how to control the human mind.

The mention of Canada caught my interest, so I continued to read. The story said that in the late forties, when the Cold War with the Soviet Union had become the main preoccupation of the American Central Intelligence Agency, concerns were raised about brainwashing. Joseph Cardinal Mindszenty's trance-like testimony at his treason trial in Budapest was hard to understand.

> The CIA was convinced that his confession had been wrung from him while he was either under the influence of some mind-bending drug or that he was standing before the dock in a post hypnotic trance.

The fears the CIA had about Communist mind-control techniques were intensified during the Korean War, when captured American soldiers appeared in film clips spouting the Marxist line. The Agency poured more money into research, using prison inmates, then mental patients, in an attempt to bring about the personality changes they'd seen in the American POWs. In their zeal, it seemed that some of the doctors involved neglected to gain the consent of the patients participating in the experiments.

Interesting stuff, but so far Canada hadn't been mentioned. I turned to page sixteen, where the article was continued, and what I saw stopped me cold. The entire page was devoted to the story, but boxed at the top in bold print was a list of the names of the doctors involved in the brainwashing research. One of the names leapt out at me.

DR. EWEN CAMERON
Allan Memorial Institute
McGill University, Montreal

The CIA and Dr. Cameron? I couldn't believe it.

> Dr. Ewen Cameron of the Allan Memorial Institute of Psychiatry at McGill University in Montreal conducted several experiments on behavior control including the effects of isolation and sensory deprivation on humans for the CIA.

A sense of betrayal shook me. Had my mother been one of those patients? Had she been a human guinea pig? Deeper into the story an Allan researcher, Leonard Rubenstein, spelled it out.

> "It was directly related to brain-washing," he said about the project in a telephone interview. "They had investigated brainwashing among soldiers who had been in Korea. We in Montreal started using some of these techniques, brainwashing the patients instead of using drugs."

I'd always believed that at the Allan Memorial my mother had the best care available at the time. This belief consoled me whenever I thought about her death. The doctors had done the best they could and suicide was an acceptable way out because her case was hopeless. That certainty dissolved as I read on. Had Cameron been more interested in brainwashing my mother than in curing her? Might she still be alive if we'd chosen another doctor?

I thought back to the years when she'd made those trips to the Allan two or three times a week seeking help. I knew some of the treatments she'd undergone had been experimental, but they had been done with her consent. Or so I had always understood. Was it possible she'd been duped?

And then I remembered. The Deep Sleep Therapy. The interview I'd done with Dr. Cameron. Psychic Driving. Jesus Christ ... had I been duped too?

I put in a call to the Allan and asked for Evelyn Morrison. As I waited on the line I reviewed what I knew about the recent history of the Institute.

Cameron had resigned as director in 1964. The move had been sudden, but no one had thought to question it at the time. He had left to head up a research team in Albany studying mental health in the elderly. It did seem a step down.

Was it possible that the tie-in with the CIA was the real reason for his departure? It would be hard to pin down; Cameron died of a heart attack while mountain climbing in 1967. I might never know the truth about his decision to leave, but I was determined to find out more about my mother's treatment.

There had to be a record of her case, a file buried somewhere in the Allan archives.

MONTREAL, 1977

"HAVE YOU SEEN today's *New York Times*?" I asked, when Evelyn Morrison called back from the Allan.

"No, I haven't. Is there something I can help you with?"

I read her parts of the story, fighting to keep the anger from my voice. When I had finished there was silence. "Well?"

"I don't know what to say. This is the first I've heard of any of this. Can I get back to you?"

"As long as it's within the next hour."

"It may take me a while ... " Her voice trailed off.

"We'll be running the story at six." I looked at my watch. It was 3:10 p.m.

"I'll see what I can do," Evelyn promised.

I put my personal concerns aside and concentrated on getting the story to air. I dialed the film library and asked them to dig up everything they had on the Allan Memorial and Dr. Ewen Cameron. There was no return call from Evelyn, but we managed to resurrect some of the Psychic Driving film for a brief piece on the news that evening.

On my ten-minute walk from the CBC building to the train station all of the concerns about my mother came flooding back again. From the newspaper story it seemed that Cameron's link with the CIA began in 1955, two years after Mom's death. I hoped this was true, but even if it was, my faith in my mother's doctor was shaken. What kind of a man would participate in this sort of thing? I was no longer sure she'd had the best care available.

The story also had me second-guessing myself. Why had I been so accepting of the positive spin Cameron put on the Psychic Driving story? I tried to remember if the subject of brainwashing had come up at the news conference. I wasn't sure. It had been fifteen years since that story had run. I knew times were different back then, journalists were less aggressive, but I think the real reason I let Cameron's explanations go unchallenged was that I'd been afraid to ask him anything tough. His answers might have disturbed the theory I'd carefully constructed around my mother's death.

I caught the seven-thirty CPR commuter train and was fortunate to get a window seat. In the Laprairie Basin of the St. Lawrence River I could see sailboats picking up the last rays of the setting sun, tiny triangles of white light on an expanse of blue-grey water. In another hour it would be dark and they'd be moored for the night, many of their owners safely home in St. Lambert, the town where I grew up, the place where my mother died.

The train dropped a few of the commuters at the first stop in

Westmount. Then, just as we began to move again, I felt a sudden wave of panic sweep over me. I was sure something horrible was about to happen. I had an almost uncontrollable urge to get off the train, to jump. I felt sweat beading my forehead. I was trembling; it seemed my emotions had broken free from my reason and were running wild, out of control.

The trip from Westmount to Montreal West, where I would be getting off, was a mere ten minutes. But I wasn't at all sure I could make it. I looked around desperately for the emergency brake. There it was. A glass box high on the wall a few seats down the aisle. I took comfort from this knowledge. If the panic got any worse, I told myself, I could always shatter the glass and pull the brake. The fact that this might be embarrassing, or even criminal, did not enter my mind. It would be an escape from the fear that was steadily tightening its grip, making it impossible to breathe, hard to swallow.

My eyes darted to other passengers; they were oblivious to my discomfort. My hands gripped a rolled-up copy of *The Montrealer* magazine. I leaned forward and rocked ever so slightly. I wanted to scream, but didn't dare. That I might scream, lose control, was more frightening to me than the prospect of pulling the emergency brake. The door at the far end of the carriage opened and the conductor pushed through.

"Montreal West, Montréal Ouest."

I could feel the train beginning to slow down. This was my stop. I got up and hurried down the aisle to the space between the cars, where the steps had already been lowered to allow passengers to get off. It was fortunate that another conductor was in the stairwell, blocking the way. Otherwise, I felt sure, I would have been tempted to leap from the train while it was still moving.

When we finally came to a halt, I pushed past him and along the station platform to a wooden bench. I sat down, hugged my arms tightly across my chest, and leaned over at the waist, my head almost touching my knees, my eyes fixed on the ground. The other disembarking commuters were a parade of feet passing before me. Then I heard the train begin to leave. I remained where I was, until slowly, very slowly, the waves of panic subsided and I was able to breathe again, although not the deep satisfying intake of air that I so desperately craved. I got to my feet slowly, shakily, and started the short walk home. I was weak, as if I had just recovered from some debilitating illness. Although I hadn't had a drink in years, I felt hungover and exhausted.

I knew the day's revelations had brought on the panic attack, but I wasn't sure exactly why. Lots of theories, but nothing that felt quite right. I also knew I was going to follow up the story. I had no choice; it was simply something I was going to do, even if the emotional price was high. I just hoped I could get it right this time. My mother deserved that.

Dr. Bikadoroff listened patiently to my account, his hands steepled beneath his chin. The faint hum of the air conditioner masked the sound of traffic from the street. It had been a year since my last visit. When the behaviour modification treatment enabled me to travel the sixty miles to our cottage, I cut back on my appointments. I had been keeping things under control with a combination of relaxation exercises and tranquilizers.

"What do you think?" I'd finished my story.

"When did you say you had the first attack?"

"A week ago. The evening the story broke."

"And since then?"

"I had another attack the next night. Nothing since then, but I've been taking tranquilizers earlier, during the afternoon, trying to stop things before they start."

It was the first time I'd done that. Until then I'd always used medication in the evening. Bikadoroff picked up a notebook from the pile of papers on his desk. "I'll prescribe something else for now, but I don't think the answer is more medication."

"What then?"

"It may be time to try psychoanalysis." The doctor wrote on a prescription, handed it to me. "Qualude," he said, and leafed through the pages of the notebook. He found what he was looking for, wrote something on a slip of paper, and handed it across the table.

"What's this?"

"The name and number of an analyst."

"You don't do it?"

"No, it's a specialty. Not my area of expertise, I'm afraid."

"What about getting my mother's records from the Allan?"

Bikadoroff closed the notebook and stood up. "I'd leave that to the analyst. They won't release them to you, but they might to him."

"This is it, then?" I asked, glancing around, wondering if it would be my last visit to this office.

"Could be." His tone was neutral.

I reached across the table and we shook hands.

"Good luck," he said.

"Do you think I'll need it?"

"A little luck never hurts." He smiled.

THE CAMERON-CIA SCANDAL "had legs," journalism jargon for any story that runs longer than a day or two. Details of the doctor's work during the period in question began to emerge. Val Orlikow, the wife of a Winnipeg member of parliament, was the most prominent patient treated by Cameron during the late fifties and early sixties. She was the first to speak out publicly, appearing on *Ninety Minutes Live*, the CBC's nightly current affairs TV program.

"Were you ever asked to sign a consent form?" The question came from Peter Gzowski, the show's host.

"Never," Val Orlikow stated emphatically. She was a plump woman in her late fifties, and except for a slight nervousness, normal for live television, she spoke clearly and lucidly.

Gzowski directed his next question to David Orlikow, who was sitting beside his wife on the set. "And you had no idea that the treatment she was receiving was experimental?"

"No." Orlikow shook his head. "We kept getting assurances from Cameron, from the staff, that in time Val would get better."

"When did you learn they were using LSD?"

"Not until recently, until we had a chance to review the records," Orlikow said.

"I knew they were giving me something strange," Mrs. Orlikow added. "I began to hallucinate. In all the time I was depressed I'd never had hallucinations. I begged them to stop the injections, but they insisted. Dr. Cameron told me I had to expect some discomfort if I was to get better, but I had a hard time believing it."

"It makes me sick," Orlikow said, "to think that they were using Canadians as guinea pigs."

"Do you think the Canadian government knew anything about it?" Gzowski asked.

"As far as I know they didn't, but if I find out they did ... "

We carried clips from the Gzowski interview on our local news the following day. In Ottawa a spokesman for the justice department promised an inquiry. The hospital was refusing all requests for interviews. In Washington the CIA wasn't answering the phone calls from our correspondent there.

In time more and more former patients came forward with stories. We learned that many had been put to sleep for weeks, even months at a time.

They were often reduced to incontinent, babbling zombies. It was felt that their flawed personalities had to be erased, like so many words on a blackboard, so that more positive characteristics could be put in their place. Electroshock, a dangerous last resort at the time, was used indiscriminately. Instead of a series of six to twelve treatments spaced over a period of weeks, Cameron's patients were often subjected to a barrage, a dozen or more, in a single day. The shocks provoked seizures and left patients weak and disoriented, with extensive memory loss.

With each new development I was more and more upset. The foundations of acceptance I'd built around my mother's death were being torn apart. In the past I'd often felt her timing was lousy, that if she'd just held on a little longer the tranquilizers that revolutionized the treatment of mental illness in the late fifties would have been available to her. But the more I heard about Cameron's methods, the more I was thankful she'd died when she did. Had she lived, she would have become just one more guinea pig.

MONTREAL, 1979

"DID YOU KNOW you're a dead ringer for Adolph Krupp?"

Silence filled the somewhat shabby office on the sixth floor of the Medical Arts building on the corner of Sherbrooke and Guy Streets.

"He's the German industrialist who built tanks and artillery for Hitler during the war."

I was lying on a couch and behind me, out of my line of sight, sat Dr. Brian Hunt, listening. Or so I hoped. When he didn't respond I continued.

"After the war Arnold Newman photographed Krupp for *Fortune* magazine. Posed him with the roaring fires of his steel mills in the background. Strange lighting. Made him look like the devil. It was years before the Germans would let Newman back into the country."

Silence.

"Krupp looks a lot like you."

It was true. Dr. Hunt could have passed as Krupp's double: tall, in his mid-fifties, his grey hair combed straight back off a high forehead. He was clean-shaven and his solid jaw balanced a prominent nose. His handshake had been firm that first day and his voice was soft, carrying an English accent.

"How can I help you?" He'd looked at me questioningly from across the desk, his eyes neither green nor blue, but somewhere in between.

I gave him a summary of my problems and he listened patiently, without comment, occasionally making notes. I itemized the drugs I was taking now—the Valium and Qualude prescribed by Dr. Bikadoroff, and a new medication, Halcion, suggested by my GP.

"You take these every day?" If he seemed surprised, he hid it well.

"Every night."

He wrote this down.

"I'd like to get off them."

"Of course."

"But not right away."

"No."

Relief. I'd been terrified he might ask me to quit.

"How long does psychoanalysis usually take? I mean how long will I have to continue seeing you?"

He shook his head. "There's no telling."

I pressed for an answer. "On an average?"

"That depends on a number of things." He clicked the gold ballpoint pen he'd been using. "I never like to guess, but based on what you've told me it could be a couple of years."

I hadn't been surprised. I'd done some research on psychoanalysis; it wasn't going to be a quick fix. I made a number of phone calls after that first appointment. I learned that Dr. Hunt had done his graduate work in London and had come to Canada in the sixties, choosing to practise in Montreal because of McGill University's growing reputation for medical innovation. A friend from university had become a neorologist, so I asked him for an insider's opinion. "He's the best," he said simply.

So here I was, six months later, telling this respected doctor he looked like a Nazi industrialist. It's hard to insult someone when you are lying flat on your back.

"The couch is a tool, not a rule," Dr. Hunt had said during that first appointment. Maybe, I thought, but I was pretty sure he liked his patients lying down. The few face-to-face sessions I'd tried since that first interview had been awkward, the conversation stilted and difficult. Most of my words were now spoken from the couch.

So Dr. Hunt wasn't going to take the bait about his resemblance to Adolph Krupp. I decided to let it go. Should I tell him I'd found his address, had driven by his home in Westmount? I was determined to find out all I could about this new silent partner of mine. He volunteered very little information about himself. I knew he played tennis because I'd occasionally spotted a racket and an equipment bag behind his desk.

"What are you thinking?" he asked.

His voice had surprised me. I was usually the first to break the silence. "I was thinking about tennis." I said, "I know you play. I've seen your racquet, your stuff ... "

That was the way it was done, I'd learned. I was supposed to give him a play-by-play account of my thoughts, uncensored.

"I bet I could beat you, beat the living shit out of you as a matter of fact." I paused.

There was no reaction.

"And I was thinking about the house you have in Westmount. You must make a lot of money."

These thoughts were blurted out and I felt uncomfortable. I wasn't sure why I'd mentioned money; my medical insurance was paying most of the bill. I shifted my position on the couch and changed the subject.

"I feel particularly lousy today," I said into the silence. "And I don't know why. Maybe it's because winter seems to have gone on forever this year." I snuck a glance at my watch. "It's March twenty-third for Christ's sake ... it's supposed to be spring. We're still getting snow."

There was no response.

"I don't know why I'm so down."

"Does the date have any significance?"

So he wasn't asleep.

"The twenty-third of March? No, I don't think so. "

I watched as a spider, high up in one corner of the office, made its way carefully across a web. Then, suddenly, it came to me.

"Oh my god ... March twenty-third was my mother's birthday." I calculated the years in my head "She'd have been sixty-five today if she'd lived."

Sadness swept over me as I spoke the words and I began to cry, just tears at first, then sobs in great gasps. Dr. Hunt was forgotten for the moment.

It was a while before I regained my composure. This was the first time I'd had to use the Kleenex that was always there on a table beside the couch. "I think I'm beginning to understand this process," I said, wiping away the tears.

"Do your feelings surprise you?"

"No, I guess not." I shook my head. "I'm a little surprised I didn't figure it out sooner. I mean my own mother's birthday ... it's pretty obvious. It makes me wonder how many of my attacks are triggered by memories I haven't acknowledged."

"Well, that's something we can consider on Friday."

This was his way of ending the session. I sat up and he moved to his desk, where he picked up a manila folder.

"I have your mother's records from the Allan."

"Oh." Fear flooded in.

I'd asked Evelyn Morrison to see if she could get me a copy of Mom's files.

"As much as I'd like to, I can't do it. The Institute won't allow it."

"Damn."

"But I can release them to your doctor."

"Bless you." I'd given her Hunt's name and address.

"Have you had a chance to look them over?"

Dr. Hunt nodded.

"What do you think?"

"Hard to say." He handed me the folder. "It was a long time ago. A lot has changed since then." He opened the door to the waiting room. "Read through it, let me know what you think."

MONTREAL, 1980

I WAITED UNTIL I was back home before opening the file. I sat down in a rocking chair by the dining room window, my hands shaking. The first document was a letter from Ewen Cameron to our GP, written in the summer of 1948.

> Dear Dr.
>
> I am writing to you regarding your patient Mrs. Gertrude Little, who was admitted to the Allan Memorial Institute on June 24th, 1948, and who was discharged on June 27, 1948. On admission the patient's primary difficulties consisted of anxiety which has been present for almost 20 years, but which has become progressively more severe in the last twelve years, and still more so in the last four years. The reasons for its intensification was the patient's marriage 14 years ago against the advice of her parents, the subsequent loss of his job by her husband during the Depression, and his lack of initiative in seeking another occupation. The patient was pregnant at the time, and felt exceedingly insecure, and there was intensification of her guilt feelings over having gone against the advice of her parents, and more especially since she had been having sexual relations with her husband prior to marriage. When the family's economic situation became better adjusted, the patient found herself still lacking confidence in her husband, and able to respond to him sexually only to a limited degree.

One sentence in that first paragraph set off an explosive charge in my mind and the echo reverberated throughout my body.

> On admission the patient's primary difficulties consisted of anxiety which has been present for almost 20 years, but which has become progressively more severe in the last twelve years, and still more so in the last four years.

My mother had told Cameron in 1948, when I was twelve, that she'd had the problem for twenty years. This meant she suffered from anxiety long before my birth. Until now I'd been sure that all Mom's troubles began when I was born. I'd believed it since that summer evening long ago when I overheard my aunts discussing her condition. The whispered words, "never the same again," had been my guilty verdict. The difficult pregnancy, the prolonged labour, and the forceps used to extract me from her womb: somehow all these had been my fault. I was responsible for her nervous breakdown. If it wasn't for me my mother might have had her own network radio program like Dinah Shore, might have even become a movie star like Judy Garland.

Now, all of a sudden, I knew this wasn't true. It wasn't my fault. It had never been my fault. She'd been sick long before I was born. A few simple words typed on a routine medical report more than twenty-five years ago had overturned the guilty verdict and granted me a pardon. The sense of responsibility, the one I'd carried around so long I'd been unaware of its existence, released its grip. My body felt as light as a child's helium balloon and as likely to disappear into the sky if accidentally released. I got up from the chair and paced the room with excitement. I don't know why, but I turned on the radio. Fiddle music filled the room and I did a silly little improvised jig, tears running down my cheeks. I caught sight of myself in the mirror and laughed. I was glad I was alone. I could be as foolish as I liked. I was free.

When the music finally ended I collapsed back into the chair, exhausted. Part of me wanted to close my eyes and just savour the moment. But there was still the question of Cameron's competence to consider. Had he been experimenting on my mother without her consent? Something drew me back to that first paragraph of the letter.

> When the family's economic situation became better adjusted, the patient found herself still lacking confidence in her husband, and was able to respond to him sexually only to a limited degree.

Why hadn't things improved after Dad found work? I could understand her fears when he was laid off. Times were tough for everyone during the Depression. But Dad had landed a job with the CBC in 1937. It was a responsible, secure position and he brought home decent money. What else had been troubling my mother? Perhaps the answer lay in the rest of the letter.

> She sought advice at the Institute about four years ago, at which time depression as well as anxiety was present. She was put on adrenaline desensitization. Under this she showed slow gradual improvement and it was eventually possible to re-

> establish her in a part-time occupation as a nursery school teacher, carrying on her household duties at the same time. Further relapses have been dealt with by means of somnolent insulin to which the patient has shown a good response.
>
> In the winter of 1947/48, she decided to have herself sterilized since neither she nor her husband wanted more children, and the possibility of pregnancy had made her exceedingly anxious. This step was agreed upon, and she entered the Woman's Pavilion of the Royal Victoria Hospital on May 31st, 1948. After successful surgery she showed acute anxiety, so was transferred to the Institute.

I'd sought these records originally because I was afraid Dr. Cameron might have been experimenting on my mother without her consent. But so far there was nothing to indicate he'd stepped over any ethical line.

> Following admission, the patient was put on Veronal grains 2 1/2 T.I.D. and nightly sedation. To this she showed good response. At the time of discharge, she was much less anxious, but remained at home on Veronal grains 2 1/2 T.I.D. nightly sedation, and with the recommendation that she should return to the Institute for a weekly somnolent insulin treatment, starting a week later.
>
> Our final diagnosis was that of chronic anxiety of long duration with the intermittent depressive episodes.
>
> Yours sincerely,
> D. Ewen Cameron, M.D.

Outside, a squirrel ran along the white picket fence that enclosed our backyard. A moment later another squirrel followed, and soon they were both scrambling up a maple tree, chattering as they climbed the branches. I reread the letter. It had been written in 1948, before the Korean War, long before Cameron's drift into the dark world of CIA-funded experiments had begun.

MONTREAL, 1980

THE NEXT DOCUMENT in the folder was a Rorschach test, taken a year before her death. Maybe it contained the answers.

Allan Memorial Institute of Psychiatry,
Department of Psychology

Name: LITTLE, Mrs. Trudy,
Case No: 52 - 11004
Address: 361 Merton Ave, St. Lambert, Quebec.
Admitted: July 2nd 1952.
Age: 41
Birthdate: March 23, 1911
Education: Teaching Certificate, University of Toronto.
Test administered: Rorschach
Date of Acquisition: July 3rd, 1952.
Date of Examination: July 11th, 1952.
Referred by: Ewen Cameron
Exam by:

EXAMINATION ANALYSIS: The Rorschach protocol was a productive, fairly rich record of 43 responses produced quickly, easily and with some originality. The personality structure presented here is complex.

The patient is a sensitive, intelligent woman who tries too hard to attain lofty goals to fulfill her extremely high social prestige needs. She employs obsessive compulsive techniques to insure her success. Failure makes her extremely guilt ridden and she withdraws in a depressed manner to save face. She tries to analyze herself and the motivations of others. She has some insight but in the main her critical judgment is clouded by her extremely powerful emotional drives. It is to be noted that at the present time she is more depressed than superficially seems to be the case.

There are components of marked anxiety, obsessive compulsiveness, hysterical and depressive trends in this aggressive, ambitious individual. There are however, pre-psychotic features. In fact there is some question whether this case would not more suitably be called a "pseudo-neurotic schizophrenia". She has a vivid fantasy life, to the extent that she often gets carried away from reality. There are periods when she becomes quite paranoid, projecting her own mounting hostility. She is a domineering individual who becomes stubborn, negativistic, and belligerent when she is thwarted, and develops marked anxiety and panic attacks.

SUMMARY:

Complex personality structure. Components of strong anxiety, hysteria, obsessive compulsiveness and underlying psychotic features. An extremely vivid fantasy life often carries her way from reality so that she thinks in an original, somewhat bizarre fashion. Periods of paranoid feelings surely exist. She is a bright, ambitious woman whose goals are set very high. Failure results in strong feelings of guilt and depression.

July 11, 1952.

"Pre-psychotic, pseudo-neurotic schizophrenia?" Was it possible my mother had been a psychotic? Or schizophrenic? I had never seen any hint of this, at least not as I understood it. She didn't hear voices; her behaviour was never such that I questioned her judgment. She may have been a little paranoid, but that didn't make her psychotic. If she had a vivid fantasy life, I'd never seen it take her away from reality. The summary of the report, as disturbing as it was to read, had held no surprises. But I felt my perception of the facts shift, as if the ground had moved ever so slightly beneath my feet.

MONTREAL, 1981

I DIALED THE NUMBER for the Allan Memorial and asked for Evelyn Morrison. It was a Monday ritual. As evidence mounted against Ewen Cameron there was increasing pressure on the hospital for some sort of explanation. The longer the Institute remained silent, the more speculation grew that it was hiding something.

"Evelyn Morrison here." Her voice was tentative, wary.

"Good morning, it's Andy." Our weekly conversations had broken down the need for formality.

"Oh, good morning." Her voice relaxed a little.

"Any luck?" I knew Evelyn was pushing the people at the Allan to hold a news conference or at the very least issue some sort of statement.

"Not yet," she sighed. "But there is another meeting this morning to consider our position."

It had been a public relations disaster for the Allan and Evelyn was doing her best to limit the damage.

"You'll let me know if anything develops?"

"You'll be the first," she laughed. I'd been a bit of a pest, but to her credit Evelyn had never lost patience with me. I think she understood that I had more than simply a journalistic interest in the story.

Shortly before lunch she called back. "Good news. The director is going to meet the press at two this afternoon."

"All right!" Finally someone was going to talk.

"Two o'clock in the main boardroom."

"I'll be there." I hung up the phone and paged a cameraman.

More than a dozen reporters and photographers crowded the room—a much better turnout than there'd been for Cameron's explanation of Deep Sleep Therapy fifteen years ago. Evelyn handed me the press release and smiled when I gave her a silent thumbs-up.

The room fell silent as the man who succeeded Cameron as director of the Institute entered the room. Tall and rangy, he was in his sixties, with a crop of unruly grey hair and the rugged features you might expect to find on an early Viking explorer. He folded himself into the chair at the head of the boardroom table and cleared his throat.

"Good afternoon," he said, and took a pair of half-moon reading glasses from his pocket. "Thank you all for coming." Cameras rolled and flashbulbs popped. "I trust you all have copies of my statement?" He held up a single sheet of paper questioningly. When no one responded he looked down and began to read.

"In light of the recent publicity about the work of the late Dr. Ewen Cameron, we at the Allan Memorial Institute have initiated an exhaustive search of our records and have found no evidence to support the claim that the American Central Intelligence Agency directly funded any of our research."

The doctor took a sip of water from the glass before him.

"We have also reviewed Dr. Cameron's files and cannot find any justification for the charges that patients under his care were subjected to experiments without their expressed consent, or the consent of next of kin."

He paused to survey the room, then adjusted his glasses and continued.

"Any criticism leveled at Dr. Cameron or the Allan must be filtered through an historical perspective. When Dr. Cameron came here in 1943 the treatment possibilities for those suffering from mental illness were limited, to say the least. In the light of what we now know it is easy to be critical of some of the procedures used, but you must remember that we were still working in the dark, the drugs that revolutionized psychiatry weren't refined until the sixties. It is our belief that Dr. Cameron was doing the best he could, given the tools he had to work with at the time. We stand behind him and regret that the recent publicity has cast a shadow on his remarkable achievements and the reputation of the Allan Memorial."

The new director removed his glasses, tucked them back in the breast pocket of his blue pinstriped suit, and rose from his position at the head of the table. A chorus of overlapping questions came from the reporters. He raised a hand like a traffic cop and the room fell silent.

"I'm afraid that's all I have to say. Because there is the possibility this matter may come before the courts I don't want to say anything that might prejudice the case. I hope you'll understand." He gathered his papers and left the room.

"Stonewalling," muttered CJAD's Sydney Margolese as he turned off his tape recorder. The room swelled with the sound of other reporters complaining. They'd been denied the chance to ask questions and weren't at all happy. Evelyn Morrison, who had been left to deal with them, could do little more than echo the party line that as long as there was possibility of a legal challenge her hands were tied.

I waited until the room had cleared and then spoke to her privately. "Well, at least you persuaded him to break the silence."

She smiled. "It wasn't easy, believe me."

"Off the record," I asked, "what is your take on things?"

She looked at me for a moment and I knew she was trying to decide if I could be trusted. "Frankly," she said, "I'm not sure. We've been over the records. There doesn't seem to be anything there that smacks of CIA involvement."

"What about Val Orlikow?"

"Hard to say." She paused. "Off the record?"

I nodded. "Off the record."

"Well, she was Cameron's patient and was part of the Deep Sleep program, but her case isn't that remarkable. There were dozens of others undergoing the same treatment. Her doctor now thinks her problem was acute and extended postpartum depression. She simply didn't respond positively to the care Cameron provided."

I decided to leave it there. As co-operative as Evelyn Morrison had been, she didn't have the answers I needed. My mother's case had been before her time.

"You'll let me know if anything more develops?"

"Of course."

MONTREAL, 1981

AT MY SESSION the next morning I told Dr. Hunt about the Allan's position. Was it possible my mother's illness was just postpartum depression? Lying on the couch, I waited for his answer. I could hear the rustle as he sorted through papers.

"In your mother's records from the Allan there is mention of a showdown she had with her father."

"Yes."

"Did you know about this? Did your mother ever mention it?"

"Sure. She told me Dr. Cameron wanted her to confront JB, have it out with him. It was no secret how much she hated her father. The confrontation was during one of our summer vacations. I was fifteen. It was the main reason we went to see our relatives that year; those trips were difficult for my mother."

"What do you remember about that day?"

"Dad drove Mom to Essex. My aunt had made up some excuse to make sure my grandmother was out of the house. I can't remember what it was. After my folks left, my cousin and I went swimming at a community pool in Detroit. It was well after lunch when Mom and Dad returned."

Dr. Hunt was silent.

"She seemed okay when she got back. She went into a bedroom with my aunt and they talked for a long time. After a while Alice came back and told us Mom was taking a nap.

"The next morning my mother told me she'd followed her doctor's suggestions and told JB exactly what she thought of him, even lost her temper and swore at him. She wasn't sure if it had done any good; it seemed the hate was still there, but at least she wasn't afraid of him any more."

Dr. Hunt remained silent. High on the ceiling the solitary spider was hard at work on another web. I guessed the cleaning staff must have swept away the earlier creation.

I thought back to the events of another visit to Essex, three years later. That was when I talked over the poison-pen letter with Aunt Alice and learned the details of Mom's breakdown. Cousin Joan had driven me to Leamington, but we'd stopped in Essex and had a short visit with my Grandma Champion.

"It was on that trip that I learned JB had been committed."

"Committed?"

"Yes, he'd become more and more difficult. I'm not sure what the problems were. He was apparently more than my grandmother could handle. My aunts got together and signed the papers."

"Do you remember when that happened?"

"I'm not sure. My cousin said it was shortly after Mom's death. I know the hospital was in St. Thomas. He was never released. He died there less than a year later."

"How did you feel about your grandfather?"

The question surprised me. I tried to recall the impressions I'd had. "I didn't see a lot of him, you know. I knew he'd been against my parents' marriage and I guess I just inherited their dislike for him." I tried to visualize JB. "I always felt he was kind of gloomy."

"Gloomy?"

"Yes, he was tall and I have this image of him looming in a doorway watching me. I know he wore dentures ... I can remember the smell on his breath. And I know he had constipation, he used to complain about it during meals. That would really piss off my grandmother."

"What else?"

"The few times I was in their house it seemed dark and gloomy. Almost haunted."

After another silence Hunt spoke. "The Allan records also indicate your mother had a miscarriage."

"I guess that's when the subject of adoption came up. They asked me if I would like a brother or sister."

"Nothing came of it?"

"No. When they learned about Mom's mental problems they turned us down."

"Were you disappointed?"

"It's funny, but I can't remember. I know I was excited when they brought up the possibility. Excited and a little frightened, I guess. I overheard them talking after they'd been turned down. Mom was angry, but I think I was probably relieved. It would have meant a big change for me."

"The records show she had an operation later to prevent pregnancy. Did she discuss that?"

"I was told she was going in to have a small tumour removed, but I didn't know that she'd had her tubes tied until I read the notes from the Allan. At the time she tried to assure me it wasn't a big deal. They did the operation while I was away at Scout camp and it wasn't until much later that Dad told me she'd had a breakdown following the surgery."

"What did he say?"

"Just that the operation had been successful, but there were complications during her recovery. It wasn't until the surgeon called in Dr. Cameron that they got things under control. I guess it was a repeat of what happened after I was born."

"Do you see any similarity in the two situations?"

I thought about it. "She was in hospital both times," I said, but I was having trouble finding any other connections. "I suppose she was in a lot of pain."

Then something surfaced.

"The first time she was having a baby, the second time she was making sure she wouldn't have another. Both situations involved babies ... having them or not having them."

Hunt lit a cigarette.

"Does it have something to do with sex?"

No answer.

"The Allan papers mention her guilt about having sex before marriage. Knowing her parents disapproved."

In the silence that followed a series of images flashed through my mind like a high-speed slide show.

Her fit of anger on a day she learned JB had taken me squirrel hunting without her permission. It was one of the few times I'd seen her actually lose her temper.

Aunt Alice's words of caution to her daughter as a child: "Make sure you're never alone with him."

The hulking silhouette of my grandfather coming down the hall. I'd wanted to run, but something prevented it. Was it a dream or had it happened? I wasn't sure.

Mom's naked, bleeding body lying on the floor in our house in St. Lambert.

"Is it possible my mother was sexually abused by her father?" I didn't know where the words came from, but they were mine.

Silence. For once I didn't mind. I was trying to sort things out.

"If that was the case, wouldn't it have come out during her treatment at the Allan?"

More silence.

"Wouldn't that be one of the first questions they'd ask?"

Dr. Hunt cleared his throat. "I don't think it was the sort of question they asked at the Allan, at least not in Dr. Cameron's day."

The idea fit so neatly into what I knew of my mother's life, I couldn't understand why I hadn't seen it before. If it was true, it explained so much. Was this the real reason behind my mother's hatred for her father?

"Why didn't she tell Cameron?" I asked. "Over the years she confided so many things to him, why did she draw the line at incest?"

Dr. Hunt thought a moment, then spoke. "Have you heard of the repressed memory syndrome?"

"Yes, I've heard the term, but I'm not sure what it means."

"What it means," Hunt said, "is that your mother may have blocked the memory from her mind."

MONTREAL, 1981

AFTER THE SESSION with Dr. Hunt I called my Aunt Alice. We'd kept in touch with Christmas cards and the occasional letter. She'd moved to Florida a few years after her husband died. But I hadn't actually talked to her since my second year in college, after Mom died.

"Aunt Alice?"

"This is Andy."

"Andy Little?"

"Yep, your nephew."

"Oh, my goodness." There was a pause. "It's been so long. How are you? I hope you're not calling with bad news."

"No, no," I assured her.

We chatted for a few minutes, bringing each other up to date on our respective families. I learned that my cousin Joan now lived in Cleveland, and with her three children raised had recently gone back to work. I filled my aunt in on the details about my three children, but decided not to tell her about psychoanalysis.

"The reason I'm calling is I'm thinking of writing a family history and I need your help." It was as good an excuse as any.

"Sure, I'd be glad to do what I can. I should warn you though, my memory isn't what it used to be." She laughed.

"What can you tell me about JB?"

Alice paused. "Hmm," she said. "Well, I know he was born in Prince Edward Island. His folks were farmers. There were four children in the family, three boys and a sister. I don't know what became of his sister but one of his brothers was a doctor and I think the other became a Baptist minister."

"Baptist?"

"That's odd, isn't it? With JB a Methodist."

"Must be a story there," I said.

"Oh, I'm sure there is," Alice said laughing again, "but I haven't a clue what it is."

That wasn't the story that interested me. But I wanted to ease into the real reason for the call, the details of JB's commitment. So I asked my aunt about her memories of my grandfather, what it had been like growing up with a difficult father. I knew my aunt shared my mother's dislike for JB.

"It wasn't easy," she said, "but I think your mom got the worst of it."

"How?"

"Well, she was the youngest. There was another child born after Trudy, a little boy, but he died within a few days of his birth. I don't think JB ever got over that."

"Do you remember when this happened?" This was news to me.

"I think it was a year or two after Trudy was born. I was about seven."

"It must have been hard on Blanche, too."

"Yes, it was. I'm only guessing now, but I think that's when she decided she didn't want any more children. I know it was then that she moved into a separate bedroom. I remember, because I had to double up with your Aunt Edith."

"Not with Mom?"

"No, she was still a baby, she was in the nursery."

Alice told me about the family's move from the Maritimes to Ontario and how JB was particularly hard on Uncle Wendell as a boy because he wasn't much of a student. "He got regular beatings," she said, "whenever his grades were poor."

"Did the other kids get beatings too?"

"Oh, sure. We all took our share of lickings whenever we messed up, but Wendell got the worst of it. JB believed that if you spared the rod, you spoiled the child. Funny, though, I don't remember him going after Trudy."

Interesting, I thought. No beatings. Something more sinister?

"But you said Mom got the worst of it?"

Alice paused. I wished I could read her mind. "Well, Dad and Blanche were both depressed after they lost the baby. For a while your Aunt Edith and I had to look after your Mom. Eventually Blanche came around, but not JB. Things were never the same between them, between JB and Blanche. So Trudy grew up in a pretty tense situation. JB always seemed angry."

"Joan told me JB was eventually committed."

"Oh, that was awful. It was years later, mind you. About a week after your Mom died. JB had become increasingly difficult. He was more and more paranoid, convinced Blanche wanted him out of the way. We got a call from her in the middle of the night. A noise had wakened her and when she turned on a light JB was standing at the foot of her bed with a hammer in his hand swearing at her. He was blaming her for Trudy's death. Claimed it was all her fault and that she was now trying to poison him. Well, somehow she managed to get by him and ran to a neighbour's house next door. She called me and I told her to stay put and I phoned your Aunt Doris, who lived near-by. She got in touch with the police and they took JB into custody.

"The next day we drove over and Doris and I conferred with JB's doctor. It was pretty clear JB was a threat to Mother, so we had very little choice. She agreed, we signed the papers, and he was sent off to the mental hospital in St. Thomas. He refused to see anyone from the family, claiming we were all ganging up on him."

I could hardly believe my ears. This was such damning information.

"Why didn't you tell me all this the summer after Dad died, when I visited you in Detroit after I got that poison-pen letter?"

"Oh, Andy, you'd been through so much, I didn't want to burden you with more bad news. What difference could it have made? JB had a history of mental illness. He had some sort of breakdown in 1934, had to give up preaching. He eventually got back to it, but it was years later."

1934. The year my parents married. The pieces of the puzzle were falling into place. I needed time to think things over.

"When did JB die?"

"It was 1954. Suffered a stroke. I can check for you. I have the exact date written down somewhere."

"I'd appreciate that. Why don't you put down whatever else you can remember and send it along to me."

"Sure," Alice said. "It's good to hear your voice again. I hope I've been some help."

"You have, and thanks." More than you know.

I broke the news to Dr. Hunt at our next appointment. "It may not be the smoking gun," I said, "but the circumstantial evidence is pretty compelling. My grandmother moves out of their bedroom after they lose their last child. She cuts off sex with JB and he turns to my mother for relief. It begins when she is very young and that would support the repressed memory theory. Mom left home as soon as she could, went off to Toronto to study music when she was just sixteen. JB had some sort of breakdown in 1934, the year of my parents' marriage. Maybe he saw Willis not as a son-in-law, but as a rival for his daughter's affection. Then, ten days after my mother kills herself, he blames his wife. She has him committed. Paranoid, but some reasons for feeling the way he did."

"What about your grandmother, Blanche?"

"I don't know much about her. I think the family name is Colpitts. They're from a little town outside Moncton. Her father was a blacksmith."

"It might be worth checking out her background."

"Why?"

"Well, in cases like these the wife usually knows, at least on some level, that there is something going on."

"Hard to believe Blanche would allow that to happen."

"It's almost parallel to the repressed memory of the child. There's usually a good deal of denial involved. If your grandmother cut off sexual relations with her husband she might also be feeling guilty about that, about denying him his pleasure."

"If that was the case, wouldn't she be even more suspicious?"

"You'd think so, but it doesn't always work out that way. Wives often feel they are to blame for the abuse, particularly if they aren't sexually responsive. So they'll go to great lengths to avoid facing the truth. From what you've told me your grandfather wasn't the model of fidelity. If your grandmother could turn a blind eye to that sort of behaviour, it wouldn't surprise me if she applied the same approach to anything involving JB and your mother."

"Well, I'll see what I can find out about Blanche. Is that my homework this week, teacher?"

Dr. Hunt smiled. "I guess that's one way to look at it."

MONTREAL, 1981

WHERE TO START? Aunt Alice said she didn't know much about the Colpitts family. But who did? I wondered about Aunt Doris, the eldest of the Champion children—perhaps she could fill in some of the blanks. She lived in Essex, where my grandmother spent her last years, and had been involved at the time they committed JB. My mother never liked Doris, so I hadn't seen much of her while I was growing up.

According to Mom, Doris had "run off" when she was seventeen and pregnant, married some "ne'er-do-well" and had two sons. The marriage didn't last and Doris returned home, over JB's protest, bringing one son, my cousin Don, with her. I didn't know what had happened to the other son, didn't even know his name, although I realized that he, too, would be a cousin. A few years later Doris married again, this time to a well-to-do local merchant in Essex, Jack Elsley. They had no children of their own, but Jack was, by all accounts, a good stepfather to my cousin Don.

The last time I'd seen Aunt Doris was at my mother's funeral. The summer after Dad died, when Cousin Joan and I stopped in Essex to see our grandmother, we didn't visit Doris, even though she lived in the same town. I wasn't sure why. I called Essex information to see if there was a listing for her, and sure enough, there was a D. Elsley on Centre Street. My hands were sweating as I dialed. With luck I'd be talking to an aunt I hardly knew, an aunt my mother hadn't liked.

A woman answered.

"I'm calling Doris Elsley."

"This is Mrs. Elsely." The voice was that of an older woman. My aunt would be in her eighties.

"Aunt Doris, this is your nephew, Andrew Little."

There was a pause. "Who?"

"Trudy's son, Andy."

"Gertrude's son?" It was Doris all right. Mom hated her given name and I'm sure Doris knew that. So the dislike had probably been mutual.

"Yes, that's right."

"My, my ... where are you?" Her question was tentative. "Are you here in Essex?"

"No, I'm calling from Montreal."

"Goodness me." Relief. "It's been such a long time since we've heard from you."

"I know. I'm afraid I've fallen out of touch with most of the family."

"Well, how are you?"

"I'm fine, Aunt Doris." I wanted to ease into the reason for my call. "How are things with you?"

"Well, I'm okay I guess, all things considered."

I wasn't sure what she meant and didn't respond.

"I'm alone now. Jack passed on two years ago."

"I'm sorry, I didn't know." I remembered Aunt Doris visited us briefly in Ottawa during the war. My cousin Don was in the Air Force and trained near Ottawa.

"It must have been difficult for you."

"I manage the best I can. Life does go on."

"The reason I called," I said, choosing my words carefully, "I'm doing a bit of genealogy, putting together a family tree. I have quite a bit of information about the Champion side of the family, but not much about Grandma's."

"The Colpitts."

"Yes."

"Well, let me see." She paused. "Our grandfather, Henry, was a farmer and a blacksmith. Grandma Nancy's maiden name was O'Neill. They lived in a little town called Harrisville, outside Moncton. It's actually part of Moncton now. Blanche was an only child. She was adopted, you know. They called her Blanche because it snowed the day before she arrived."

"Oh?" This was news. "Adopted?"

"Yes, I'm not sure why they couldn't have children of their own. My mother never explained that."

"I didn't know she was adopted. Mom never mentioned it."

"Blanche never talked much about her family. I think maybe she was a little embarrassed that she'd been adopted. It was only later, when she was in her nineties, that she told me."

"What else do you know about the family?"

"Grandpa Colpitts died before I was born, but Grandma eventually remarried. A man named Charlie Woodling."

"Did they have children?"

"No, that was much later. Charlie had two children by a previous marriage.

"So Blanche had step-brothers and sisters?"

"Well, I guess you could say that, but by that time she'd already married JB."

"I see." Interesting, I thought. "Do you know anything about Blanche's real parents?"

"No," Doris laughed. "That was always been a bit of a mystery. But it's quite the story."

"I love stories," I said encouragingly.

"Well, the way my mother told it, she wasn't officially adopted till later, but as a very young baby she'd been left on the steps of Grandma and Grandpa's house. Unwed mothers often did that back then, if they couldn't take care of the child themselves. It must have happened during the night, because when they woke up in the morning there she was, in a basket. It was raining and Blanche was crying to beat the band."

As Doris continued, I tried to imagine the scene. I'd been to Moncton and seen pictures of my great-grandparents, so that helped.

A light rain falls in the pre-dawn gloom, misting the gentle hills that roll down to the shores of the Bay of Fundy. There'd had been a cover of snow on the ground the night before, when Henry and Nancy Colpitts went to bed. This morning it's gone, pulled from beneath the wooden garden furniture on the lawn like a magician's parlour trick, leaving tables and chairs undisturbed.

"According to Mother," Doris continued, "it was my grandfather who discovered her that morning."

Henry is up and his slippers make a shuffling sound as he moves across the cold hardwood floor in the kitchen, carrying his morning cup of tea. Through the window, his blacksmith shed is an impressionist painting, its outline blurred and softened by tears of rain running down the steamed panes of glass.

The tea is hot and Henry, who had burned his tongue too many times in the past, resists the urge to sip it. He waits. The only sounds are the occasional crackle of wood burning in the cook stove, and the gentle sigh of the sea as the tide moves in.

"Grandpa used to tease Blanche," Doris said. "She was small, barely five feet tall, but he said she could make a lot of noise when she wanted to. I guess she wanted to that morning."

Then there is another sound. A muffled cry. At first Henry thinks it must be a barn cat, complaining in the rain. He listens ... the cry comes again, more insistent now. Henry leaves his teacup on the kitchen table and makes his way along the hall, past the dining room and parlour to the front door. When he opens the door, the sound is louder. Out on the porch, near the steps to the yard, he sees a small wicker basket.

Inside the basket, tightly wrapped in a pink blanket, is a baby, the tiny face red from the exertion of crying.

"What is it?" Behind him, his wife Nancy stands framed in the doorway. She holds a flowered robe tightly closed at her throat as if fearful her husband might glimpse more of her than she cares to show.

"You won't believe it," he says, lifting the basket so she can see the baby.

"Oh my God!" says Elizabeth. "Where ... where did you find it?"

"Here on the porch ... near the stairs."

"Poor little thing," says Elizabeth, looking down at the child. She takes the basket from Henry, carries it into the kitchen and puts it on the table. Then she lifts the baby out, cradling it against her breast.

"Fetch me some milk, Henry ... Lord knows when this little one last ate."

"You have to remember," Aunt Doris said, "my grandparents wanted children. But they'd been married ten years and I guess they'd just about given up hope."

Nancy sits down at the kitchen table, humming softly to the child, gently rocking it in her arms. She wonders how a mother could abandon a newborn baby this way. But looking down at the tiny pink face, Nancy Colpitts realizes her prayers have been answered.

"The ways of the Lord are mysterious to behold," she whispers quietly to herself.

"That's quite a story."

"Yes," Doris laughed, "it certainly is."

"I wonder why the mother chose to leave the baby with your grandparents."

"I'm not sure. But with the blacksmith shop and the farm they were pretty well off. And it was no secret they wanted children."

I needed time to absorb this. "Well, thanks, Aunt Doris."

"You're more than welcome. If you get down this way be sure to drop in. We'd love to see you. It's been such a long time."

"Yes, it has."

"Too long."

We said our goodbyes and I hung up.

Left unsaid was something else. I knew that when unwed mothers left children, they often did so at the doorstep of the father who refused to marry them. Was Blanche actually Henry's illegitimate child? Perhaps that was why she had kept her adoption secret from the family for so long. Had her mother, Nancy, realized this? If so it might have made for a strained relationship between mother and daughter. Is it possible Blanche knew? Carrying this emotional baggage into her marriage with JB might explain why she refused to acknowledge incest.

MONTREAL, 1981

THE EARLY MORNING SUNSHINE slanted through venetian blinds, creating a zebra-striped pattern on the wall of the office. The familiar surroundings no longer seemed shabby, merely practical. I'd been coming here three days a week for two-and-a-half years. I sat down opposite Brian Hunt. I wasn't worried about my choice of the face-to-face approach versus the couch today. This was to be my last session. Drug-free now, I no longer needed tranquilizers. My anxiety and phobias had vanished, and I knew they wouldn't be back. I wasn't sure exactly how these changes had come about and didn't care. I simply accepted them.

"It isn't really a science, is it?"

"What isn't a science?"

"Psychoanalysis."

Across the desk from me Dr. Hunt sipped his coffee. True to form, he remained silent.

I chuckled. I knew now what power that silence held.

"It's as much an art as it is a science. You don't sit there listening to me, looking for symptoms so you can make a diagnosis."

He smiled. "I don't?"

"No, you free associate along with me, letting your mind wander the same way mine does. I've never asked, but I bet you close your eyes as you listen."

"Some of the time," he acknowledged.

"The main difference, as I see it, is that while I verbalize my feelings you don't. Or when you do, it is only to prompt me, keep me going."

He nodded and reached for a cigarette.

This time I remained silent.

He inhaled and blew smoke at the ceiling. "What about now? What are you feeling now?"

"I don't know. Glad ... sad. Glad I won't have to come here three times a week. Sad that it's over."

"It isn't over, you know."

"What do you mean?" I was a little confused, a little afraid. "I thought we decided it was time to wind it up?"

"We did. When I said it wasn't over, I merely meant that when you run into difficulties in the future, you can apply some of the insights you've learned here."

"Oh, for a moment there you had me worried. I thought you were going to suggest that I might eventually need more therapy."

"No, I doubt that will be necessary. You have the tools to help yourself." He put his cigarette in the ashtray and rose. I reached across the desk and we shook hands. It seemed such an inadequate way to conclude something that had meant so much to me.

Hunt smiled reassuringly. "Of course, in the future, if you ever feel the need to talk things through, I'll be here."

Tears of gratitude filled my eyes.

"Goodbye then," I said, "and thanks."

I walked through the waiting room, out the door, and down the corridor to the elevator. When I reached the street, I walked slowly to my car, got in, and headed for the city's East End. It was a bright spring day and that morning I caught every green light on my way to work.

ESSEX, ONTARIO, 1989

AS A MEASURE OF HOW complete my cure was, my fear of flying had disappeared, and I found I could travel anywhere without worrying about a panic attack. My apprehension about live TV had vanished as well, and I went back on the air, eventually hosting a weekly current affairs television program in Montreal. When budget cuts forced its cancellation, I was hired as a field producer for *On the Road Again*, a CBC network show that originated in Ottawa. This not only meant moving my family from Montreal, but the work itself involved one week of travel each month. Where once I'd been paralyzed at the prospect of driving more than fifty miles, I was now flying without fear to places as remote as Baffin Island and the Yukon. The travel also took me to New Brunswick, Prince Edward Island, and Southern Ontario, where I was able to research my family history. I visited the church where my mother was baptized, saw her name written in JB's hand in the registry.

I'd long ago shed any guilt I felt about my mother's death. But I remained curious about the events that led her to take her own life. While I was convinced that incest was at the root of her problem, there was no proof, no smoking gun, and that bothered me. Where to turn? Aunt Alice was dead, but I discovered that Aunt Doris was still alive, in her nineties and living in Essex. So I arranged to produce some stories for *On the Road Again* in Southern Ontario. While I was there I took an extra couple of days and visited my aunt.

I parked the rental car on the street and walked up the steps. My palms were moist and my mouth dry. I rang the bell. There was no mistaking the woman who opened the door. It had been forty years since I'd last seen Doris, but I recognized her at once and knew in that instant how my mother might have looked if she'd managed to live into old age.

"Andy?" Her voice was tentative.

"It's me, Aunt Doris," I leaned forward and kissed her lightly on both cheeks. The faint scent of Lily of the Valley hung in the air between us.

She held me at arm's length and looked me up and down. "Trudy's boy." The tentativeness was gone from her voice. "Come in, come in."

We sat facing each other in the living room, or what Aunt Doris still called "the parlour." The formalities were observed; tea was served by the housekeeper and the dishes cleared away. My aunt wore a red blouse, a cameo broach at the throat, a navy blue skirt, and sensible shoes. Her hair, freshly permed, was streaked with grey. The eyes, when she looked at me, were my mother's eyes.

"Now, what brings you here, after all these years."

I explained that I was in the area, shooting an *On the Road Again* video. Then I used the "family history" cover story again.

"It's for my children," I explained. "They never met any relatives from my side of the family. I thought maybe you could fill in some of the blanks."

Doris relaxed. She began to talk about her own children and grandchildren. I let her ramble on. When she finally seemed to run out of things to say, I said, "You were pretty young when you married for the first time, just eighteen."

She looked at me for a long time, as if weighing what she was about to say next. Then she dropped her gaze and her voice. "I had to get away from him."

"From him?"

"From JB ... your grandfather."

"Why?"

Doris sighed. "It's hard to explain. He was smothering me. I couldn't go out with the boys I wanted to date. I couldn't go anywhere or do anything without a thousand questions."

"So you eloped?"

"Yes" she said. "And it created quite a scandal."

"Your folks wouldn't give you their blessing?"

Her head was down, staring at her lap, fidgeting with a wedding ring. I wasn't sure if she was going to continue, but after a moment or two she looked up at me. "No." Her laugh was harsh. "But there was another reason."

I waited.

"I've never told anyone," she said, her eyes now cold with hate, her stare fixed on me. "But I'm not going to be around much longer and someone should know the truth."

I remained silent.

"I had to get away," Doris said. "JB wouldn't leave me alone. He would slip into my bedroom in the middle of the night ... " She let her words trail off.

The smoking gun. Although I'd expected abuse, her words stunned me. Not just my mother.

"Couldn't you tell Blanche?"

Doris shook her head. Tears replaced the hate I'd seen in her eyes. "I was pretty sure mother knew what was going on."

"Why didn't she do something?"

"I don't know. Maybe she didn't want JB after her ... "

"Wasn't there anyone else you could tell?"

Doris gave a dry chuckle, devoid of humour. "Who would I tell? Who would believe me? JB was a minister."

She fixed me with that same intense stare she'd used earlier. "I blame Blanche almost as much as JB. She had to know what was going on. Why do you think he hated her so at the end? He blamed her for your mother's death. He was babbling about it when they put him away, but no one would listen. Folks put it down to the ravings of a madman, but I knew better." Her eyes dropped again. "I knew better," she said. "Blanche did too."

"So you think ... JB and my mother?"

Doris smiled sadly and nodded. "I was back home by then. My marriage had fallen apart. I moved in, brought my son with me. JB didn't like it, but he knew if he made a fuss I'd let the truth out. And he knew better than to try anything with me."

"So he turned to your sisters ... to Mom?"

Doris shook her head. "Alice and Edith were out on their own so I don't know about them. I never asked. And I'm not sure about Claire."

"But you are sure about my mother."

"I'm afraid so."

We sat in the silence.

I wanted to ask her why she didn't do anything, but I knew the answer. She'd returned home because she had no choice. She had a young son to raise and no means of support. She didn't want to rock the boat. My mother told me she'd always felt uneasy around Aunt Doris, but never explained why. She probably didn't know herself. More repressed memories. Now it all made sense at last.

Doris broke the silence. "Of course if you write any of this I'll deny it." She was the old Doris again, her eyes hard—the survivor.

"Then why tell me at all?"

"Because Trudy was your mother and I think you have the right to know the truth."

Doris got up and put the teacups back on the tray with the cream and sugar. She left me alone and I could hear her rinsing out the dishes in the kitchen. I had come here in search of the truth. I'd found it. I felt a lifetime of tension leave my body and silent tears streamed down my cheeks. It was finally over.

EPILOGUE

VAL ORLIKOW, WITH HELP from her husband David, led the long and complicated legal battle against the authorities, seeking compensation for her treatment by Dr. Cameron. In 1981 she reached an out-of-court settlement of fifty thousand dollars in her suit against the Royal Victoria Hospital. In 1988 nine victims of the doctor's hubris, including Orlikow, received one hundred thousand dollars each from the CIA in another out-of-court settlement. The suit against the Canadian government was resolved in 1992 when an Order-in-Council granted all former patients involved in the Deep Sleep Program an *ex gratia* payment of one hundred thousand dollars.

To date, seventy-seven victims have received this form of compensation. All were required to sign depositions promising not to take any further legal action against the Royal Victoria Hospital or the Allan Memorial Institute. But Cameron's experiments at the Allan on behalf of the CIA still haunt the Institute.

In the latest lawsuit, the son of a mother who was pregnant at the time of her treatment is claiming personal damages. He says his life was compromised by Cameron's experiments on his mother when he was still a fetus. There has never been any formal acknowledgement of guilt by the CIA, the American government, the Canadian government, the Hospital, or the Institute.

Cameron's program and its legal consequences have been the subject of a number of books. The first was Don Gillmor's *I Swear by Apollo: Dr. Ewen Cameron and the CIA Brainwashing Experiments,* published in 1987. A year later Anne Collins won the Governor General's non-fiction award for *In the Sleep Room: The Story of the CIA Brainwashing Experiments in Canada.* The CBC based its 1997 miniseries on the Anne Collins book. Harvey Weinstein's *A Father, A Son and the CIA,* published in 1988, is a son's account of his father's treatment at the Allan. Elizabeth Nickson based her 1994 novel, *The Monkey-Puzzle Tree,* on the experiences of her mother, also patient of Ewen Cameron's in the late fifties and early sixties. A much earlier work, *The Search for the Manchurian Candidate,* by John Marks, published in 1980, provided an overview of all the CIA's mind control programs.

My stepmother had retired and moved in Florida, where she was caring for an invalid sister. So on a winter vacation I found myself sitting opposite Grace in a little restaurant not far from her condo in Clearwater. It was hard to believe that this tiny woman was over eighty years old. She had changed very little over the years.

"I have to ask you something." She looked up expectantly, a spoonful of ice cream poised over her dish. "Do you know of anyone who was upset by your marriage to Dad?"

Grace lowered the spoon and her gaze. "I know you weren't too thrilled with the idea," she said with a hint of bitterness.

This answer caught me by surprise. I'd thought I'd hidden my animosity at the time. But now I knew better. Of course she'd sensed how I felt. Everything I'd done had signalled disapproval.

"I mean ... anyone else?"

She looked up at me with a puzzled frown. "I can't think of anyone. Why do you ask?"

My college roommate's words from long ago came back to me. Carl MacCallum had urged me to confront Grace the day I received the letter. "I guarantee you'll be able to tell from her reaction whether she was fooling around with your father."

"A few weeks after Dad's death," I plunged on, determined to get it over with, "I received an anonymous letter from someone." I sipped some water, preparing my next words carefully. "They said you'd been having an affair with Dad, that Mom found out, and that was the reason she killed herself."

Grace's expression was one of puzzlement and confusion. Not guilt, not even hurt. "But your father and I didn't meet until months after Trudy's death." She shook her head. "I thought you knew that."

"That's what Dad told me, but for a long time I wasn't sure. Then I met Bobbie Vale, Mom's college friend, and she confirmed it."

Grace nodded. "That's right. Willis was looking for Bobbie's number when we met, quite by accident, in Toronto. He wanted to let Bobbie know about your mother's death."

"I just thought you should know that someone in St. Lambert was upset when you married Dad ... upset enough to write me a poison-pen letter." I felt a little ashamed now that I'd even brought the issue up.

"I can't imagine who that would be. I was there less than a year." Grace still seemed more puzzled than hurt. "It was all so long ago." She shook her head.

I was feeling closed in; I just wanted to pay the bill and get out of the restaurant. "I guess it doesn't matter." I signalled the waiter.

I drove Grace back to her condo. "Maybe I'll see you again next year," I said, and bent and kissed her lightly on both cheeks.

"Next year the lunch will be my treat."

"It's a date." I got back into my car. I could see her in the rear view mirror waving as I pulled out of the parking lot.

I waved back.

PENUMBRA PRESS

Cover and book design by Tammy d'Entremont. The cover photo was taken by Andrew Clyde Little.

The text of the book and the running heads are set in Cartier Book 11/13 at Penumbra Press in Manotick, Ontario.

The Penumbra Press logo was designed by Carl Schaefer, OSA, RCA (1903-1995).

For a complete list of Penumbra Press memoirs, visit our website www.penumbrapress.com